GW00778790

Paternalism and Politics

Studies in Modern History

General Editor: **J. C. D. Clark**, Joyce and Elizabeth Hall Distinguished Professor of British History, University of Kansas

Titles include:

Bernard Cottret (*editor*)
BOLINGBROKE'S POLITICAL WRITINGS
The Conservative Enlightenment

Philip Hicks
NEOCLASSICAL HISTORY AND ENGLISH CULTURE
From Clarendon to Hume

William M. Kuhn
DEMOCRATIC ROYALISM
The Transformation of the British Monarchy, 1861–1914

Kim Lawes
PATERNALISM AND POLITICS
The Revival of Paternalism in Early Nineteenth-Century Britain

Nancy D. LoPatin
POLITICAL UNIONS, POPULAR POLITICS AND THE GREAT REFORM ACT OF 1832

James Muldoon
EMPIRE AND ORDER
The Concept of Empire, 800–1800

W. D. Rubinstein and Hilary Rubinstein
PHILOSEMITISM
Admiration and Support for Jews in the English-Speaking World, 1840–1939

Lynne Taylor
BETWEEN RESISTANCE AND COLLABORATION
Popular Protest in Northern France, 1940–45

Studies in Modern History
Series Standing Order ISBN 0–333–79328–5
(*outside North America only*)

You can receive future titles in this series as they are published by placing a standing order. Please contact your bookseller or, in case of difficulty, write to us at the address below with your name and address, the title of the series and the ISBN quoted above.

Customer Services Department, Macmillan Distribution Ltd, Houndmills, Basingstoke, Hampshire RG21 6XS, England

Paternalism and Politics

The Revival of Paternalism in Early Nineteenth-Century Britain

Kim Lawes
Associate Lecturer
School of Classics, History and Religion
University of New England
Armidale, NSW
Australia

First published in Great Britain 2000 by
MACMILLAN PRESS LTD
Houndmills, Basingstoke, Hampshire RG21 6XS and London
Companies and representatives throughout the world

A catalogue record for this book is available from the British Library.

ISBN 0–333–74474–8

First published in the United States of America 2000 by
ST. MARTIN'S PRESS, INC.,
Scholarly and Reference Division,
175 Fifth Avenue, New York, N.Y. 10010

ISBN 0–312–23116–4

Library of Congress Cataloging-in-Publication Data
Lawes, Kim, 1958–
Paternalism and politics : the revival of paternalism in early nineteenth-century
Britain / Kim Lawes.
    p.   cm. — (Studies in modern history)
Includes bibliographical references and index.
ISBN 0–312–23116–4
1. Great Britain—Politics and government—1830–1837. 2. Paternalism—Great
Britain—History—19th century. I. Title. II. Studies in modern history (St. Martin's
Press)
DA530 .L38   2000
320.51'3'094109034—dc21

99–056310

This book is printed on paper suitable for recycling and made from fully managed and sustained
forest sources.

10   9   8   7   6   5   4   3   2   1
09   08   07   06   05   04   03   02   01   00

Printed and bound in Great Britain by
Antony Rowe Ltd, Chippenham, Wiltshire

For Ray, Ian, Dorothy, Susan and Wendy

Contents

Acknowledgements

I would particularly like to thank Associate Professor David Kent, whose guidance, encouragement and unfailing support played no small part in the completion of the doctoral thesis on which this book is based. My thanks must also go to Professor Alan Atkinson, who provided some valuable comments and suggestions on some of the earlier chapters. I am also sincerely grateful to Professor Harold Perkin, Professor John Vincent and Dr John Gascoigne for their encouraging remarks and suggestions. During the research for this work, I received a lot of help from staff at the Bodleian, British Museum and Leeds Central Libraries, the British Library of Political and Economic Science and the West Yorkshire Archives, and from archivists at Leeds and Nottingham Universities. Finally and above all, I wish to thank Dr Ray Bale, who has provided and continues to provide the kind of support that is too precious to be reduced to a trite phrase or two.

List of Abbreviations

Blackwood's	*Blackwood's Edinburgh Magazine*
BLPES	British Library of Political and Economic Science
PR	*Cobbett's Weekly Political Register*
ER	*Edinburgh Review*
PD	British Parliamentary Debates
PP	British Parliamentary Papers
Thorseby	*The Publications of the Thorseby Society*

Introduction: Michael Thomas Sadler and 'the Revival of the Aristocratic Paternalist Ideal'

This book is a study of the revival of paternalism and its implications for the development of social policy in early nineteenth-century Britain. It focuses on the period 1815 to 1833, during which attention shifted from foreign to domestic issues and demands for reform – social, political and economic – invigorated political debate. To many historians, this is the age of liberalism, characterized by the 'triumph of individualism' and the popularization of political economy and utilitarian, *laissez-faire* thinking. In the face of the country's transition from a predominantly rural, agricultural and community-based society to an industrial, urban, capitalist nation-state, eighteenth-century ideas about hierarchical responsibility, deference and reciprocal obligation seem anachronistic. Yet, it will be argued here, that paternalist thinking remained crucial to the discussion and formulation of social policy in this period. As the term 'revival' suggests, this was not just a continuation of eighteenth-century ideas, however, it was a resurgence of paternalist thinking that had far more significance than simply nostalgia for the past or a reactionary response to the rise of the new economy. By focusing on the paternal responsibilities of government and parliament, the early nineteenth-century paternalists sought to accommodate the changing social and political climate. In the tradition of protectionism, they looked to the state for solutions to social as well as economic problems. This substitution of governmental for familial and community responsibility not only distinguishes nineteenth- from eighteenth-century paternalist thought, but is important to understanding the paternalist origins of the Victorian collectivist state.

The inspiration for this study came from Harold Perkin's discussion of 'the revival of the aristocratic paternalist ideal' in *The Origins of*

Modern English Society 1780–1880 (1969). This examines the genesis of class consciousness, arising from the conflict between the different interests groups or, to use Perkin's phrase, from the 'struggle between the ideals', in the first two decades of the nineteenth century. During this period, explains Perkin, three essentially economic-based visions of 'the ideal society' – the entrepreneurial, the working-class and the aristocratic – influenced social and economic discourse and determined relations between individuals and between the different social orders. The paternalist revival was largely a response to the *laissez-faire* economists' highly successful promotion of the entrepreneurial ideal.[1] However, as Perkin points out, the 'aristocratic ideal never quite died':

> At its weakest, in the agitation for the abolition of the poor laws between Waterloo and the Queen's trial, an etiolated sense of responsibility for the lower orders managed to survive amongst the aristocracy.[2]

It was through the efforts of paternal idealists like Michael Thomas Sadler and the group of Tories who wrote for *Blackwood's*, the 'the main channel' of the paternalist 'current of social thought', that the aristocratic vision of society was not only kept alive but emerged with a renewed sense of purpose.[3] This was as much a reaction, adds Perkin, 'against the betrayers of paternalism as against the new entrepreneurial ideal'.[4]

Sadler – 'the key figure' in the revival of paternalism[5] – occupies a minor place in the historiography of this period. Most accounts of Sadler focus on his involvement in the 1830s phase of the factory reform campaign and his association with Richard Oastler and the Yorkshire Tory Radicals. In 1832 Sadler headed the parliamentary campaign for factory reform. He was the instigator and chairman of the 1832 Committee on Child Labour. But his role as its parliamentary spokesmen for the factory movement was short-lived. Parliament was prorogued before the Committee had completed its report and Sadler was unsuccessful in his efforts to secure a seat in the newly reformed House of Commons. He was succeeded by Lord Ashley, about whom considerable more has been written, of course, for his career as a humanitarian reformer spanned some 60 years. There are a few references to Sadler in relation to the late 1820s conservative backlash against liberal reformers and economists. For some historians, *The Law of Population*, in which Sadler attempted to overturn Thomas Malthus's thesis and provide an alternative theory of population growth, was his greatest achievement.[6] Others note his outspoken opposition to Catholic emancipation and his political association with the reactionary 'Church and King' party. Again, however, Sadler is seen as a minor player and largely under the influence of the Duke of Newcastle to whom he owed his political career.[7] Some notice is taken of Sadler in analyses of the intellectual climate of the early nineteenth century and in connection with the Tory Romantics' critique of the materialists' concept of progress.[8] Finally, there is an outdated, but none the less fairly comprehensive, biography of Sadler, published in 1842 by the well-known bookseller and publisher, Robert Benton Seeley.

It is not just Sadler's place in history that needs to be further examined. The impact of the revival of paternal thought in this period has likewise either been overlooked or treated almost as an aberration.[9] Arguing that ultimately, in the struggle between the ideals, the entrepreneurial ideal proved triumphant, Perkin notes that the revival of the aristocratic paternalist ideal 'has suffered the neglect and misunderstanding of most lost causes'. It was 'signally defeated by the Reform Act (which overthrew Sadler himself), by the New Poor Law, and by the triumph of free trade, and then dissipated in the romantic feudalism of Disraeli, Lord John Manners and "Young England". Yet in the 1820s', continues Perkin, acknowledging the underlying progressiveness of the revival,

> it produced, quite apart from Sadler's contribution, a counterattack on aristocratic 'abdication' and the entrepreneurial ideal which not only rejected outright the whole canon of classical economics but anticipated in great measure both Keynesian economics and the social outlook of the Welfare State.[10]

The historiography of the eighteenth and nineteenth centuries has recently been placed under the spotlight by J.C.D. Clark's provocative critique of the standard left-wing view of social and political history laid down by historians including the Webbs, the Hammonds, G.D.H. Cole, Harold Laski and more recently continued in the work of E.P. Thompson and the generation of social historians whom he inspired. Emphasizing the continuity of ideas in history, Clark contends that many historians, in dwelling on transition and the 'triumph of individualism', have imputed too much to the material changes brought about by the industrial revolution.[11] These materialist-inspired interpretations overstate the extent and pace of industrialization, particularly in its eighteenth-century phase.[12] More importantly, for this analysis, Clark questions the assumption that material changes were sufficient in themselves to transform ingrained philosophical, religious, political and social beliefs. 'It is by no means clear', writes Clark,

> that the sort of material changes witnessed by the vast majority before 1832 were enough in themselves to necessitate or effect immediate and basic *transformations* of outlook and belief: only the slow passage of generations did that.[13]

'The values of nineteenth-century industrial society', he adds, 'owed far more to the values of the ancien régime than the Victorians were prepared to admit.'[14] The aristocratic and patriarchal social outlook continued to shape British society well into the nineteenth century.[15]

David Roberts' study of paternalism in the nineteenth century supports Clark's continuity thesis. 'In early Victorian England', writes Roberts, 'no social outlook had deeper roots and wider appeal' than the paternal or patriarchal.[16] As a study of paternalism in early Victorian England, Roberts focuses on the 1830s and 1840s but includes Sadler in his examination of the origins of Victorian paternalism. In seeking to formulate an alternative – paternalist – social and economic theory, Sadler was part of the broad intellectual movement that had begun to examine the social implications of the new economy, particularly in its effect upon the lower orders and the undermining of social harmony and stability. 'Men as different as Oastler, Sadler, Digby, and Chalmers', writes Roberts, 'joined the romantic poets Southey, Coleridge, and Wordsworth to form a pre-Victorian generation of intellectuals who sought to work out a theory of paternalism.'[17]

As 'diffuse and varied as it was widespread and popular', the paternal social outlook was, in Roberts' opinion, an amorphous, incoherent, 'cluster of ideas and attitudes' with no positive theoretical basis.[18] Similarly, John Stuart Mill wrote of a mind-set deeply rooted in instinctive and customary behaviour. It 'exercises an unconscious influence', he explained, 'on the opinions and sentiments' of individuals, who do not 'consciously guide themselves by any ideal'.

> It makes its appeal to our imaginative sympathies in the character of a restoration of the good times of our forefathers ... It is an

idealization, grounded on the conduct and character of here and there an individual.

Referring to it as the 'theory of dependence and protection', Mill identified its chief characteristics:

> The relation between rich and poor, according to this theory ... should be only partly authoritative; it should be amiable, moral, and sentimental: affectionate tutelage on the one side, respectful and grateful deference on the other. The rich should be *in loco parentis* to the poor, guiding and restraining them like children. Of spontaneous action on their part there should be no need. They should be called on for nothing but to do their day's work, and to be moral and religious. Their morality and religion should be provided for them by their superiors, who should see them properly taught it, and should do all that is necessary to ensure their being, in return for labour and attachment, properly fed, clothed, housed, spiritually edified, and innocently amused.[19]

The idea was implicit in his reference to the authority and duties of the higher classes, but Mill did not refer specifically to the paternal responsibilities of the state.

For Roberts the paternalists' view of government was highly ambiguous and their references to a 'parental government' and the 'Protective State' were too vague and rhetorical to be taken literally. They looked to legislation that would give local authorities, the landed classes and the traditional ruling élite more power to guide, protect and control the dependent classes. But they did not seek the centralized, bureaucratic administrative role for government associated with the Benthamite tradition.

The present work considers Sadler and the Tory paternalists' notion of paternal government and arguments for a more interventionist state in the light of Roberts' claim that the 'paternalist writers were not statists, and they did not look to the state for panaceas'.[20] By focusing on the 1820s revival and the nature and development of Sadler's thinking in particular, it demonstrates that the Tory paternalists' rejection of the individualistic, *laissez-faire* doctrine encouraged a reappraisal of the social responsibilities of government and parliament which provided a new context for the paternal ideal. This was manifest in a shift in the locus of paternal authority and responsibility from the family and the community to the state. As the Tory

paternalists became more conscious of their fundamental protectionist, paternalist beliefs, the paternal social outlook acquired a more
coherent and systematic form. For Sadler the notion of governmental
responsibility assumed greater importance after he entered parliament
and began defending the interests of the labouring poor. By 1830 it
had become a central aspect of his thinking, and both critics and
supporters of the 'Sadlerian school' recognized this. Sadler's Tory
paternalist philosophy is examined in detail in Chapter 2. Chapter 1
outlines the ideas and attitudes which underpinned the revival of the
aristocratic paternal ideal and demonstrates the extent to which high-
profile conservative thinkers and social commentators of Sadler's
generation were prepared to defend old-world, paternalist, protectionist and community-based values against the new individualistic,
laissez-faire philosophy.

1
Continuity and Change in the Revival of Paternalist Social Thought

> [Sadler] was the channel rather than the originating spring of the revival. He belonged to a widespread current of social thought, which was flowing strongly in the 1820s before it carried him to the top, provided him with a pocket borough seat in Parliament, and chose him as its leader.
>
> Harold Perkin, 1969[1]

Focusing on some of the leading social commentators of the early nineteenth century, this chapter outlines the principal themes underlying the revival of paternal social thought in the 1820s. It is not an exhaustive, systematic analysis of paternalist thought, for that has already been undertaken by David Roberts in his study of Victorian paternalism. Instead, it identifies a number of high-profile, mainly conservative members of the intellectual community, people like Samuel Taylor Coleridge, Robert Southey and the group of high Tories associated with *Blackwood's*, whose vision of society was essentially paternalistic. Importantly, for this study, it is in these writers' defence of interventionist, protectionist policies and focus on the social responsibilities of the state that we see the germ of the idea of the Victorian collectivist state. Not only did these demands for a more active social and protective role for the state represent a radical departure from the eighteenth-century minimalist view of government, they also ran counter to the individualistic, *laissez-faire* philosophy underpinning the new economic doctrine of the nineteenth century. Fundamental to these arguments for social and economic intervention was, among conservative paternalists, in particular, a belief in the need for governments to ensure a balance and harmony of interests. The aggressive competitiveness and self-interest underlying the commercial spirit, the driving force of the manufacturing system, was felt by these social commentators to be the root of all social and economic evils.[2] In particular, it was blamed for widespread unemployment and distress among the labouring poor. But while they questioned the economists' preoccupation with commerce and material progress and repeatedly voiced concerns about the impact of industrialization upon the labouring classes, the paternalists were not necessarily seeking to turn the clock back and arrest the pace and scope of change. Rather, they sought to restore a balance between the interests of the old world of agriculture and landed property and the new world of manufacturing and commerce. These concerns, to a large extent, were governed by humanitarian feeling. At the same time, the spectre of the French Revolution and a discontented labouring class still loomed large, and demands for government intervention and regulation of social problems were frequently justified in terms of the national interest and social stability.

The emphasis on the state's social responsibilities was reinforced further by the influence of Rousseauian determinism. In opposition to liberal arguments about individual responsibility, the paternalists maintained that social and economic problems were not the fault of the individual but a consequence of misguided policies. As a corollary to that argument, they refused to accept that social problems were inevitable or incapable of being remedied. Indeed, they were optimistic that it was well within the state's power to restore to the people a degree of prosperity and contentment. A determinist perspective also lay beneath many of the paternalists' proposals for a national system of education. Designed to inculcate notions of civic duty and reinforce deferential attitudes among the lower orders, these educational schemes generally had more to do with social unity than individual improvement. To appreciate the reason for this, we need to consider the relationship of the individual to the state in paternalist thought. Its understanding of that relationship was grounded in an organic or holistic view of society. Like the principle of balance and harmony, it was a view of human relations founded on the hierarchical, great chain of being idea depicted in Alexander Pope's *Essay on Man* and central to Edmund Burke's *Reflections on the Revolution in France*. The paternalists looked on the interests of the individual as being inseparable from those of the state, and stressed the importance of social and economic interdependence. Conversely, the political economists viewed the state atomistically as an aggregate of individuals and valued policies which promoted independence and self-help.

While concepts such as harmony, balance and interdependence illustrate the continuation of ideas between the eighteenth and nineteenth centuries, demands for a more active social role for the state belong to the nineteenth and twentieth centuries. In the 1820s, paternal social thought seemed poised between these two worlds.

I

As one of the most important articulators of conservative philosophy in the early nineteenth century, Samuel Taylor Coleridge helped lay the theoretical groundwork for a more expansive and active social role for the state. His seminal prose work, *On the Constitution of Church and State* (1830), focused on the conflict emerging between the old and the new worlds, or what Coleridge termed the forces of permanence and the forces of progression. *The Statesman's Manual* (1816) and *A Lay Sermon* (1817) considered hierarchical responsibility in relation to social harmony and stability.[3] Addressed to the upper and middle classes, these two tracts provided a foundation for his theory of the state.

Unashamedly élitist and with little trace of his youthful Jacobinism, *The Statesman's Manual* outlined Coleridge's concerns about the dissemination of radical and revolutionary ideas among the lower orders. For Coleridge, harmony and stability depended on people being educated according to their social status. With the growth in the number of pauper schools, expansion of the periodical press and increased availability of literature through circulating libraries, 'we now have a READING PUBLIC', exclaimed Coleridge. He was worried about the effect that this improved access to political and philosophical ideas might have on people who read about rights without understanding that these carried responsibilities. From Coleridge's conservative, hierarchical social and political perspective, the privileged classes had the leisure, the moral sense and that 'sound book learnedness' needed to comprehend complex, political, philosophical and theological principles. 'From you we have a right', he declared, 'to expect a sober and meditative accommodation to your own times and country of those important truths declared in the inspired writings "for a thousand generations".' As for the labouring classes, they

> are not sought for in public counsel, nor need they be found where politic sentences are spoken. It is enough if every one is wise in the working of his own craft: so best will they maintain the state of the world.[4]

William Hazlitt concluded that Coleridge's labouring classes were destined to be mere 'hewers of wood or drawers of water'.[5] Without the enlightened and paternal influence of their social superiors, Coleridge feared that education of the lower orders would do more harm than good. It was a mistake, he believed, to assume that 'a national education will have been realized whenever the People at large have been taught to read and write'.

> Now among the many means to the desired end, this is doubtless one, and not the least important. But neither is it the most so. Much less can it be held to *constitute* Education, which consists in *educing* the faculties, and forming the habits; the means varying according to the sphere in which the individuals to be educated are likely to act and become useful.

Requiring a greater commitment from the 'rich and powerful' than a yearly subscription to the local pauper school, for Coleridge the utility of a national system of education for the lower orders lay in its improvement of their character, moral sense, practical skills and in promoting an awareness of social responsibilities and duties. Its purpose was to serve national rather than individual ends.[6]

In the *Lay Sermon*, Coleridge delved deeper into the social and economic problems confronting the postwar generation. Mindful of the effect of economic distress in breeding social discontent, he was concerned about the impact of widespread unemployment. During these period, the labouring classes were receptive to the propaganda of radicals, demagogues and other 'misleaders of the multitude', intent upon undermining the authority of the state and the existing social order:[7]

> Where distress is felt tales of wrong and oppression are readily believed, to the sufferer's own disquiet. Rage and Revenge make the cheek pale and the hand tremble, worse than even want itself: and the cup of sorrow overflows by being held unsteadily.[8]

The 'Overbalance of the Commercial Spirit', encouraging speculation, unrestrained competitiveness and extravagance, was in Coleridge's view the underlying cause of the postwar economic crisis.[9] Under the influence of rationalistic, *laissez-faire* arguments people were too inclined, he believed, 'to look at all things thro' the medium of the market, and to estimate the Worth of all pursuits and attainments by their marketable value'.[10]

I cannot persuade myself, that the frequency of failures with all the disgraceful secrets of Fraud and Folly, of unprincipled Vanity in expending and desperate Speculation in retrieving, can be familiarized to the thoughts and experience of Men, as matters of daily occurrence, without serious injury to the Moral Sense.[11]

Coleridge identified three 'natural counter-forces' to the modern materialistic, commercial spirit. The first was 'the feeling of ancient birth and the respect paid to it by the community at large'. The second lay in the pursuit of philosophical inquiry, for the 'pursuit of Truth for its own sake and the reverence yielded to its professors, has a tendency to calm or counteract the pursuit of wealth'. The third came from the teachings of Christianity. In order 'to tame mankind and introduce a sense of virtue, the best human means is to exercise their understanding, to give them a glimpse of a world superior to the sensible; and while they take pains to cherish and maintain the animal life, to teach them not to neglect the intellectual'.[12] These, essentially moral, intellectual and religious precepts, constituted the spirit of the State:

> I feel assured that the Spirit of Commerce is itself capable of being at once counteracted and enlightened by the Spirit of the State, to the advantage of both.[13]

Above all, Coleridge was concerned about the change in social attitudes that had accompanied the expansion of commerce and industry. In Cobbett-like fashion, he portrayed the new breed of capitalist farmers as men driven by materialism and self-interest, with little regard for the social duties and responsibilities attached to wealth and property.[14] In traditional high Tory fashion, he equated the interests of the landed classes with the national interest. Taking into account the social as well as the financial decisions made in the management of large estates, he suggested that property in land represented something more tangible than trade or commerce, where 'no distinction is or can be acknowledged between Things and Persons'.[15] Landed property stood for permanence, continuity and stability:

> That Agriculture requires principles essentially different from those of Trade – that a gentleman ought not to regard his estate as a merchant his cargo, or a shopkeeper his stock – admits of an easy proof from the different tenure of Landed Property, and from the

purposes of Agriculture itself, which ultimately are the same as those of the state of which it is the offspring ...

'If the continuance and independence of the State be its object', added Coleridge, then 'the final causes of the State must be its final causes.'[16] Essentially, Coleridge believed that the landed classes had abdicated their social responsibilities. Since the rise of commercialism, the connection between the landowner and his tenantry had been seriously weakened and, in many cases, completely severed. Leaving the management of their properties to agents and overseers, landowners were unaware of the social decay and deep sense of alienation felt by small farmers and labourers employed on their estates. As a consequence of the commercialism driving the enclosure movement, peasant farmers were suffering from the dispossession of smallholdings and common pasturage. Because agents and overseers were governed by pragmatic and administrative concerns and lacked an understanding of social responsibility, this trend had continued unchecked.[17] 'Our ... gentry must regard their estates', declared Coleridge, 'as offices of trust, with duties to be performed, in the sight of God and their Country.' In addition to the weakening of social bonds, a growing number of labouring people were psychologically as well as physically remote from the land. They depended on the produce of the land for survival, and yet had no direct connection with its cultivation or production.[18]

In his promotion of a more positive, interventionist role for the state, Coleridge's idea of hierarchical and paternal responsibility parted company with traditional Tory views. According to his understanding of government, it existed, first, 'to make the means of subsistence more easy to each individual'; second, 'to secure to each of its members THE HOPE of bettering his condition or that of his children'; and third, to encourage 'the development of those faculties which are essential to his Humanity, i.e. to his rational and moral Being'.[19] In a subsequent essay he insisted that, 'in addition to the necessaries of life', the individual

> should derive from the union and division of labour a share of the comforts and conveniences which humanize and ennoble his nature; and at the same time the power of perfecting himself in his own branch of industry by having those things which he needs provided for him by others among his fellow-citizens; including the tools and raw or manufactured materials necessary for his own employment.[20]

This enlarged view of governmental responsibility was far removed from the eighteenth-century minimalist idea of the state. 'To provide for us in our necessities', Burke had declared, 'is not in the power of government. It would be vain presumption in statesmen to think they can do it.'[21] It was also completely at odds with the non-interventionist position underpinning nineteenth-century *laissez-faire* doctrine. In addition to ensuring peace and security, Coleridge's idea of government implied that the state was responsible for securing the moral, social and economic needs of the people. By implication, therefore, the state was entitled to intervene in practically every sphere of an individual's life.

The idea central to *Church and State* was equipoise – or the resolution of tension and conflict. Published in 1830, it was written in response to the Catholic emancipation crisis. In addition to establishing the interdependence of church and state and reconciling the temporal with the spiritual world, Coleridge aimed to restore balance and harmony between the forces of permanence and the forces of progression. The landed classes, the guardians of 'the institutions, rights, customs, manners and privileges' of the state, stood for permanence and continuity. Progression, manifested 'in the arts and comforts of life, in the diffusion of the information and knowledge', and in the 'rights and privileges of citizens', was identified with the mercantile, manufacturing and professional classes.[22] One of the principal functions of Coleridge's national church, or clerisy, was to reconcile these two opposing forces. Like Plato's philosopher-king, an informed clerisy would act as the nation's paternal guardians – the instructors of moral and social behaviour – and thus provide a counterpoise to the materialistic, commercial ethos. 'I hold it the disgrace and calamity of a professed statesman', he declared,

> not to know and acknowledge, that a permanent, nationalized, learned order, a national clerisy or church, is an essential element of a rightly constituted nation, without which it wants the best security alike for its permanence and its progression; and for which neither tract societies nor conventicles, nor Lancastrian schools, nor mechanics' institutions, nor lecture-bazaars under the absurd name of universities, nor all these collectively can be a substitute.[23]

The other area of tension identified by Coleridge was in the relationship of the individual to the state. From the foregoing discussion, it is clear that the idea of balance and harmony was fundamental to his understanding of progress. The interests of permanence and progression were 'at once supporting and counterpoising'.[24] The interests of the individual and the state were likewise inexorably connected. Indeed, the whole purpose of his 'National Clerisy' was

> to form and train up the people of the country to obedient, free, useful, organizable subjects, citizens, and patriots, living to the benefit of the state, and prepared to die for its defence. The proper *object* and end of the National Church is civilization with freedom; and the duty of its ministers, could they be contemplated merely and exclusively as officiaries of the *National* Church, would be fulfilled in the communication of that degree and kind of knowledge to all, the possession of which is necessary for all in order to their CIVILITY. By civility I mean all the qualities essential to a citizen, and devoid of which no people or class of the people can be calculated on by the rulers and leaders of the state for the conservation or promotion of its essential interests.[25]

This integration of individual interests with the interests of the state was in keeping with the Rousseauian Romantic tradition.[26] In contrast to the Benthamite idea of the administrative state, Coleridge's state was not merely a social and economic entity, it was an organic whole, with a moral and spiritual life of its own.

Coleridge's contribution to the development of paternalistic social thought lay mainly in his theoretical and philosophical writings. Because he was not writing for a popular audience, he did not enter into social debate with quite the same vigour as Southey, but there were two areas in which he took an active interest, namely the slave trade and child labour. In 1818, during a week of intense debate on Sir Robert Peel's cotton factories bill, Coleridge circulated two pamphlets, *Remarks on the Objections Which Have Been Urged Against the Principle of Sir Robert Peel's Bill* and *The Grounds of Sir Robert Peel's Bill Vindicated*.[27] Based on the view that manufacturers were too much governed by the politics of *laissez-faire* economics and self-interest to be trusted with self-regulation, Coleridge argued for government regulation of the industry. In an anonymous letter to *The Courier,* he urged that it was

> necessary that the poorer classes should be undeceived and know their real friends; and such proofs of inconsistency fairly brought forward, will go far to convince them, that they are not to be sought for among such as would use them merely as tools for their

ambitious as well as mercenary views; but among those who are
unostentatiously striving to improve their condition, and to make
them happy by preserving *each* in his station, that he may be best
able to promote the welfare of the *whole*.[28]

As John Colmer observes, this marked a turning-point in Coleridge's
view of legislative regulation. It was the first social issue in which
Coleridge attributed 'sufficient importance to legislation as an instrument of reform'. Prior to that, and the slave trade issue is a case in
point, he had rested his hopes upon the enlightenment of the individual. He had in fact been highly critical of William Wilberforce's
handling of the slavery issue, claiming that his 'application to the
Legislature was altogether wrong'. At that time, Coleridge thought
that the way to conquer the slave trade was to appeal to people's
consciences and persuade them to refrain from indulging in sugar,
rum and other products of the iniquitous trade.[29]

II

Southey shared Coleridge's distrust of liberal, *laissez-faire* economics.
'Too long', he wrote, 'has that foul philosophy prevailed, which
considers men either as mere machines ... or as mere animals, whose
animal wants are all that are to be taken into the account of statistic
economy.'[30] He likewise believed that the materialistic, commercial
spirit, accounting for the rapid growth of the manufacturing system,
was largely to blame for the prevalence of distress among the labouring classes.[31] It fostered selfishness, destroyed the social order and was
an affront to the genuine spirit of Christianity.[32] In 1809, he painted
a grim picture of the inequality arising from the homage paid to
commerce, 'the queen witch':

A happy country indeed it is for the higher orders; no where have
the rich so many enjoyments, no where have the ambitious so fair
a field, no where have the ingenious such encouragement, no
where have the intellectual such advantages; but to talk of English
happiness is like talking of Spartan freedom, the Helots are overlooked. In no other country can such riches be acquired by
commerce, but it is the one who grows rich by the labour of the
hundred. The hundred, human beings like himself, as wonderfully
fashioned by Nature, gifted with the like capacities, and equally
made for immortality, are sacrificed body and soul.[33]

Twenty-two years later his views were unchanged. In the *Colloquies*, his ghost of Sir Thomas More declared,

> But that cannot be a durable state of things in which the increase of riches in a few, occasions an increase of poverty in the many. National wealth is wholesome only when it is equitably diffused.[34]

Southey believed that the labouring people were not only relatively but absolutely worse off than they had been 40 years previously, and regretted, as much as Cobbett, the gradual disappearance of the old familial, patriarchal and community-based social hierarchy.[35] His idealistic and romantic view of traditional face-to-face society was strongly reminiscent of Cobbett's nostalgic depiction of old England in *Rural Rides*. 'The small farmer', wrote Southey,

> or, in the language of Latimer and the old English feeling, the yeoman, had his roots in the soil: this was the right English tree in which our heart of oak was matured. Where he grew up, he decayed: where he first opened his eyes, there he fell asleep. He lived as his fathers had lived before him, and trained up his children in the same way. The daughters of this class of men were brought up in habits of industry and frugality, in good principles, hopefully and religiously, and with a sense of character to support. Those who were not married to persons of their own rank, were placed in service; and hence the middle ranks were supplied with that race of faithful and respectable domestic servants; the diminution and gradual extinction of which is one of the evils (and not the least) that have arisen from the new system of agriculture.[36]

Thus, under the old system, the principle of social and economic interdependence determined individuals' relations with one another. Conversely, under the new manufacturing system there was no sense of community or of reciprocal obligation. The manufacturing poor

> have necessarily less of that attachment to their employers which arises from long connexion, and the remembrance of kind offices received, and faithful services performed; an inheritance transmitted from parent to son: and being gathered together in herds from distant parts, they have no family character to support in the place to which they have been transplanted.[37]

Southey rejected the liberal view of social responsibility and self-help. Individuals, and particularly the labouring poor, were neither responsible for the social and economic problems which beset them nor were they in a position to resolve them. As did Coleridge's, his paternal understanding of hierarchical responsibility translated into a comprehensive view of government's social role. The 'two main ends of government were the security of the subjects and the improvements of the nation'.[38] Its first responsibility was 'to provide relief for those upon whom the pressure of the times bears hardest'. Contemptuous of Malthusian claims about the poor, Southey explained that 'the true policy of governments is not to prevent their subjects from multiplying, but to provide uses and employments for them as fast as they multiply':

> If in any country they increase faster than means, not merely for their existence, but for their well-being, are provided, in that country there is a defect of policy; the error is in human institutions, not in the unerring laws of nature; in man, not in his Maker.[39]

The difficulty for Southey and other social commentators lay in the need to convince statesmen that legislation could make a difference, that social problems could be overcome. 'Statesmen in this point are like physicians', acknowledged Southey, 'afraid, lest their own reputation should suffer, to try new remedies in cases where the old routine of practice is known and proved to be ineffectual.'[40] And yet, with the involvement of parliamentarians in the abolition of the slave trade and reformation of the harsh criminal code, considerable progress had already been made towards a more interventionist and socially responsible state. The parliamentary select committee was an increasingly important device in identifying the extent of the country's social and economic problems; indeed, in 'no other country', observed Southey, 'have the wounds of the commonwealth been so carefully probed'.[41]

Nineteenth-century critics recognized the paternalist implications of Southey's broad understanding of the state's social responsibilities. In a caustic review of the *Colloquies*, Lord Macaulay referred to 'the omniscient and omnipotent State' as Southey's idol.[42] Highly authoritarian, it implied,

> that no man can do any thing so well for himself, as his rulers, be they who they may, can do it for him; that a government

approaches nearer and nearer to perfection, in proportion as it interferes more and more with the habits and notions of individuals.[43]

John Dennis, a late nineteenth-century editor of Southey's works, suggested that he was, in many respects, ahead of his time. 'He thought as, by a curious turn of the tables, Radicals think now, that the diseases of society can to a large extent be remedied by State interference.' Dennis agreed with Southey's son 'that his father was one of the chief pioneers of most of the great improvements taking place in our time'.[44]

Southey defended a more activist government at a time when the political economists were increasingly opposed to the legislature meddling in business or social affairs. In Macaulay's view,

> Our rulers will best promote the improvement of the people by strictly confining themselves to their own legitimate duties – by leaving capital to find its most lucrative course, commodities their fair price, industry and intelligence their natural reward, idleness and folly their natural punishment – by maintaining peace, by defending property, by diminishing the price of law, and by observing strict economy in every department of the state. Let the Government do this – the People will assuredly to the rest.[45]

For his part, Southey accepted that

> Interference may often be dangerous, but it is certain also that neglect, not unfrequently, is fatal. They whose aim, and it is the wise and proper aim of statesmen in well ordered communities, is to keep things as they are, should bear in mind, that such conservation can only be effected by constant vigilance and care; that human affairs never remain stationary, but are always taking their course.[46]

Notwithstanding statements like this, there was still some way to go before the notion of a paternal, interventionist or collectivist welfare state, wholly responsible for social and economic affairs, would be acceptable even to conservative paternalists. While Southey promoted a more expansive role for the state, he was not necessarily in favour of an authoritarian, centralized government and he did not want to undermine the existing parochial hierarchy. Referring to the vexed issues of rising poor rates and increasing pauperism, he suggested that 'more may be done by benevolent individuals, and by making parishes sensible of their true interests, than by parliamentary interference'.[47]

At the same time, Southey saw an urgent need for legislation and government intervention in areas where there was no community support; either because the old paternal social order had disintegrated under the weight of commercialism or because of unprecedented circumstances brought about by the emergence of the new, tightly regulated, textile factories and the expansion of densely populated and socially divided urban centres.[48] In 'large cities, and more especially in the metropolis', he observed, 'there is much to be done which cannot be accomplished without parliamentary assistance.'[49] Child labour was one of the areas in which Southey felt that there ought to be tighter legislative controls. He supported the campaign to abolish the use of children to sweep chimneys, and fervently hoped that the government would intervene to limit the hours worked by children in cotton factories.[50] However, for the most part, his proposals for more extensive legislative regulation were aimed at improving the quality of life of the labouring classes as a whole. He argued for decriminalization of the game laws, for legislation to prohibit 'brutal sports' like bull-baiting, for a restriction on the number of licences for public houses and he applauded the efforts of men like Henry Grey Bennet, MP for Shrewsbury, for better treatment of felons and improvement of conditions in prisons.[51] Finally, to alleviate the problems of widespread unemployment, Southey strongly approved of 'a liberal expenditure in national works ... [for this was] one of the surest means for promoting national prosperity'.[52] It was also necessary to the maintenance of social stability and harmony. 'Let us not deceive ourselves!', he exclaimed, 'governments are safe in proportion as the great body of the people are contented, and men cannot be contented when they work with the prospect of want and pauperism before their eyes.'[53]

As a substitute for notions of familial authority and responsibility characteristic of traditional, pre-industrial, society, Southey looked to a paternal government. This shift in the locus of authority and responsibility from the family and the community to the state was fundamental to the development of paternalistic social thought in the early nineteenth century. In order to revive that community of feeling and understanding of reciprocal duty and responsibility which existed in close-knit, rural communities, it was necessary to reinforce the authority and legitimacy of the state. For that reason, Southey advocated a national system of education.[54] Similar to the clerisy of the Coleridgeian theocratic state, he anticipated that it would act as a unifying force, a bulwark of church and state. Its primary purpose was to guide and direct the lower orders to be useful and responsible members of society. Poverty 'will be diminished and want will disappear in proportion as the lower classes are instructed in their duties, for then only will they understand their true interests'.[55]

III

The conservative paternalist advocated education as a means of reinforcing an identity of interest between the different orders in society and ultimately between the individual and the state. Robert Owen was similarly influenced by eighteenth-century holism and Rousseauian determinism. But his scheme for improvement of the lower orders, with its authoritarian-paternalist emphasis on social conditioning and repression of individuality, went beyond what the conservative paternalists had in mind. After visiting New Lanark, Southey was left with the impression that Owen

> keeps from out of sight from others and perhaps from himself that his system, instead of aiming at perfect freedom can only be kept in play by absolute power ... The persons under him happen to be white, and are at liberty by law to quit his service, but while they remain in it they are as much under his absolute management as so many negro slaves.[56]

In time, Southey grew even more wary of Owenite-type education schemes. In 1833, to satisfy the Benthamites' concerns about the lack of education among the poor, Lord Althorp's Factory Act included a provision for making factory proprietors responsible for providing their child labourers with some elementary schooling. Twelve months after its implementation, Southey wrote disparagingly of its effects on familial relations:

> Unhappily some of the best intended efforts for mitigating the wretched consequences of this system have a sure tendency to deprave still further the very persons for whose relief they are designed. I allude to infant, and even to Sunday schools. Teach a mother to teach her children what all mothers used to teach theirs fifty years ago, and the instruction is given in love and received in

love, and is wholesome for the whole family. The duty is undertaken *for her* now – nay, it is *taken from* her, for the sake of making
display, and the Sunday school is made, for the children the
longest school-day in the week.[57]

In Owen's view, the fact that parents, relieved of the responsibility of
caring for their children, were 'more usefully occupied, both for themselves and the establishment' in the mills, was one of the chief
attractions of the New Lanark Institution. For the same reason, he
provided children who were too young for formal instruction with a
supervised play area. This freed parents from the necessity of having
to watch over their children; it also ensured that 'their young minds
were properly directed', for he had found that the

> tempers of the children among the lower orders are generally
> spoiled, and vicious habits strongly formed, previous to the time
> when they are usually sent to school; and, to create the characters
> desired, these must be prevented, or as much as possible counter-
> acted.[58]

Thus, from the time they were able to walk, the children of New
Lanark were placed under Owen's care.

Located in the centre of New Lanark, his Institution for the
Formation of Character was designed to promote community activities. His aim was to create a happy and relaxed environment
conducive to learning. It was to be a place where adults as well as children would acquire the necessary skills and education to 'make them
valuable members of society'.[59] To that end, he organized evening
lectures on raising and training children, on household economy and
prudent management of weekly incomes. The young girls were
instructed in the virtues of cleanliness and order, and trained in the
arts of sewing, knitting and cooking.[60]

Owen's philosophy of education was based upon the idea 'that character is universally formed *for* and not *by*, the individual'.[61] Provided
individuals were given the necessary instruction and guidance and
placed in surroundings favourable to their mental and moral improvement, it was possible for 'those who have influence in society' to
mould and fashion any character, 'from the savage to the sage'. With
the supreme confidence of a successful master manufacturer, he
believed that characters could be refined and adjusted in the manner
of a machine or factory organization.[62]

If ... due care as to the state of your inanimate machines can produce such beneficial results, what may not be expected if you devote equal attention as to your vital machines, who are far more wonderfully constructed?[63]

Inspired by the regimental monitorial system of schooling, devised by Joseph Lancaster and others, Owen's experiments with education were of particular interest to liberal social reformers and educationists.[64] However, as did Coleridge, Owen believed that a universal system of education required a greater commitment from the upper classes than the provision of elementary schooling. With a heavy emphasis on social control, its ultimate purpose was to improve the character and disposition of the lower orders. The children of the lower orders must learn 'the habits', explained Owen, 'of obedience, order, regularity, industry, and constant attention, which are to them of more importance than merely learning to read, write and account'.[65]

The Owenite view of education and of social reform in general required a highly structured and planned social environment. Owen looked to the government to establish a national system of education, to provide work for the unemployed and to regulate conditions in factories. He proposed a system of education that was to be funded and, more importantly, managed by the state. Indeed, it was remarkably prescient in that it called for the establishment of a new department of government responsible for maintaining national educational standards. Under the direction of 'those individuals who possess the highest integrity, abilities, and influence in the state', a department of education would oversee the appointment of schoolmasters and determine the best programme of instruction for the schools. The schoolmasters would receive their training at one of a number of seminaries to be established and funded by the state for the purpose of ensuring that the new schools provided the right sort of instruction and guidance.

Notwithstanding the contribution of Owen's proto-socialist ideas to the growth of centralized government, he did not vizualize a hierarchically structured paternal state. Fundamentally, his new view of society rested on a concept of community and, in opposition to the liberal principle of individual interest, he posited the principle of co-operation. Based on a holistic view of society, Owen believed in an 'inseparable connection ... between individual and general, between private and public good'.[66] To Bentham and other liberals, for whom a community was simply an aggregate of people, the notion of

community interest made no sense.[67] The political economists,
observed Owen,

> have assumed it as an incontrovertible position, that wealth is
> created of a superior kind and more abundantly, is more wisely
> distributed, better preserved for future consumption or reproduced
> and more advantageously used under the present System of sepa-
> rate and opposing interests, than it would be under one of mutual
> Aid and Co-operation, or of united interests. And although the
> reverse were the case, they have also supposed, that it is impossible
> to unite mankind to act cordially and beneficially for the general
> good; in short, that human beings could not be stimulated to exer-
> tion, except through the influence of individual, separate and
> opposing interests.[68]

Owen's theory of education and many of the reforms implemented at
New Lanark were geared to promoting unity, co-operation and mutual
respect. The interests of the community were placed above those of
the individual, whose self-fulfilment and happiness would come from
serving the community.[69]

None the less, Owen's philosophy of education and his faith in
environmental determinism did contain the belief that, ultimately,
individuals would attain independence of thought and action. The
final objective, he explained, was 'to make knowledge universal, and
thence to bring the right of private judgement into general practice'.[70]
But he evidently felt that society had a long way to go before that
objective would be realized. Referring to radical demands for political
reform, he questioned whether the 'advocates of that measure, well-
intentioned and patriotic as many of them are', had

> shown one good practical effect to be derived from it in the present
> state of ignorance in which the mass of the British population is
> now allowed to be trained? On the contrary, can any rational being
> attentively observe the scenes exhibited during every general elec-
> tion, and wish for those scenes to be extended? That, indeed, would
> be to wish anything but a reform of the manners, habits and prin-
> ciples of our abused and deluded fellow subjects.[71]

Owen's communities of co-operation were not intended to threaten
the existing social order. On the contrary, a more equitably organized
society would be a more stable one. Poor men would be content with

their station in life and would cease to be jealous of the 'supposed privileges' of the higher classes. Once the working classes understood their real interests, they would 'have no desire for any of the fancied advantages now possessed by the higher classes'.[72]

IV

On a tour of New Lanark, William Cobbett was struck by the artificial nature of the community. He accepted that Owen possessed a sincere and benevolent regard for the welfare of his workers, but 'was not the less convinced'

> that it was a melancholy thing to behold; that it was the reverse of domestic life, that it reversed the order of nature, that it made minds a fiction; and, which was among the greatest of evils, it fashioned the rising generation to habits of implicit submission.[73]

Somewhat enigmatic, but indicative of the interplay between change and continuity in the 1820s, Cobbett's paternal social outlook combined radicalism with conservatism. For the ideal society, he looked to the eighteenth-century and the existence of a predominantly rural, community-based, hierarchical and integrated social structure; a society where obedience, duties, obligations and reciprocal relations were paramount. This traditional aspect of Cobbett's thinking is viewed by some historians as backward-looking; his opposition to progress is considered to be one of the fundamental weaknesses of his radicalism.[74] Yet, Cobbett was not so reactionary as to oppose all advances in technology. In an address to the Luddites, he argued that machines were 'not naturally and necessarily an evil'. They were 'the product of the *mind* of man; and, their existence distinguishes the civilized man from the savage'. He also dismissed proposals for restoring labour-intensive practices and make-work schemes for the poor as absurd. If the answer to unemployment lay in grinding corn by hand or threshing with a flail, then one might just as well, he exclaimed, 'resort to Robinson Crusoe's *pestle and mortar*'.[75]

In similar fashion to the Romantics, Cobbett viewed unrestrained progress in terms of its effect on the labouring classes. He could not reconcile talk of vast improvements and prosperity with evidence of rising poor rates and increasing distress.[76] When trade was depressed or crops failed labourers were expected to carry the burden. They either had to accept a drop in wages or their jobs were taken from them. It seemed as if those who had reaped the rewards of these 'industrious and ever-toiling creatures', never made any sacrifices.[77] To Cobbett, labourers were the victims of circumstances and should not be blamed if they were unable to procure work or adequately maintain themselves. 'It is nonsense', he declared, 'to rail against the poor for being paupers. The fault is not theirs. It is the system that has degraded them'.[78] If there was no work available, how could they help it? They did not have 'the management of the affairs of the nation'.[79]

Cobbett wanted the labouring classes to be treated fairly, with respect and kindness. This did not mean that he desired equality: there 'must be different ranks and degrees in every civil society'. It was 'necessary', he reasoned, 'to the very existence of a people, that nine out of ten should live wholly by the sweat of their brow'.[80] With Burke, he believed that social and economic inequality was part of the natural, divine, order of things, for God sees

> with *equal eye* the rich and the poor; but he interferes not *to make them equal*. That is a plain case or you would be as rich as your Master ... God views rich and poor with an equal eye: that is to say, he gives *reason* and *bodily faculties* to both; and it is for both to make use of these for the maintenance or the acquirements of their rights. God acts by 'general, and not by partial laws'.[81]

In conjunction with fair treatment, he was persistent in asserting the rights of the common people. Above all, he defended their right to an adequate reward for their labour. In defence of that right, he maintained that, first, labour was the source of national wealth and, second, land was originally *'one man's as much as another's'*.[82] Again, he was not suggesting that wealth or land should be apportioned equally among all members of the community. But, since labourers had assisted in the creation of wealth and in making land productive, they were entitled to a reasonable share, and that share was guaranteed in part by the system of poor relief. Cobbett's claim that the poor not only had a right to relief but that land ownership was contingent upon that right rested upon a contractarian view of the origins of civilized society.[83] In an address to the stocking weavers, 'You must have assistance', he declared,

> ... and whence are you to have it, but from *the land*, that out of which all arises, that which is held by individuals upon the *condition*, that they provide for the indigent and helpless. You are to live:

you are not to be starved: you have a *right* to food and raiment if helpless, or if, by due labour, you cannot obtain it. This is the condition upon which land is held; and, if the Landlords, they who have and who always must have, the powers of Government in their hands, wish that the demands of the poor should be *light*, it is for them to take care not to suffer the poor to be so burdened with taxes as to compel them, when able and willing to work, to come for relief.[84]

Like most early nineteenth-century paternalists, Cobbett's social criticism hinged on the idea of a balance and harmony of interests. The government's chief priority was 'to take care, that one part of the people do not cause the other part to lead miserable lives'.[85] It was said to be an age of prosperity, yet a large proportion of the labouring classes did not enjoy its benefits. Indeed, society seemed to be in a worse condition than it had been in his youth, when the 'whole of the people' of 'this once happy nation' had decent clothing and an abundance of good food.[86]

It was not the advent of new technology, but the accompanying change in people's values and attitudes which accounted for much of Cobbett's ambivalence towards the new society. With the Romantics, he felt that there was no longer a 'community of feeling, between the farmer and the labourer'. In a well-managed estate the landowner exercised a humane and paternal regard for his labourers who, in turn, were content, obedient and respectful.[87] The principle underlying Cobbett's idealized, golden age view of pre-industrial society was economic and social interdependence:

Each considerable farmer used to have one head carter, and one under carter at the least, a couple of threshers, a shepherd, a cowboy, a couple of young women, and a girl or two, *all in the house*; and all *sitting at the same table with the master and the dame*. These took the head of the table, had the first cut, perhaps; but all sat at the same board. Here was a group of young people bred up under the eye and in the company of those who were so well able to teach them their various duties, and whose *interest* it was to see them perform those duties with regularity, and in the very best manner, and whose *example* must necessarily be powerful. Here was *education*. Here was early rising, industry, good hours, sobriety, decency of language, cleanliness of person, due obedience, all taught, and that, too, by competent teachers, who had a deep interest in the success of their teaching. This was *England:* this was an English farm-house ... From this arose the finest race of people that the world ever saw. To this the nation owed its excellent habits. All was in order here. Every one was in his place. These were the breeding places of sober and able workmen.[88]

The relationship between masters and their servants was both a social and an economic one. With the advent of the new breed of entrepreneurial farmers, the 'farming aristocracy', labour had become a commodity.[89] The extent to which the economic dimension of the master/servant relationship had assumed pre-eminence, was to Cobbett evident in the rise of 'newfangled jargon', the use of appellatives like 'employer' and 'operative'. 'When *master* and *man* were the terms, every one was in his place; and all were *free*. Now, in fact, it is an affair of *masters* and *slaves*.'[90] In an analysis of Cobbett's life and works, Ian Dyck uses statements like this (and one can find many examples) to support his argument that 'Cobbett was edging from a vertical to a horizontal perspective of rural society; in other words exchanging his countryman consciousness for class consciousness'. In the postwar years, claims Dyck, he 'came to recognize that all relations in English rural society were class relations'.[91] Dyck's Cobbett is a thorough-going radical, divested of all romantic Tory ideals and nostalgia for the past.[92] By forcing Cobbett's ideas into a framework of class consciousness, Dyck seems to obscure much more than he reveals. When Cobbett referred to masters and slaves he was, as Dyck suggests, making a distinction between horizontal and vertical relations, but he made such distinctions because he wanted to restore vertically integrated social and economic relations.[93] Social and economic interdependence was the hallmark of Cobbett's thinking. To Karl Schweizer and John Osborne he was a 'deep-dyed reactionary', but they come much closer to the mark than Dyck in claiming that Cobbett 'would allow no separate working class: all true Englishmen were of one country'.[94]

In *Cottage Economy*, Cobbett wrote of how he despised the 'man that is poor and contented; for such content is a certain proof of a base disposition, a disposition which is the enemy of all industry, all exertion, all love of independence'. With the aim of raising expectations and improving the quality of the lives of the labouring poor, *Cottage Economy* provided guidelines for efficient domestic management. But Cobbett's ideas about self-help fell well short of encouraging labourers to take matters into their own hands by organizing friendly societies or savings banks. He did not see labourers' interests as class-based or independent of the community at large.[95] By 'independence' he meant that labourers should be independent of parish relief, not of their masters:

> After all the talk about independence, we must still be dependant upon one another. You do not call the labourers of your parishes; you do not actually call them members of your family: but, in fact, from the very nature of things, the connexion between you is little less strict than if they were related to you by the ties of kindred.[96]

When referring to the discontent prevailing among stocking weavers in the early 1820s, Cobbett spoke of the '*unnatural* strife between masters and men'. Although scathing criticism of greedy farmers or indolent masters frequently accompanied such observations, he was not above appealing to labourers and journeymen not to blame their 'poor devils of masters' if they were unable to pay adequate wages.[97] In an address to journeymen and labourers, Cobbett defended employers and cautioned labourers against taking any rash action, action that could prove detrimental both to their and their employers' interests. 'When journeymen find their wages reduced, they should take time *to reflect on the real cause*', he explained, 'before they fly upon their employers, who are, in many cases, in as great, or greater, distress than themselves.'[98]

Where Cobbett's familial and patriarchal-based paternalism seemed to diverge from the ideas of people like Southey and Coleridge, was in his view of government intervention and the role of the state. Abdication of hierarchical responsibility was a key theme of his writings and many editions of the *Political Register* were openly critical of government policy. But it was the abdication of the governing classes rather than of the government itself that troubled Cobbett. Indeed, he was extremely wary of government intervention and, like many of the political economists, usually regarded it as unwarranted interference. 'The proof of the existence of distress is by no means', he declared, 'sufficient to warrant any legislative measures for the removal of that distress, even supposing such measures to be within the power of the legislature.'[99] Toward the end of his life, he wrote of a government that had become increasingly more intrusive. 'I liked not the never-ending recurrence to Acts of Parliament. Something must be left and something ought to be left, to the sense and reason and morality and religion of the people.'[100] This suggests that Cobbett would have regarded the notion of a paternal state as abhorrent. However, taking into account his belief in the need for government to ensure a balance of interests, his views on this subject appear somewhat ambiguous.

Cobbett wanted to restore patriarchal and self-sufficient communities. He was opposed to anyone – tax-eaters, cotton lords, stock-jobbers, Methodists, Jews, entrepreneurial farmers – who undermined the social structure. The factory system, with its monopolization of wealth and assemblage of large numbers of working people under one roof, was 'a most unnatural state of things'.[101] Ideally, manufacturing should be spread throughout the country and integrated with farming. Women should be engaged in domestic industry and men in agriculture. In an article addressed to landowners 'On the evils of collecting Manufacturers into great masses', Cobbett entreated them to restore 'the blessings of domestic manufacturing' to their estates. 'What is to prevent you from causing the spinning-wheel and the knitting-needle to come back again, and to enable me, once more in my lifetime, to get a pair of worsted stockings that will not be out at the toes at the end of the first week?' Conversely, he had little faith in parliament's ability to effect any lasting improvement in the condition of the labouring classes. 'We have paid for the printing of hundreds and thousands of volumes of Reports upon this subject, the whole of which have had not the smallest effect.'[102]

V

The main impetus for the revival of paternal social thought in the 1820s was the popularization of the liberal *laissez-faire* philosophy. In 1820, James Mill began writing *Elements of Political Economy*, a simplified account of David Ricardo's economic theories. His aim was 'to compose a school-book of Political Economy'.[103] Having extraordinary faith in his friend's philosophy, Mill was determined to ensure that society would benefit not only from the publication of Ricardo's ideas but from his active participation in political debate. 'When I am satisfied', he declared,

> that you can very greatly improve a science on which the progress of human happiness to a singular degree depends; in fact that you can improve so important a science far more than any other man who is devoting his attention to it, or likely to do so, for Lord knows how many years – my friendship for you, for mankind, and

for science, all prompt me to give you no rest till you are plunged over head and ears in political economy.[104]

Mill offered to edit and organize Ricardo's writing and, after much cajoling and prodding, eventually succeeded in persuading him to enter parliament as the spokesman for political economy.[105] Ricardo was MP for Portarlington, Ireland, from 1819 until his death in 1823. Throughout his short parliamentary career, he was regarded as the authority on economic doctrine and was accordingly treated with great respect, even among high-ranking parliamentarians with well-established political credentials. In a study of political economy in this period, Barry Gordon maintains that this was because

> Ricardian theory offered aristocrats and professionals a rational basis for a voice in economic policy making. It equipped them with a set of general principles which they could use to compete, for influence in that area of government, with the partial analysis that constituted the wisdom of most men of business. Hence Ricardianism was a tool welcomed by some of those unfamiliar with the ways of economic enterprise and the inner life of the structures of commerce and industry.[106]

Together with Mill and, indeed, most of his closest allies, these parliamentarians treated Ricardo's interpretation of classical economic theory as indisputable. Ricardo and 'his disciples', writes Gordon, 'had started a secular version of an intellectual holy war to reform the conduct of public policy in the light of the truths of their recently formulated creed.'[107] Founded in 1821, the Political Economy Club was set up in order to propagate this '*accepted* doctrine'. Drafted by Mill, its rules stipulated: 'It shall be the duty of the Society to study the means of obtaining access to the public mind through as many as possible of the periodical publications of the day and to influence as far as possible the tone of such publications in favour of just principles of Political Economy.'[108] The extent to which free trade principles and the 'science' of political economy had become articles of faith was perhaps nowhere more explicit than in Nassau Senior's lectures on economics, delivered to students at Oxford University in 1826. 'I hope in the course of these Lectures', he announced,

> to prove the truth of my statement, that the theoretic branch of the science, that which treats of the nature, production and distribu-

tion of wealth, – is capable of all the certainty that can belong to any science, not founded exclusively on definitions; and I hope, also, to show that many conclusions and those of the highest importance, in the practical branch, rest so immediately on the conclusions of the theoretic branch as to possess equal certainty and universality.[109]

Senior was as keen as Mill to propagate the free trade gospel.[110]

In May 1817, *Blackwood's Edinburgh Magazine*, founded earlier that year, published an extremely favourable review of Ricardo's *On Principles of Political Economy and Taxation*. A 'more than ordinary interest must be excited by the appearance' of this work, observed the reviewer,

in which this able economist has explained his opinions respecting some of the *fundamental* doctrines of the science, and in which, as it appears to us, he has established some highly important principles, and rectified many prevailing errors.[111]

Within a year *Blackwood's* had completely renounced Ricardianism.[112] The article in which this renunciation appeared was characteristic of the journal's high Tory paternalist sentiments, which became noticeably more pronounced as Ricardian political economy gained in popularity. The correspondent was alarmed by the *Edinburgh Review's* inference, drawn from Ricardian principles, 'that the interests of the landlord were always opposed to that of every other class of the community'.[113] Stressing the importance of hierarchical responsibility and interdependent social relations, *Blackwood's* observed in reply that

the wealthy man has many wants, and none of them can be satisfied without the assistance of the poor. Even when the poor cease, from age and infirmity, to be able to contribute to the other enjoyments of the rich, there is still one remaining to which they can contribute, the indulgence of a benevolent disposition.[114]

What the *Blackwood's* reviewers found particularly disagreeable, indeed ominous, was Ricardo's theory of wages and profits; according to which, a rise in wages invariably led to a diminution of profits and a diminution of wages to a rise in profits. This doctrine was not, from a Tory-paternalist perspective, conducive to social stability and harmony:

If this theory to its full extent be maintainable, a theory which teaches, that by the nature of human society, there is a constant and irremediable contrariety of interests between its different members, and that a general amelioration, in which all should participate alike, is impossible, we could only regret that such an obstacle to national harmony should exist, and that men should be constrained to repine at the good fortune of one another.[115]

The *Blackwood's* circle was concerned about the influence of the *laissez-faire* doctrine on William Huskisson and his liberal-Tory colleagues. The popularization of Ricardian economics coincided with the government's programme of trade liberalization. This involved the lifting or easing of import and other restrictions across a range of manufactured goods and raw products. Believing that Huskisson's system was largely responsible for the recessions of the mid- and late 1820s, *Blackwood's* became a staunch defender of paternal, protectionist policies.[116] One of the journal's most trenchant critics of liberal-Toryism, David Robinson, thought that it was 'the most monstrous of all monstrous things, to suppose that the trade and industry of this country could thrive without laws for their regulation and protection'.[117]

The social implications of the free trade doctrine was a predominant theme in Robinson's numerous articles criticizing government policy. In 1825, he strongly defended the combination laws, arguing that they reinforced hierarchical authority and the social order. The fact that the proposal for their repeal had been initiated by Joseph Hume, one of the most outspoken proponents of *laissez-faire* principles, was, for Robinson, indicative of the political economists' command of economic and social debate in parliament. From a tyranny-of-the-majority perspective, he insisted that the repeal of the combination laws had inverted the master/servant relationship. With 'combiners' able to dictate terms and conditions of pay, it 'was now for the servant to command, and the master to obey'. As a consequence of this, declared Robinson, the 'old feelings of reciprocal good-will and regard for each other's interests, are destroyed, and replaced by strife and animosity'. As did Cobbett, he saw the diminution of patriarchal authority and erosion of interdependent social and economic relations manifested in the substitution of 'employer' and 'the working classes' for 'the good old English words – servant and master'.[118]

It was concern about the lower orders acquiring too much independence of thought and the growing disunity between the different orders in society that underpinned Robinson's criticism of liberal education schemes advocated by Henry Brougham and the *Edinburgh Review*.[119] Robinson believed that the training and guidance which labourers received from their masters was important in cementing social ties and in maintaining harmonious relations. In line with Coleridge, he believed that education for the working class should be confined to improving, first, morals and, second, professional and practical skills. Thus, it was

> essential for the good of the labourer, as well as for the good of the state, that he should be under the authority of his master in respect of general conduct as well as labour; that his master should instruct him in what constitutes a good member of society, as well as in the mysteries of his calling; and that his master should coerce his bad morals, as well as his idleness and bad workmanship.[120]

Robinson was suspicious of the liberal reformers' motives. He shared Coleridge's anxiety about 'shallow visionaries' and 'petty demagogues' inculcating the labouring classes with ideas that, 'dissolve the bonds between the poor and the rich, create insubordination, and ferment those animosities which unfortunately prevail so much already between servants and masters'.[121]

In attacking the new economy, the *Blackwood's* journalists set out to expose what was, from their perspective, a mechanistic, self-interested and cold-blooded doctrine. Toward the end of the 1820s and with the onset of recession, they became increasingly concerned about widespread unemployment among the lower orders and the general deterioration in the quality of labouring people's lives. They repeatedly urged the ministry and parliament to adopt measures that would alleviate distress and protect the interests of the poor against the avarice of the rich. As well as demonstrating that free trade policies were directly to blame for the downturn in manufacturing, *Blackwood's* wanted to make its readership aware of the insidiousness of the *laissez-faire*, competitive ethos. Under its influence, the upper and middle classes were said to be increasingly intolerant and insensitive towards the lower orders. In responding to this change in temperament, the *Blackwood's* journalists became more self-consciously paternalistic. In an articulation of 'true Tory principles', William Johnstone outlined their central maxim:

> As Tories, we maintain that it is the duty of the people to pay obedience to those set in authority over them: but it is also the duty of

those in authority to protect the people who are placed below them. They are not to sit in stately grandeur, and see the people perish, nor, indeed, are they ever to forget that they hold their power and their possessions upon the understanding that they administer both more for the good of the people at large, than the people would do, if they had the administration of both themselves.[122]

Undoubtedly, the political implications, the need to maintain social harmony and stability, rated high among the paternalists' concerns about the governing classes' neglect of the poor. At the same time, they clearly felt that working people, from both a legal and moral standpoint, were entitled to a decent living.

Primarily, Johnstone was concerned about the inequitable distribution of wealth and the widening gap between the rich and the poor. At a time when a great many working people were unemployed and suffering from extreme privation, the upper classes seemed to be enjoying a period of unparalleled prosperity. He was particularly critical of landlords who neglected their social responsibilities. Admonishing them for their extravagant and self-indulgent displays of wealth and grandeur, he suggested that the money spent on one night's lavish entertainment would be sufficient to provide a small plot of land and a cow for some of the needy poor in their districts. The growing disparity between the rich and the poor was a product, he believed, of the free trade system, which increased national wealth but not general prosperity. Under the new system, explained Johnstone, capital, 'instead of being generally diffused amongst the people', had tended 'to accumulate in large masses'. The small farmer and the domestic manufacturer had been 'swept away' by the advances in technology and the substitution of machine for manual labour.[123]

Where, then, is the improvement? Of what advantage *to us* these prodigious means of extending our manufactures without the aid of men, when so many of our own population are thereby left to idleness and starvation?[124]

For Johnstone, therefore, the separation of interests was the fundamental issue. The 'great machinery of society', he observed, operated 'smoothly hitherto, only in consequence of a connexion of its parts'. To those who accused him of advocating 'dangerous and levelling principles', he replied that the right of the people to a subsistence was in conformity with the spirit of the constitution.[125] The duty and 'business of Parliament is to consider *how*', he stressed, 'the resources of the country may best be made available for the people's support'.[126] He was optimistic, given the country's potential and vast untapped resources, that the unemployment problem could be easily alleviated. Johnstone's suggestions for dealing with it were typical of someone who was closely identified with the landed interest. He thought that the legislature ought seriously to consider projects for the reclamation and cultivation of waste land, and the establishment of 'horticultural villages' into which 'the poor may be drafted, and where, under due regulation, they may be made to dwell very much happier than they have hitherto been'. The crucial thing was for parliament and the government to demonstrate a willingness to help the labouring poor. For 'the people know very well that the means are within the country to make them all comfortable' and, unless they were given some reassurance that the government was concerned about their welfare and prepared to protect their interests, they would not submit to its authority.[127]

The *Blackwood's* circle regarded the poor as victims of the political economists' system. Because of the fluctuation in the demand for manufactured products and the seasonal nature of agricultural work, labourers frequently found themselves 'deprived, from no fault of their own', explained Robinson, 'of employment'.[128] In addition to the loss of work arising from the implementation of free trade policies, many labourers had been forced to accept considerable reductions in their earnings. Even though they might work as many as 16 hours a day, they could not support their families without parish assistance.[129] In highlighting the inequitable treatment of labourers, the Tory paternalists emphasized that this practice of paying labourers starvation wages was in conformity with the teachings of the political economists. The fact is, wrote Edward Edwards, 'the self-styled Economists of England regard the poor merely as animals to be driven to death; their aim is to get out of the poor the largest possible quantity of labour for the most scanty remuneration upon which they can be made to subsist'.[130] This had been the experience of workers in the recently liberalized silk industry. Exposed to foreign competition, domestic silk manufacturers had been forced to reduce their prices. This had operated in favour of the wealthy, who were the principal consumers of silk goods, but at the expense of labourers, whose wages had been reduced to starvation levels.[131] Under the old system of restrictive laws, explained Edwards, both the property of the rich and the wages of the poor were protected:

> These laws gave to every man a full scope for the exertion of his skill, or the application of his property to any pursuit or occupation which held out to him the promise of the greatest return of profit; exacting from him in return no condition, except that he should consent to share his advantages with his fellow-citizens. These laws secured profitable employment to the poor, and restrained the rich from seeking enjoyments to be derived from foreign sources, when these could have been supplied at home.

'They administered to the wants of the needy', added Edwards, 'rather than to the craving desires of the affluent.' Together with the Poor Laws, the old paternal, protectionist policies had served to reinforce the state's social role, which was to protect and to nurture. Under that system, 'so long as one human being could be found destitute of the means of providing for his own subsistence, the state, like an affectionate parent, watched over and protected the beginnings of his humble industry'.[132]

It was wrong, argued Robinson, for economists to assume that displaced labourers could easily transfer their skills to other avenues of employment. Generally speaking, the labourer 'knows only his own calling, and he must therefore follow it', and without the means to pay for alternative training for his children, they were destined to pursue the same occupation, irrespective of its prospects or monetary reward.[133] In opposition to the Ricardian theory of wages and profits, he posited the proto-Keynesian idea that consumption directly depended on incomes; that wages, in other words, affected profits and that the two rose or fell simultaneously. In order for labourers to purchase the products of agriculture, and more particularly of manufacture, they needed a surplus income. It was thus essential for the health of the economy and for general prosperity that labourers be rewarded with more than subsistence wages.[134] 'The rise of wages', he explained, 'will make these classes consume better goods, and this alone will raise the manufacturer's rate of profit.'[135] These arguments appeared in a series of articles, published between September 1829 and January 1830, in which Robinson styled himself 'One of the Old School' and strongly defended protectionist policy against the new *laissez-faire* doctrine. Objecting to the status which had been accorded the teachings of political economy at Oxford and other leading educational establishments in England and Scotland, Robinson addressed his articles to 'the heads of the University of Oxford'.[136] He was appalled that a system, founded upon erroneous principles, which 'wars against all the best feelings and possessions of human nature', was being taught to the 'rising statesmen' of the country:

> In obedience to it, the Ministry and Legislature have in late years displayed such flinty indifference to public misery, and such savage cruelty in the production of it, as were never before witnessed in any civilized nation.[137]

In this climate of antagonism between *laissez-faire* and protectionism, between liberalism and paternalism, the *Blackwood's* journalists greeted Sadler's rise to prominence in parliament with considerable enthusiasm. In addition to being an able advocate of the paternalist, protectionist creed, he effectively challenged the *laissez-faire* doctrine and was instrumental in keeping social issues to the forefront of political debate. Hierarchical responsibility and the need for balance and harmony between competing interests were fundamental to *Blackwood's* argument for a more active social role for the state, which became more pronounced towards the end of the 1820s when Sadler first entered parliament. These ideas, particularly the emphasis on the state's social role, were pivotal to Sadler's contribution to social and economic debate and subsequently to the development of social policy. From the outset of his career, the *Blackwood's* writers recognized that Sadler's sense of political and civic duty was in keeping with their idea of disinterested representation. He combined a genuine humanitarian concern for the poor with a commitment to protectionist policies. Disappointed by the direction which liberal-Toryism had taken in recent years, *Blackwood's* hoped that Sadler would lead the way and succeed in convincing his colleagues that for stability to be maintained government must revise its economic and social policy and pay more attention to the interests of the lower orders.

2
Sadler's Protectionist, Paternalist Social System and the Foundation of his Social Agenda

> [Mr. Sadler's] system cannot, it appears to us, be better described than as the *Paternal or Productive*: its leading characteristics being, to foster, protect, cherish, encourage, promote: its chief means of operation, the presenting to human beings the motives of benevolence and *hope*.
>
> Robert Benton Seeley, 1842[1]

Before examining Sadler's paternalist philosophy, a brief sketch of the influences which shaped his social and political outlook during his formative years will help explain why a linen merchant of Leeds should champion not the ideals of the entrepreneurial class but those of the aristocratic and leisured classes. Although Sadler spent most of his adult life in Leeds, he grew up in a small village and farming community in Derbyshire. His father, James, owned a small estate in the neighbouring villages of Snelston and Doveridge; his mother, Frances, was granddaughter of Henry Wrigley of Langley Hall, near Middleton in Lancashire. This estate was entailed upon her and her three sons, Joseph, Benjamin and Michael, who was the youngest. Sadler was born at Doveridge in 1780. From the age of six, he was placed under the tutelage of a local schoolmaster, named Harrison. Sadler acquired competency in Latin and Greek and the rudiments of French, Italian and German. He also developed an interest in history, science and mathematics. When Sadler turned 12, the family intended sending him to a public school but Harrison persuaded his father not to send the boy away. He remained with Harrison until he was 14 or 15 and had exhausted his tutor's fund of knowledge. After that, he was more or less left to his own devices. He spent many hours in the family library, becoming well acquainted with many of the leading works of literature and philosophy.[2] His writing and speeches are replete with references to classical authors, including Bacon, Hobbes, Locke, Paley, Montesquieu and Sir Thomas More. 'Leisure, and such a course of reading', wrote Seeley somewhat disapprovingly,

> soon produced one very common result, in a mind of an imaginative and enthusiastic order. He began to indulge in a poetic vein to a considerable extent.

Extant are two unfinished manuscripts, entitled 'Parts of Alfred' and 'Darius's Feast', which display a penchant for the heroic epic poem made fashionable by Scott and the Romantics. Sadler also enjoyed recomposing the Psalms and a sample of his shorter pieces is reproduced in Seeley's biography, together with a sentimental ballad entitled 'The Factory Girl's Last Day'.[3] Sadler did not, however, possess much artistic talent. His inclusion of a number of unknown and unsourced stanzas of poetry in his works on Ireland and population drew considerable derision from Lord Macaulay, who suspected, probably rightly, that they had come from Sadler's own pen.[4] Seeley was evidently pleased that 'Alfred' remained in its unfinished state and that the author's feelings of dissatisfaction with it drove him from such idle pursuits 'to labours of far higher value and more enduring utility'.[5]

Sadler's first political tract was 'An Apology for the Methodists', published in 1797. This was addressed to the vicar of Doveridge, Rev. Henry Stokes, who had sought to discredit Sadler and his family for their involvement with the Methodists. The family's conflict with Stokes, who tried to prevent publication of Sadler's broadside, is mentioned in Mary Howitt's autobiography.[6] The Methodists 'had first appeared in the neighbourhood [of Uttoxeter] in our grandfather's day', wrote Howitt,

> and this through a respectable family of the name of Sadler, dwelling at the old Hall in the near-lying village of Doveridge. These Sadlers were most earnest in the new faith; and a son named Michael Thomas, not then twenty, a youth of great eloquence and talent, preached sermons, and was stoned for it. Sir Richard Cavendish and the clergyman of Doveridge countenanced their farm-servants and some rough fellows pelted both the boy-preacher and his listeners. Michael Thomas Sadler wrote a stinging pamphlet that was widely circulated. It shamed his persecutors, and almost, I think, wrung an apology from them.[7]

Clearly, Sadler's family encouraged tolerance and open-mindedness, even if it meant alienating fellow church-goers and earning the opprobrium of the local minister. The Sadlers' active encouragement of the Methodists did not, however, lead to formal withdrawal from the Anglican church; rather, it was indicative of the earnestness of their faith.[8] The family joined with those devout and zealous members of the Anglican church who had welcomed the Methodists' influence in regenerating its spiritual and moral energy. In his broadside to Stokes, Sadler defended the movement's purpose as spiritual, not political:

> If by the Church, you mean the Church of England, I still deny that the Methodists endeavour to overthrow it; they only wish to reform its members, and surely any one must own the necessity of this and applaud the design.[9]

The turn of the century marked a watershed in Sadler's life. Its closing years were marred by the unexpected death, first of his mother and then of his father. On the death of his wife, James Sadler decided that it was time for his youngest son to learn more about the world beyond Doveridge. Sadler left home to join Benjamin in Leeds and, under his guidance, soon became acquainted with the world of trade and commerce. The two brothers operated a drapery business. In 1810, they entered into partnership with Fentons, an established Leeds firm and a major importer of Irish linen.[10] Sadler later married the Fentons' eldest daughter, Ann. In time, both Michael and Benjamin were to become not only respected businessmen but prominent public figures in Leeds. In her biography of Charlotte Brontë, Elizabeth Gaskell described a game played by Charlotte and her sisters, on a cold December evening in 1827. Each of the girls chose an island and then listed the men whom they would want as leaders of their respective domains. Anne's first choice was Michael Sadler.[11]

Notwithstanding Sadler's aptitude for figures, it was his brother who was the more proficient businessman. Sadler did not have the temperament for business; he was too easily distracted by literary interests, especially poetry in which, frequently, he became 'so absorbed ... as to forget all other affairs for days and even weeks together'. This romantic sensitivity, coupled with notions of civic and religious duty, carried Sadler into more high-minded and socially conscious endeavours than business had to offer. Soon after settling in Leeds, he became an active member of the Strangers' Friend Society. He also joined the Leeds' board of management for poor relief and, for several years, served as its treasurer. As well as the physical state of the poor, he was concerned about their moral and religious well-being and to that end became superintendent of one of the Sunday schools in Leeds. Through these philanthropic and religious activities Sadler learned a great deal about the life of the urban poor of Leeds. Later, as a parliamentarian, he was able to speak with the authority and confidence of someone who had seen for himself the human and social cost of economic distress.

One of the earliest records of Sadler's political activities in Leeds is of his involvement with the anti-slavery movement and William Wilberforce, whom he assisted in the contest for Yorkshire in 1807.[12] Sadler remained interested in the slavery issue, but in parliament concentrated upon domestic issues.[13] Highly suspicious of liberal economic principles, both he and Benjamin were closely allied to the Tory interest in Leeds. The Leeds Corporation, the governing body of the city, was a Tory stronghold.[14] Benjamin joined the Corporation in 1817 and Michael in 1820; later, in the 1830s, Benjamin was appointed mayor of the city.[15] The brothers were also prominent members of the Leeds Pitt Club.[16] At its anniversary meeting in 1813, Sadler spoke against Catholic emancipation. Widely publicized in the Yorkshire press, this speech secured his reputation as a defender of high-Tory principles and served as a stepping-stone for his parliamentary career. He was also a regular contributor to the city's principal Tory newspaper, *The Leeds Intelligencer*.[17]

A Tory sense of duty and concern for the stability and safety of the nation prompted Sadler to join the Leeds Volunteers. This was one of the many citizen militia groups organized to preserve domestic peace following the 'Peterloo' débâcle. In Leeds, as elsewhere, the period 1816–20 was a time of 'extraordinary privation'.[18] The political reform movement was very active in Leeds and several meetings of between 300 and 500 people took place during October and November 1819. Although peaceful, the *Intelligencer* viewed these gatherings with much foreboding; and its concerns were shared by many of the leading members of the Leeds community, including the Sadler brothers. In early January 1820, a 'very numerous and respectable meeting' was convened at the court house to consider organizing a citizen militia for Leeds. Training commenced in May, and in October the new regiment appeared in public for the first time, and marched in military finery through streets crammed with enthusiastic spectators. The regiment boasted five companies and Sadler, who appeared with his brother at the top of the list of volunteers for the organization, was a captain of the 2nd battalion. The military ethos and aristocratic spirit of the Volunteers accorded well with Sadler's high-Tory perspective.[19]

Of course, this enthusiasm for the Volunteers was not unanimous and, given the events – the public rallies – which led to the formation of the militia, it comes as no surprise to find that support for the organization divided on class and party lines. The *Intelligencer* was strongly supportive and reported the Volunteers' progress and activities in glowing term. The Pitt Club was also full of encouragement. At its anniversary meeting in 1820 numerous toasts were proposed in honour of 'the worthy citizens who have so nobly stood forward in support of the Civil Power'.[20] For the *Leeds Mercury*, on the other hand, 'the idea of raising soldiers, not to encounter a foreign enemy, but to war against their own countrymen, was abhorrent to every Liberal mind'.[21] Understandably, among the working-class communities of Leeds, the Volunteers met with considerable hostility and resentment. On several occasions members of the militia were ambushed on their way home from drill practice. On Coronation Day a group of Volunteers was accosted by a mob of between 200 and 500 people. Ultimately the Volunteers 'preserved the peace of Leeds by discreetly keeping out of the way', suggests Emily Hargrave, author of a short history of the Leeds Volunteers. For several years, the Pitt Club continued to toast the Volunteers at its annual meetings but 'Leeds remained tranquil' and their services were never required.[22]

An important forum for the development of Sadler's political ideas and his public speaking skills, was the Leeds Philosophical and Literary Society, which was set up in 1818, after the *Mercury* published a series of anonymous letters (reputedly written by the proprietor's son, Edward Baines Jr) outlining the benefits of such an organization for the 'promotion of intellectual and literary improvement'.[23] The idea was well received by the city's intellectual community and within two months a society had been established. Its founder members envisaged an organization that would occupy a prestigious place in the Leeds community.[24] The Society's membership consisted of a cross-section of Whig, Tory, manufacturing, commercial and professional interests. At the inaugural meeting, the members agreed to steer clear of topics that were too controversial or emotive, and banned discussion of religion, politics and ethics.[25] In most cases, the papers presented to the society were of a scientific, historical, literary or philosophical nature; however, the 'no politics' rule was sometimes broken. Edward Baines' paper on 'The Moral Influence of Free Trade' was heavily biased in favour of liberal principles.[26] Practically all of Sadler's contributions were politically motivated. It was during this period that he began to formulate a coherent social philosophy to counter the increasingly popular *laissez-faire* doctrine.[27] An emerging sense of purpose was evident in the topics he selected for discussion. The population issue, social improvement and the Poor Laws were among his principal themes. In 1824–5, he prepared discussion papers on 'The Principle of Population, considered in connection with the Poor Laws' and 'The Best Means of Improving the Conditions of the Poor in Large Towns'. In the same period, he gave a series of eight public lectures on the English Poor Laws. In 1827, he presented a dissertation on 'The Balance of the Numbers and Food of Animated Beings'. Couched in pseudo-scientific language, this was a thinly disguised critique of Malthus's thesis on population.[28] His last contribution, as President of the Society and newly elected Member for Newark, was entitled 'The Necessity for Exertion, as promoting the Progress of Civilisation'.[29] A clear pattern had begun to emerge in Sadler's writings and speeches. A combination of high-Tory beliefs and paternalist, protectionist ideals was the central unifying theme.

While Sadler's paternal social outlook grew more progressive, his position on constitutional questions, particularly Catholic emancipation, remained immutably high-Tory. The revival of the Catholic disabilities issue in Parliament in 1813 provoked a public outcry, and across the country defenders of the Protestant constitution organized anti-Catholic protest meetings. A rally held at Leeds' Parish Church in early February 1813 attracted some 2,000 people. Organized by the mayor, the 'object of this meeting was to petition parliament against the proposed concessions'. As one of the principal speakers, Sadler seconded the motion for the petition.[30] Between his public address on Catholic emancipation at Leeds in 1813 and his parliamentary maiden speech on the Catholic Relief Bill in 1829, a space of 16 years, there was no substantial alteration in his convictions.[31] While he did not seek to encourage intolerance by denying the individual's right to religious freedom, he was convinced that concessions to Catholics would endanger the authority of the state and upset the constitutional balance.[32] 'Does it need a proof', he observed in 1813, 'that it is calculated for the support of Arbitrary Power?'

> We should ... reject it, as a Principle that saps the very foundation of Political Morality by recognizing an Authority that can dispense with the most sacred duties and absolve the most solemn obliga-

tions: As being hostile to every other profession of the Christian faith, made up as it were of Intolerance and Exclusion. And, above all, as being dangerous to the interests of all Protestant Governments, by yielding allegiance to a power out of the Country, always at variance with its views, and often in open hostility to it.[33]

The dire consequences that Sadler anticipated Catholic relief would have for the church–state relationship and the threat it posed to social harmony and stability were in keeping with the standard Tory view of the issue.[34] His evident distaste for popish doctrines and what was generally regarded by critics of Catholicism as superstitious idolatry was also in keeping with popular Protestant feeling. Sadler's allusions to Protestant martyrdom, in particular, underline the difficulty which he, and indeed many Protestants of his generation, had in separating the emotional from the rational or political dimensions of the issue. 'The spirit of Popery', he urged in 1829,

> when dominant ... dragged the objects of its resentment to the stake; that spirit still survives; its advocates at this moment would willingly inflict on its conscientious opponents a martyrdom still more grievous to generous minds, in aiming at the moral and intellectual character and attainments of those whom they mark out as their victims.[35]

In 1813, he spoke of 'Spiritual Tyranny, of Priestly Domination, destroying the native freedom of the soul and freezing up its faculties – 'Tis dumb amaze and list'ning terror all! but the gloom of its dreadful superstition', continued Sadler,

> has been indeed awfully illuminated by the fires it kindled throughout this land, in which expiring martyrs, writhing in agony, slowly yielded their souls to God in torturing flames.... It is in vain our opponents assure us these days of persecution are for ever past.[36]

From this distance, it is difficult to appreciate fully the depth of Protestant feeling but, as Linda Colley demonstrates in her analysis of Protestantism in the eighteenth century, it was an irrational and to a great extent a nationalistic response that had been renewed, reinforced and reinvigorated over many generations.[37] John Foxe's *Book of Martyrs* (1563) had left an indelible impression on Protestants from all walks of life. Colley suggests that there was a strong correlation between the forging of a Protestant national identity in Britain and the century of prolonged conflict with France.[38] Sadler grew to manhood as the war raged against France. Indeed, it could be argued that war was the ever-present reality as his view of the world took shape.

II

Sadler's protectionist, paternalist social system was among the first systematic attempts to formulate, in the words of John Stuart Mill, a 'theory of dependence and protection'.[39] Sadler was by no means a sophisticated thinker and close scrutiny of his arguments reveals weaknesses and inconsistencies. Indeed, in his day, they were subjected to considerable criticism, particularly from the *Edinburgh Review*. None the less, through his persistent criticism of Malthusian, *laissez-faire* doctrine and vigorous defence of the interests of the labouring poor, Sadler's writings and political activities contributed to the development of paternal social thought in this period. His emphasis on the responsibilities of the state helped to provide the paternal ideal with a new coherence and clarity of purpose; because of his political associations it became more closely allied to high Tory doctrine. Together with Southey and Coleridge, Sadler advocated a more active social role for government. Referring to William Paley, who had claimed that 'the care of the poor ought to be the principal object of all laws', Sadler maintained that, in addition to ensuring security and reconciling competing interests, government should be concerned with economic, social and moral improvement; the protection of the labouring poor ought to be its first priority.[40] It was not until Sadler entered parliament, however, and began to consider practical solutions to the problems affecting the labouring classes, that the argument for governmental responsibility and the idea of a paternal state began to emerge as the central aspect of his thinking. Increasingly, he felt that parliament had lost sight of its moral and social obligations.[41]

The evolution of Sadler's thinking in relation to the state's social role is taken up in subsequent chapters which detail his parliamentary career. This chapter examines the fundamentals of his paternal system, outlined in *Ireland; its Evils and their Remedies* (1828, 1829) and *The Law of Population* (1830). Initially intended as an advertisement for his more comprehensive treatise on population, *Ireland; its Evils and their Remedies* was a response to the debate about the increasing instability, and growth of pauperism, in Ireland. It addressed the country's social and economic problems and argued the case for a compulsory, legislated system of relief, which Sadler believed was the only solution to Ireland's economic problems and vital to its ongoing stability and security. His main objective in publishing this work was to discourage parliament from accepting the recommendations of Sir R. J. Wilmot Horton's Committee on Emigration. This committee had proposed a government-sponsored system of emigration as the best means of dealing with Ireland's 'redundant population'. 'Fatal will it be for the patient', Sadler gravely proclaimed, 'should she be delivered over to these blind, but confident experimenters.'[42] Having called upon Thomas Malthus himself to give evidence, the committee had revealed a flagrant Malthusian bias in concluding that Ireland's distress was the result of 'a superfluous population ... increasing faster than the means of subsistence'.[43] This assertion was based on the assumption that the theory of population was axiomatic. Yet that theory, argued Sadler, was not only open to interpretation, but was also seriously flawed. We see in these two works, and in *Ireland; its Evils and their Remedies* in particular, the foundations of Sadler's paternal social agenda. He wanted, first, to rekindle a sense of responsibility and obligation among the upper classes and, second, by exposing the aridity of the Malthusian, *laissez-faire* doctrine, to impress on the governing classes the need for policies that reinforced reciprocal obligation and helped to cement the social order, combining social and moral with economic considerations.

Like most paternalists, it was concern about the impact of modern economic theories which prompted Sadler to become involved in public debate on these issues. He considered that the 'modern and fallacious principle of population' had serious implications for the question of social responsibility. The new 'science' had effectively stifled economic and social debate. More serious, however, was the fact that it had encouraged complacency and provided statesmen and the social élite with a ready excuse for neglecting the labouring poor.

> [I]t absolved in great measure, wealth and power from their deep and anxious responsibilities; excusing the sloth and negligence, if not even sanctioning the misrule of those whose elevated duty it is to mitigate or remove human miseries, by attributing those miseries to the laws of nature and of God.[44]

Indeed, as it appeared to him, the influence of the doctrine of *laissez-faire* had become so entrenched that any legislation designed to protect the labouring classes was considered to be fundamentally unsound. Referring to the widespread and uncritical acceptance of Ricardian economic theories, modern philosophers, he observed,

> embrace it on pain of forfeiting their title to their very name; peri- odical writers almost unanimously espouse it, and unceasingly spread its dogmas through every part of the earth; legislators seem on the very point of reducing the system into practice; and even many of the expounders of our religion, though they cannot pollute the well-head of revelation with its principle, yet are busily engaged in tingeing the stream with its pernicious admixture.[45]

Sadler shared with Coleridge and Southey concern about the social consequences of principles which taught 'human beings to view each other as rivals for an insufficient share in the bounties of nature'.[46] The old ideals of duty and obligation, essential for social stability and cohesion, were gradually being eroded. The callous and self-serving capitalists and industrialists were oblivious to such considerations. Commenting on the adverse effects of the growth of monopolies and the substitution of machines for manual labour, it is 'the purpose of the new school', wrote Sadler,

> to treat and regard men as animated machines, and indeed to supplant them by inanimate ones, were it possible; to pronounce them as worthless, or otherwise, just as it may please the capitalists (who in proportion as they are diminishing in number, are becom- ing more powerful) to employ them or not; instructing the latter at the same time that they are under no imaginable obligation but what selfishness dictates, to encourage the labour of those by whom themselves are supported.[47]

The inequitable distribution of wealth was a central theme in Sadler's writings. In parliament, he frequently urged members not to speak of *national* prosperity when the mass of the people were experiencing considerable hardship and deprivation. Moreover, the 'prosperous condition of some districts, or the thriving trade carried on by certain overgrown capitalists engaged in manufactures', was no proof, he believed, of the country's general prosperity.[48]

Fundamental to Sadler's argument for compulsory relief for

Ireland's poor was the redistributive, essentially proto-Keynesian, principle of consumption. The poor were 'consumers', explained Sadler, 'to the amount of their entire expenses; and, of the several millions which they cost the country, almost every fraction is redistributed amongst the industrious classes of the community; which we are not sure would be the case ... were that sum retained by the wealthy'.[49] Sadler's ideas about the labour market and consumption were closely linked to the concepts of social integration and mutual dependence. Among the many shortcomings of the political economists was their failure, he declared, to recognize

> that mankind are reciprocally producers and consumers, and that, under proper regulations, they are necessary to each other, whatever be their numbers; that mutual wants are so balanced and connected in the mechanism of the social system ... as to produce that perpetual motion which nothing but the 'feathers' of these philosophers can disturb or destroy.[50]

In addition to anti-Malthusian statements, Sadler's writings and speeches are full of disdainful remarks about monopolists and capitalists, stock-jobbers and speculators, and complaints about double standards; all strongly reminiscent of Cobbett's views. Referring to critics of the poor relief system, have any, he exclaimed,

> held forth that the ministers, the chancellors, the judges, and all other servants of the crown; that all public officers, civil, military, or naval; that all bishops and ministers of the church, of all orders and degrees; I say, have they proposed, when the health of these fails, or they have advanced far in years, so as to be no longer fully capable of performing the duties of their several callings, that they should at once resign them, and give up their emoluments, without any equivalent, half-pay, pension, superannuated allowance, or consideration whatsoever?[51]

Like most conservative paternalists of his generation, Sadler was strongly influenced by eighteenth-century philosophy. His belief in the value of reciprocal relations and mutual obligation translated into a holistic, great chain of being concept of social organization. In defence of that principle, the surest way, he urged,

> of serving even the separate interests of the country, is, resolutely

and perseveringly to support the whole: to act upon the principle which all are ready enough to acknowledge theoretically – their reciprocal dependence; and, consequently, to reconcile and re-unite in bonds of mutual good-will those pursuits which, in a country like this, can never be prosperous but when they are indissoluble.[52]

The notion of harmony and balance was central to his idea of progress. Unashamedly patriotic in his support of traditional, mercantilist, policies – policies which the Ricardian economists regarded as essentially misguided and thoroughly anachronistic – Sadler believed that the protection of domestic industries was one of the most important duties of government. Against the new free trade system, he vigorously defended the old protectionist system, claiming it was the 'true national policy'. It has 'carefully attended to commerce', explained Sadler,

> without having been dictated to by it; knowing that there are other 'things than are dreamt of in its philosophy', namely, the health, happiness, morals, and well-being of the mass of the community, without securing which, even riches would make to themselves wings and fly away. Its maxims have tended to harmonize the various interests of the community, and to secure their advantages severally, not by sacrificing them to each other, but by promoting the prosperity of the whole.[53]

Sadler was similarly defiant in his defence of the 'old-fashioned' principle of population against the 'sneers' of the new school.[54] Contrary to Malthusianism, this essentially positive view of population growth equated a country's prosperity and progress with the size of its population. It complemented Sadler's claim that labourers, as the productive classes, were the source of national wealth and prosperity.

Prior to entering parliament, Sadler's vision of a hierarchical and family-based social system was similar to Cobbett's, in that it placed more emphasis on the social responsibilities of the governing classes, particularly of landowners:

> Few, I think, who are advocates of the social system, and especially amongst those who are placed at its summit, but must be eager to acknowledge, that the duties it imposes are reciprocal, and that their due discharge becomes the more important, the more elevated and commanding the station occupied.

His reason for emphasizing the responsibility of the upper classes was to draw attention to the irresponsibility of Ireland's disproportionately high number of non-resident landlords: those 'whom civil institutions have placed in the highest rank, and invested with the most extensive influence', who have abandoned 'their proper sphere and desert[ed] their numerous and degraded dependants'. Absentees were the main target of the criticism in *Ireland; its Evils and their Remedies*. As a consequence of their desertion,

> [t]here are none to give employment to those who, in an advancing state of society, are liberated from the lowest drudgeries of life; none to excite genius, or reward merit, none to confer dignity and elegance on society; to lead in the march of civilization; to diffuse knowledge or dispense charity.[55]

In abdicating their social responsibilities, Ireland's absentee landlords had taken full advantage of the economic benefits of the enclosure movement. After many years of land appropriation and consolidation, most of the country's peasantry had been dispossessed of their smallholdings. As a consequence of the landed classes selfish disregard of labouring people's interests, they were utterly demoralized and barely able to support themselves.[56] Sadler's appraisal of the agricultural revolution and its impact upon the peasantry mirrored Coleridge's.

Sadler, like Cobbett, wanted to restore a system of small cultivators. For both men, the substitution of 'dependent' and 'servile' labourers for 'independent' and 'free' labourers was among the worst outcomes of the enclosure movement and the monopolization of industry. Sadler defended the 'superiority of that moderate and mixed system of husbandry, which leaves the deserving peasantry of the country the opportunities and hopes of ultimate advancement'.[57] In the previous chapter, distinction was made between liberal notions of independence and Cobbett's understanding of that concept. Similarly, Sadler's proposals for individual advancement were not incompatible with his belief in the value of mutual dependency and reciprocal relations. The paternalists emphasized the need for self-improvement among the lower orders, but only in the context of social and economic interdependence. In other words, their understanding of self-improvement was different from the liberal individualists'. In the latter case, the emphasis was on self-help, and the individual's interests were seen as separate from those of the community. Moreover, the underlying consideration was to minimize all constraints – social, political and economic – which were thought to hinder individual initiatives and opportunities for improvement.

Sadler regarded self-help schemes as unrealistic and misguided. 'Nothing on earth', he declared, 'can be less philosophical than the idea of making the whole of the labouring classes hoarders of money.'[58] If they were in a position to set aside a percentage of their meagre incomes, given the principle of supply and demand and the fact that labourers were both consumers and producers, Sadler doubted whether a system of 'universal saving' would be of any great benefit to the economy. On the contrary, it would diminish expenditure among a significant proportion of the population, which would impede the circulation of money and lessen the demand for both manufactured goods and agricultural products. This would have a serious impact on the market for labour and would ultimately throw the whole social system into chaos. 'You would have got rid of the poor laws, it is true', observed Sadler, but you would have 'desolated your pastures, closed your manufactories, emptied your exchequer, and spread universal idleness and beggary: in a word, after you had robbed the poor, you would have become national bankrupts, with the consolation of having richly deserved your fate.' Moreover, schemes for encouraging individual initiative and responsibility among the lower orders rested on the assumption that labouring people were motivated by the same work ethic mentality as the middle and upper classes. 'The fact is', observed Sadler, 'that nothing but the spur of necessity occasions the bulk of mankind to labour at all, and they only labour up to their necessity.'[59] Essentially, Sadler was acknowledging the charge, common among those concerned about the rising cost of poor relief, that the poor 'seem always to live from hand to mouth'.[60] Finally, Sadler questioned whether or not poverty could ever be eradicated. He did not believe so; indeed, he did not even think it was necessarily desirable to do so. 'Poverty', he urged with much evangelical austerity, 'is the great weight which keeps the social machine going: remove that, and the gilded hands would not longer be seen to move aloft, nor the melodious chimes be heard again.'[61]

When Sadler condemned self-help schemes as designs to rob the poor, he did so advisedly. The view that the 'poor have a RIGHT to relief founded in the nature of things' was one of the central planks of his social system.[62] It was a right 'prescribed by the nature of things, by the original principle of appropriation, by the institutions of God, by the dictates of Nature, by the laws of the realm'.[63] The philosophical grounding of this claim – the principle of original appropriation and the laws of nature – was derived from the theory of the social contract developed by the seventeenth-century natural law theorists, Hugo Grotius, Samuel von Pufendorf and John Locke, and taken up in the eighteenth century by such writers as Montesquieu and Rousseau.[64] The notion of a social compact was put forward by these philosophers as a rational explanation for the origins of civil society and government, in opposition to the theory of divine right. It rested on a reconciliation of what they considered to be the two fundamental principles of social organization, namely, the preservation of life and the protection of property.[65] Though 'Men when they entered into Society', explained Locke,

> give up the Equality, Liberty, and Executive Power they had in the State of Nature, into the hands of the Society, to be so far disposed of by the Legislative, as the good of the Society shall require; yet it being only with an interest in every one the better to preserve himself his Liberty and his Property.[66]

In Britain the theory was closely associated with development of liberal ideas about the nature and extent of political authority. For some theorists, it supplied grounds for resisting arbitrary, monarchical rule; for Hobbes, it served as a justification for absolutism.[67] In terms of a theory of social organization or of social relations, it rested on the individualistic axiom that 'Society is made for man, not man for society'.[68]

Paradoxically, the social contract idea was taken up in the nineteenth century by writers looking for a plausible, theoretical defence of the Poor Laws against the rationalistic objections of the Malthusian political economists and those who supported the concept of voluntary, as opposed to state-funded, relief. Quoting Sir William Blackstone on the 'rights of persons', Sadler observed, that

> the law authorizing the wretched and indigent to demand from the more opulent part of the community the necessaries of life, declares it to be 'a provision, dictated by the principles of society'.[69]

As Cobbett understood it, 'civil society was formed for the *benefit* of the whole. The whole gave up their natural rights, in order that every one might, for the future, enjoy his life in greater security.'[70] Thus, according to nineteenth-century paternalists' interpretation of the social contract, first, every member of the state had an equal right to protection and, second, it was the responsibility of the state to ensure that that right was upheld. Locke had declared that,

> As *Justice* gives every Man a Title to the product of his honest Industry, and the fair Acquisitions of his Ancestors descended to him; so *Charity* gives every Man a Title to so much out of another's Plenty, as will keep him from extream [*sic*] want, where he has no means to subsist otherwise; and a Man can no more justly make use of another's necessity, to force him to become his Vassal, by withholding that Relief, God requires him to afford to the wants of his Brother, than he that has more strength can seize upon a weaker, master him to his obedience, and with a Dagger at his Throat offer him Death or Slavery.[71]

Locke referred to men's social responsibilities in the context of individual morality and Christian values. There was no intimation of government protection nor of a legislated system of poor relief. In fact, one of the weaknesses of Locke's theory, to which George Sabine draws our attention, is that it is not clear whether the 'original compact' gave rise to society itself or to government.[72]

Notwithstanding the finer points of Locke's treatise, the nineteenth-century paternalists concluded that the mandatory system of poor relief was a practical expression of the principle of protection underpinning the social compact. Moreover, some of the later proponents of natural law, including Montesquieu and Paley, were more explicit in declaring that the legislature had a responsibility to protect the poor.[73] The right of the poor to a subsistence was the basis of numerous pamphlets published in defence of the existing system, following the 1817 Select Committee on the Poor Laws.[74] 'I know', exclaimed one pamphleteer, Thomas William,

> that the rich and the great talk loudly of their rights and let their rights be sacred! But the poor also have their rights; and life and food, in the way of honest industry, every man has a right to demand of the state to which he belongs. It is a right derived from God and nature, and which will one day be vindicated by him who gave it.[75]

Sadler adopted a similar line of argument, maintaining that the system of poor relief was the mechanism through which the labouring poor were guaranteed a 'share of the property of the country'. Again using Paley as his authority, he insisted that it was a share to which the poor 'have clearly as much a right as the rich have to the remainder'.[76]

Responding to these arguments, Malthus pointed out that while they emphasized the poor's right to relief, they gave no thought to human nature or, to be more precise, to the disposition of the labouring poor:

> If it be taught that all who are born have a *right* to support on the land, whatever be their number, and that there is no occasion to exercise any prudence in the affair of marriage so as to check this number, the temptations, according to all the known principles of human nature, will inevitably be yielded to, and more and more will gradually become dependent on parish assistance.[77]

In *A Summary View*, published 32 years after the first *Essay on Population*, Malthus examined the question of the poor's right to subsistence in the context of natural law and the protection of property, and concluded that the rights of poverty and the rights of property were incompatible. 'The existence of a tendency in mankind to increase, if unchecked, beyond the possibility of an adequate supply of food in a limited territory, must at once determine the question as to the natural right of the poor to full support in a state of society where the law of property is recognized.'[78]

Sadler did not share Malthus's concerns. One of the attractions of the contractarian idea for the paternalists was that it was not a levelling principle. The principle of equality was applicable in the case of protection and of justice, but not in the case of property. The rights of the indigent would not, Sadler insisted, encroach on the rights of property:

> It is not put forth as a right on the part of the poor, to share individually and personally in any part, however small, of the real property of the country; on the contrary, it is one urged in perfect consistency with the claims of wealth, however great, and however rigidly maintained; it simply implies, as I expound it, and shall urge it on this occasion, a real and indisputable right that, after the institutions of the country have sanctioned the monopoly of property, the poor shall have some reserved claims to the necessaries of life.[79]

For the spiritual grounds of his argument, the poor's 'sacred claim to relief', Sadler looked to the profusion of scriptural injunctions, entreating the faithful to protect and succour the poor. From both the Old and the New Testaments, but particularly from the former, he was able to extract numerous commands stipulating the poor's right to relief and to protection.[80] In terms of Christian duty and personal salvation, however, it is probable that opponents of the Poor Laws would not have disagreed with Sadler's claims about the decrees of the Bible. It was the principle connected with the public provision of *compulsory* assessment with which they took issue. Many political economists and critics of the English system, of whom the Scottish Presbyterian minister Dr Thomas Chalmers was one of the most outspoken, felt that care and ministration of the poor should be left to charitable organizations and private benevolence. The author of several *Edinburgh Review* articles on this subject, including an assessment of the 1817 Select Committee Report on the Poor Laws,[81] Chalmers was strongly influenced by Malthus's claim 'that every public and proclaimed provision, for the relief of general indigence ... has the effect of perpetuating and extending the very distress which it proposes to alleviate'.[82] Chalmers was an ardent exponent of the principles of self-help and self-preservation, and he was opposed to most forms of legislative intervention, particularly when it encroached on spiritual affairs. The English Poor Laws – 'this artificial and uncalled for process of interference' – was 'the result', he declared,

> of a very bungling attempt, on the part of the Legislature, to do that which would have been better done had nature been left to her own free processes, and man to the unconstrained influence of such principles as Nature and Christianity have bestowed upon him.[83]

Not surprisingly, therefore, he was unwilling to accept the claim that poor relief was a right. He thought it lamentable that, with 'the introduction of legal assessment, the money given to the poor has lost its original character of a free-will offering, and is now given and received in the shape of an extorted right from the wealthier to the humbler classes of the community'.[84]

Sadler insisted that a publicly funded system of relief for the poor was sanctioned by, and in accordance with, divine law.[85] 'A regular provision for the poor', he explained, 'was amongst the first of the apostolic institutions, was established wherever Christianity was spread, and will never cease till its spirit shall be utterly extinguished.'[86] Sadler took exception to Chalmers' suggestion that the English system fostered mutual suspicion and animosity between the different classes. He was also appalled by the idea, which he understood as central to Chalmers' proposal for a voluntary and parochial system of relief, that provision for the poor should be chiefly funded by the poor themselves.[87] From Sadler's paternalist perspective, the most important function of the poor relief system was that of its influence in elevating the moral character of the poor and maintaining social stability. 'We have a better right', he claimed, 'to assert that the labouring classes of England have been improved in character, conduct, and condition, by its operation, than its impugners have to assert the contrary.' Moreover, he attributed 'no inconsiderable share of the prosperity which has ... distinguished this nation from all others, to this great and constantly operating cause'.[88] At the same time, Sadler admitted, in common with most advocates of the Poor Laws, that problems existed in the administration of the system and that some reforms were necessary to accommodate the social and economic changes of the postwar period. He accepted that many abuses had crept into its operation and that insufficient notice was given to what ought to be its cardinal rule, namely that of providing relief, where possible, in exchange for labour.[89]

Concluding his argument for the 'sacred right of the poor to relief', Sadler stressed that this right did not 'rest upon the foundation of individual worthiness, nor, indeed, does personal demerit abrogate it, though such circumstances may, properly enough, be taken into due consideration in its ministration'. This remark was directed at the political economists, and at Malthus in particular, who claimed that 'dependent poverty ought to be held disgraceful'.[90] 'It is placed upon a very different basis', continued Sadler,

> upon human suffering, and the pleasure of God that it should be relieved. Indeed if there be one point more preeminently clear in our religion than another, it is, that we are totally inhibited from making merit the sole passport to our mercy; the foundation of the modern code.[91]

Clearly, Sadler did not rule out discrimination, but in making a distinction between the deserving and the undeserving poor he was perhaps less harsh in his judgements than were many of his contemporaries. Always eager to defend the character of the poor, he was appalled that, notwithstanding evidence to the contrary, 'many choose to regard the national charity as solely occupied in supporting and maintaining able-bodied and flagitious idleness'.[92] Given his paternal, holistic view of society and belief in the value of social and economic interdependence, the purpose of a national, institutionalized system of relief was not merely to assist the indigent. By combining protection with moral authority and guidance, it helped to foster a deeper sense of social responsibility and commitment among the upper classes towards the lower and that, in turn, reinforced a community of feeling and understanding between the different orders in society. The interests of the poor were inseparable from those of the nation as a whole.[93]

It was noted in the previous chapter that Rousseauian determinism was among the dominant characteristics of the paternalist social outlook. In parliament, Sadler spoke of the injustice of blaming the poor for circumstances which were beyond their control. The poor man is perpetually insulted, he declared, 'for being a pauper, when his accusers have compelled him to become such; for being idle, when his work has been taken from him; for improvidence, when he can hardly exist'. Hinting at the dire social and political consequences of ignoring the claims of the labouring poor, he 'can trace his sufferings and degradation to their true source', continued Sadler, for he

> knows they have been inflicted upon him, and he feels what would be their cure, and can calculate how little it would cost others to make him and his supremely happy. Meantime, the authors of his sufferings are those that insult him with demanding that he should be quiet and grateful, that he should be contended and cheerful under them![94]

In line with Coleridge, Southey and his high-Tory friends at *Blackwood's*, Sadler believed that responsibility for widespread unemployment and distress among the poor ultimately lay with governments, not individuals; contrary to the imputations behind some liberal economists' advocacy of individual responsibility, these things were a product not of people's moral depravity or lack of initiative and drive, but of defective social and economic policies and, as such, they were capable of being remedied. Like many paternalists of this period, therefore, Sadler had faith in government's ability to implement policies that would not only improve the country's economic prospects but resolve its social problems. This fundamentally optimistic outlook challenged the pessimism which underlay Malthusian concerns about the growth of population and poverty. One of the reasons for Sadler's objections to Malthusianism was its expediency. It attributed all of society's ills 'to the laws of nature and of God'.[95]

While Malthusianism continued to influence social and economic debate, there was very little prospect, Sadler realized, of a legal provision being introduced into Ireland. Moreover, if Malthus was correct and there was 'a constant tendency for human beings to increase faster than their means of sustenation', then questions about whether or on what grounds – moral, theological or political – relief should be afforded to the poor, were largely redundant.[96] The first step, therefore, was to demonstrate that Malthus's thesis was untenable. This critique would be more creditable, he felt, if it was bolstered by an alternative hypothesis.[97]

In opposition to Malthus's thesis, Sadler posited his 'law of human increase'. This was founded on the idea that population expansion in any given area was determined by its density:

> The fecundity of human beings is, *caeteris paribus*, in the inverse ratio of the condensation of their numbers; and, still in direct contradictions to the theory now maintained, the variation in that fecundity is effectuated, not by the wretchedness and misery, but by the happiness and prosperity of the species.[98]

The first part of this 'law' implied that, like goldfish in a pond, there was some principle in operation which prevented human beings from reproducing in excess of what their environment was capable of sustaining. Sadler acknowledged that the principle was based on his study of the reproductive processes of plants and animals.[99] Armed with a mass of statistical data, encompassing different periods of time and a variety of countries and circumstances, the *Law of Population* endeavoured to prove, in contradiction to Malthus's thesis, that in densely populated areas, such as towns and cities, there are fewer marriages and fewer children produced than in the generally sparsely populated country regions.[100] The second part of his equation suggested that there was a correlation between fertility and prosperity. Adopting what was essentially a sociological or, to use a term more appropriate to his time, an anthropological assessment of human behaviour, Sadler maintained that population increase was regulated by economic prosperity and social improvement:

Excluding, of course, cases of extreme distress, a state of labour and privation is that most favourable to human fecundity. A dispersed and scanty population invariably implies that state; but as mankind advances from the hunting to the pastoral, and from thence to the agricultural stages of existence, and ultimately rise to the highest condition of civilization, labour becomes divided and consequently diminished in its duration and intensity, and many are liberated from its drudgeries, so as to devote themselves to other and more intellectual pursuits, or are rendered independent of it altogether; while the means of subsistence become progressively augmented, and ease and luxury more generally diffused. At every step the principle of increase contracts, and, as I contend, would pause at that precise point where it had secured the utmost possible degree of happiness to the greatest possible number of human beings.[101]

It is evident that in setting forth his own theory of population growth Sadler wanted to revive a sense of optimism and to give the whole population and Poor Laws debate a more positive stance. He pointedly referred to Malthus's as the 'darker theory'. To a large extent, his argument was simply a reversal, and intentionally so, of the populationists' claims. The belief that poor relief fostered irresponsibility among the poor and encouraged procreation was fundamental to Malthusian criticism of the English Poor Laws. For Sadler, on the other hand, marriage and the number of children reared in a community were allied to the prosperity and enlightenment of its people. Again strongly suggestive of later, Keynesian ideas, Sadler's theory suggested that a provision for the poor contributed to promoting economic prosperity and economic prosperity in turn checked population growth. Of the two systems, he explained,

> one maintains that the law of human increase, if not checked by a constant and unnatural restraint, would ... 'plunge society into the most wretched and desperate state of want' and misery; the other demonstrates that, in connexion with the virtues which it calls into existence and perpetuates, it is so regulated as to elevate human beings to the utmost degree of prosperity.

'Equally opposite', continued Sadler,

> are they as to the means by which they respectively maintain the varying principle of human fecundity to be governed: the former

asserting that it is by the perpetual operation of want and misery that the numbers of mankind are 'kept down to the level of food'; the latter, that increasing plenty is the regulator.... The one teaches human beings to regard each other as rivals for an insufficient share in the bounties of Providence; the other as copartners in an abundance, which overflows as they multiply, and by means of that multiplication.[102]

At times, Sadler was inclined to project his ideas beyond the realms of rationality:

I have shown that the strong tendency of mankind in a high state of affluence and ease, is not to multiplication, in the 'geometric ratio', or in any ratio, but to diminution and *extinction*.[103]

When Sadler spoke of the 'law of increase' as a natural law he was essentially equating it with divine law. He had difficulty reconciling Malthus's thesis with its moral implications. He could not believe that God would have made such a 'grievous miscalculation', establishing one law for human increase and another for the increase of sustenance. Malthus's theory implied that the two laws were not only different, they were incompatible.[104] A 'God of infinite goodness would not', declared Sadler, 'create those whom he could not sustain'.[105] The fact that Malthus had the audacity to profess certainty about something which only God could foresee offended his sense of Christian propriety.[106] An ardent critic of the Tory paternalists, and of Sadler in particular, Lord Macaulay realized that this was perhaps the most compelling argument that could be put up against Malthus's thesis. Accordingly, his critique of Sadler's *Law of Population* begins by vigorously denying that Malthusianism was an affront to Christianity.[107]

Most of the ideas characteristic of the paternalist social outlook were given full rein in Sadler's exposition of the 'true' principle of population. The notions of harmony and balance, of mutual dependency, of hierarchical authority and responsibility, and of natural or divine law were fundamental to his thesis. Essentially, these ideas were an expression of an organic or holistic understanding of human relations. Referring to this as the 'Law of Relations', Sadler delineated the intricacies of human relations not only with one another, but with past and future generations, and with organic and animal life:

Whether we contemplate nature in those orbs which are perpetually iterating their ancient courses around us, or in those mighty
conformations or minuter particles in which matter is presented to
our closer examination; or pursue our inquiries into the vegetable
and animal kingdoms, we find all its several parts strictly relative,
and reciprocally dependent upon, and influencing each other,
forming, therefore, a connected whole; involving a series of calculations and proportions, as exact as they are immense, of which
magnitude, motion, number, space, and time itself, are essential
ingredients: thus connecting creation, from its ubiquital centre to
its boundless circumference, in one unbroken and everlasting
chain, and preserving, in all its vast and complicated movements,
the eternal equipoise of the universe.[108]

This articulation of the interrelation of human beings with their
natural environment, extending to the inner as well as to the outer
universe and ultimately to God, revealed an extraordinary depth of
passion and an intense idealism. It also demonstrated the extent to
which the two dominating intellectual trends of the period, progressive rationalism and conservative romanticism, had influenced
Sadler's thinking. The physical, objective world of scientific knowledge and discovery is enveloped in romantic feeling, subjectivity and
flights of fantasy. This glittering declamation exulting the 'immensi-
ties of creation' is a fine example of the Sadlerian holistic, paternal
philosophy:

As we gaze, we hear the hierophant of this mysterious temple of
Nature, our immortal Newton, explaining the mechanism of the
stupendous scenery, and telling us, in terms too vast for simple
apprehension, the various magnitudes, distances, densities, veloci-
ties, orbits, eccentric or concentric, of the rolling spheres, all of
them, with their various phenomena and several influences, as
having exact relations to each other, constituting essential parts of
the same system, and obeying those simple laws which preserve
them and the universe, of which they form a part, in their present
existence:– laws, by which the central ruler, the steadfast sun, not
only governs his universe, but by which himself is governed, and
whom, therefore, while in imagination we are beholding surround-
ing creation from his sphere, we feel, as it were, rock beneath us
while he rolls his planetary orbs around him, reeling beneath the
mighty rush and reaction of the complicated machine. Bodies of

such magnitude, forces too complicated and immense in their moment, were they not in all their evolutions most perfectly balanced, we may well believe, would instantly occasion the 'wreck of matter and the crush of worlds'.[109]

The extract is taken from one of Sadler's lectures to the Leeds Philosophical and Literary Society. It must have been a rousing speech and one can only speculate on its impact, but surely some members of the society would have left the hall that evening pondering over the nature of existence, perhaps more conscious than ever before of their place in eternity and in the divine scheme of things.

   Sadler's optimism complemented his single-mindedness. Although he faced considerable opposition and criticism, he was unwavering in his insistence that something must be done to ease the burden of distress and to assist those members of the community who were unable to help themselves. He argued for an extension of the system of poor relief to Ireland on the grounds that 'wealth should be *compelled* to assist destitute poverty'.[110] In parliament, he became more aware of the responsibilities of parliament and parliamentarians in addressing the plight of the labouring poor. It 'is necessary to speak the real truth', he urged,

> in order to rouse us to a sense of our duty, and quicken us in the discharge of it – this state of things is remediable – remediable by Parliament, which cannot, I fear, be held altogether guiltless of having permitted, if not produced it.[111]

In *Ireland; its Evils, and their Remedies* and *The Law of Population* there are no direct references to the paternal state or to the patriarchal responsibilities of parliament, although it is evident that his ideas were moving in that direction. His suggestions as to how Ireland's absentee landlords might be compelled to attend to their social responsibilities anticipated a number of austere government initiatives which threatened the sacrosanct rights of property. First, he would amend the law of primogeniture to allow English lords to entail any Irish estates in their possession upon junior branches of their family, who would then be legally obliged to remain residents of Ireland. Second, he would not only compel absentees to contribute to a national relief fund for Ireland but would ensure that they paid at least twice as much as resident property holders. Third, to stop the practice of sub-letting, an 'offspring of absenteeism', he would make landowners whose land had been subdivided between members of the same family pay an additional levy. 'Granting that they have a right to desert their country, if they chose, still they have not a right, while so doing, to avail themselves of the advantages of its high values, without sustaining any part of the heavy burdens which the national system imposes.'[112]

Sadler's parliamentary endeavours on behalf of Ireland's poor and arguments for a more extensive role for the state are taken up in chapters 4, 5 and 6. The next chapter examines the influence of paternalist thinking on parliamentary debate during the period when Sadler was developing his paternal philosophy and making a name for himself in Leeds. At that time, there was no dominant strand of paternalist thought in parliament and, while the idea of a paternal government was implicit in many of the arguments put forward in support of the Poor Laws or in defence of the interests of the labouring classes, the emphasis tended to be more on the responsibilities of the governing classes than of the state. Moreover, while the paternalists were struggling towards a more coherent articulation of their views, the Ricardian *laissez-faire* theorists – self-assured and eloquent in their espousal of the non-interventionist, free trade doctrine – were at the peak of their influence.

3
Parliamentary Debate of Social Issues, *c.* 1815–30: a Conflict between Liberal Utilitarianism and Aristocratic Paternalism

In the period 1815–30, intellectuals were as much influenced by parliamentary debate of social and economic issues as parliamentarians were influenced by intellectual discussion of social ideas and theories. Coleridge took his 'facts' for his pamphlets on Peel's Cotton Factory Bill from the 1816 Select Committee on Child Labour.[1] Prior to that, he had very little idea of conditions in factories.[2] Indeed, his two pamphlets added nothing new to the debate; they were simply an affirmation of the position adopted by Sir Robert Peel, Lord Kenyon and other paternalist and humanitarian-inspired parliamentarians. At this time, two areas of child employment claimed parliament's attention: the chimney sweeping trade and textile factories. In both cases, a precedent for government intervention had already been established. Legislation was introduced for chimney sweepers in 1788 and for cotton factory apprentices in 1802. The other major areas of social debate of this period were distress, unemployment and the Poor Laws. Postwar depression, coupled with the recent disbanding of the army and navy, had seen a significant increase in the numbers of unemployed and, in the face of widespread public concern about the mounting cost of poor relief, the question of whether the Poor Laws should be radically reformed or even abolished was central to the whole issue of distress and unemployment. While parliamentarians were searching for solutions to the unemployment problem, the old solutions – the regulation of wages and mediation between employers and employees – were becoming increasingly untenable in an age of *laissez-faire* and the free market. It was during this period that the Spitalfields Acts were abolished and for no other reason, it seemed to many, than that the principle of regulation was anathema to the new market-driven economists. At the same time, the traditional, paternalist outlook continued to influence and shape the discussion and formulation of social policy and the tension between the 'old world' paternalist, protectionist ethos and the new *laissez-faire* philosophy underlies much of the social and political debate in this period. The distinction between these two seemingly incompatible perspectives is not always clear-cut, however, and we find that some parliamentarians subscribed to individualistic and utilitarian ideas at the same time as they defended the community values which underpinned the paternalist outlook. In the previous chapter, we saw that the paternalist ideal could be as readily translated into progressive ideas about social control and the mental and moral improvement of the lower orders as traditional aristocratic ideas about community responsibility and safeguarding the interests of the lower orders. In parliament, this conflation of progressive with traditional ideas was most evident in the immediate postwar period. By the mid-1820s, however, when Ricardianism was at its height and the political economists were more confident of the validity of their *laissez-faire* doctrine, the non-interventionist principle was not confined to economic and trade matters. It was applied more freely to social issues. Conversely, the proponents of protectionism and old world Tory opinion became more outspoken in resisting the new non-interventionist economic doctrine. Finally, it should be noted that because of the fluidity of party politics during this period, tensions existed between not only the Whigs and the Tories, but within the conservative spectrum of thought, between the liberal and the old world Tories. It was not until after the Catholic emancipation crisis that the more distinctive Tory strand of paternalism of which Sadler was representative began to have a greater influence upon social and economic debate.

I

In an article of June 1816 on the state of the nation, 'Nothing in the whole compass of our domestic policy demands more imperiously the attention of the legislature', declared a correspondent of the *Edinburgh Review*, 'than the state of the Poor-laws; and more especially at the present moment.'[3] Between 1816 and 1820, numerous pamphlets and political tracts proposed alternative, usually self-help, schemes for assisting the unemployed and for gradually dispensing with the Poor Laws. Many of these were addressed to members of parliament. In May 1816, John Christian Curwen, Whig member for Carlisle, proposed the appointment of a select committee on the poor laws. This was after learning from Lord Castlereagh that the government had no intention of introducing any measure to reform the existing system of poor relief. 'To restore the respectability and the happiness of the inferior classes, they must be brought back', Curwen declared, 'to those manners from which they have swerved.'[4] As a solution to the problem, he proposed that the government establish a 'National Benefit Society' in which every member of society, including those likely to become recipients of relief, would participate. Based on the principle of universal poor relief assessment, the contributions 'would be nearly equal', he explained, 'from those who were to be partakers of the funds, and those who must be considered as only contributors to it'. As a country gentleman, Curwen's sympathies were clearly on the side of the landed classes. His plan represented a mixture of ideas: modern *laissez-faire* principles were combined with old-fashioned, authoritarian paternalist values. It had all the hallmarks of the individualistic, self-help doctrine popular with Malthusian political economists and anti-interventionists. At the same time, he saw it as a means of cementing community ties. Similar to the existing parish-based system, under Curwen's scheme each parish, township or group of adjacent parishes would establish its own poor relief society. These would be administered by committees, in the election of which all adults would be allowed to participate. The committees would be responsible for determining their own rules and regulations, based on local conditions and circumstances. Rather than centralized governmental control, therefore, the emphasis was on local authorities and local administration. Curwen believed that by involving the labouring classes in the management and distribution of poor relief funds, the scheme would reinforce social harmony and establish an identity of interests between the different ranks of society. There was also a strong emphasis on social control and the moral improvement of the lower orders. The societies would monitor the behaviour of the individuals and families provided with assistance and give 'rewards for good conduct'. Conversely, any behaviour deemed unacceptable would be treated as grounds for expulsion from the societies.[5]

Sir Samuel Egerton Brydges, the Tory member for Maidstone, was appalled. A sympathetic advocate for the poor, Brydges frequently complained about the costly and unwieldy settlement laws which permitted paupers to be unjustly and pointlessly shunted from one parish to another. Any individual without a settlement and unlucky enough to fall foul of the parish authorities could be dragged, literally dragged, he exclaimed, 'from the home where all his connexions were formed, and the spot which had hitherto furnished him with the means of an industrious livelihood, to some remote parish where there was only a poor house to receive him, and nothing but the parish dole for his support'. On the grounds that 'no man ought to be paid less than the worth of his labour', he also strongly objected to the use of poor relief funds for topping up insufficient wages; a practice that had become common in the southern agricultural counties of England where wages were so low that labourers were unable to support their families without some form of parish assistance. If a pauper was unable to support himself, then it was the duty of the parish to provide him with work and preferably, he declared, 'of a beneficial and productive kind'.[6] There was clearly a need for some measure of reform in the administration of the Poor Laws, but he balked at the idea of radically altering a system which had become a part of the very fabric of society:

> The present laws were so widely ramified, so deeply rooted, and so intimately interwoven with the whole system of the institutions of the country; they were the result of such a long series of generations of legislative and judicial talent, acting on the successive experience of the numerous and changing facts in the condition of life of the lower orders; and in this last collection of enactments, and provisions, and judgements, had become so familiar to the understanding and habits of those who were dispersed everywhere, even to every corner of the kingdom, that for his part he must hesitate and pause, before he could reconcile his mind to a change so immense, a theory so untried, as that now proposed.[7]

After four months of investigations, the findings of the select committee instigated by Curwen and chaired by William Sturges Bourne were published in July 1817. It was the first comprehensive inquiry into the operation of the Poor Laws and it was far from favourable. It coincided with the publication of the fifth edition of Malthus's *Essay on Population*. Taking advantage of mounting public concern over the rising cost of relief, Malthus had inserted a new chapter ('Of Poor-Laws, continued'), which recommended a gradual abolition of the Poor Laws, and in the appendix he included commentary on some of the alternative poor relief schemes recently put forward by Curwen and others. Chiefly, Malthus was concerned about the demographic effects of equalizing the poor rates. An increase in the funds available for relieving the poor would lead to an increase in the number of paupers, who were mainly responsible, he believed, for the recent accelerated growth of the population. Under the existing parochial system, country parishes bore most of the cost of relieving the poor, but the individuals who contributed to those funds had a vested interest, explained Malthus, in keeping the rates as low as possible.[8]

Most of the main points of Malthus's thesis were reiterated in the 1817 Report on the Poor Laws. Strongly influenced by liberal, *laissez-faire* principles, it concluded that the Poor Laws were largely responsible for the increase in the population and were a disincentive to self-improvement. These effects were said to be manifest in the irresponsible attitude among the labouring poor, who generally showed no regard for their own, much less their children's, future. Most controversial and damaging, however, was the claim that, ultimately, the nation's wealth and property would be entirely squandered in providing financial assistance to the labouring poor:

> Your Committee feel it their imperious duty to state to the House their opinion, that unless some efficacious check be interposed, there is every reason to think that the amount of the assessment will continue as it has done, to increase, till at a period more or less remote, according to the progress the evil has already made in different places, it shall have absorbed the profits of the property on which the rate may have been assessed, producing thereby the neglect and ruin of the land, and the waste or removal of other property, to the utter subversion of that happy order of society so long upheld in these kingdoms.[9]

The report also gave weight to some popular prejudices, including the belief that a compulsory, statutory requirement to assist the poor discouraged charitable and Christian feeling. Relief was doled out grudgingly and received with ingratitude or demanded as a rightful claim, 'and not unfrequently', added the report, 'engenders dispositions and habits calculated to separate rather than unite the interests of the higher and lower orders of the community'. Again, we see traditional paternalist ideas about mutual obligation and parochial ties coupled with modern individualistic and essentially anti-community theories.

Despite its dire predictions, the committee was wary of a change of the order proposed by Curwen. Similar to Brydges, it felt that the system had 'become interwoven with the habits and very existence of a large class of the community'.[10] There was no objection to 'Parochial Benefit Societies', organized by individual parishes in much the same way as friendly societies or sick clubs, but the concept of a national poor rate levy represented too radical a change. The report restated Malthus's concerns about the impossibility of checking 'demands upon such a fund, when every excess in parochial disbursement would be merged in the general expenditure of the empire'. If states, like individuals, were 'compelled to limit their expenditure according to their means', then the tax raised to support the poor 'is in no greater degree capable of unlimited extension', warned the report.[11] To contain the cost of relief, the committee proposed the introduction of a fixed upper limit on the total assessment for each parish, based on average expenditures for, say, the preceding ten years. The allowance system designed to assist parents over-burdened by large numbers of children attracted heavy criticism. The committee recommended placing the 'redundant' children of those families in schools of industry. Expected to work in return for the maintenance they received, these children would thus benefit, it was felt, from the inculcation of industrious habits. Again, this type of institutionalized care had strong overtones of authoritarian paternalism.[12] The committee was in fact in favour of a restoration of the workhouse system, which 'for a long time acted very powerfully in deterring persons from throwing themselves on their parishes for relief'.[13] The provision of work for able-bodied paupers was one of the most contentious features of the Elizabethan Poor Law. Beginning with labourers aged between 18 and 30, the report recommended a gradual phasing out of this practice as the labour market showed signs of improvement. The framers of the report recognized that this might prove impracticable in some circumstances, however, and in areas where work was scarce suggested that parishes be allowed to acquire land for the establishment of parochial farms or allotments for able-bodied labourers. For those worried about the poor taking advantage of the system, this 'would afford the means', the report explained, 'which otherwise might be wanting, of bringing to the test the willingness to work of some of the applicants for employment'.[14]

Soon after Bourne had introduced a series of bills to put into effect some of the committee's recommendations, Thomas Peregrine Courtenay (Totnes) published *A Treatise upon the Poor Laws*. A liberal-Tory and member of the Poor Law Committee, Courtenay was concerned that the report's sanctioning of Malthus's ideas might be carried too far. Much of the talk about the mounting cost of poor relief and the adverse social effects of the system was, he believed, grossly exaggerated.[15] Even Malthus admitted that there was some doubt as to whether the Poor Laws 'did in fact tend to the encrease of Population'.[16] While Courtenay accepted that there were defects in the system, this did not necessarily imply that it was wrong in principle or that parliament should consider abandoning an established institution of the state.[17] A paternalist of a somewhat authoritarian kind, Courtenay strongly agreed with the report's proposal for schools of industry in which the parish would act in *loco parentis* to children whose parents were unable to provide adequate support. In his treatise on the Poor Laws, Courtenay provided a detailed account of how such a scheme might operate. Its main advantage, he believed, was that it would punish parents for their lack of foresight and improvidence while affording the child some protection. Indeed, he '*hoped* that the separation of families will be felt by the Poor as an affliction' and that the dread of separation would encourage parents to strive harder in fulfilling their duties towards their offspring.[18] The children would in fact be better cared for by the state, he felt, than by 'improvident parents' who relied upon allowances. 'In the Schools, attention would doubtless be paid to health and personal cleanliness of the children, and much more filth and misery withdrawn from the habitations of the poor than the pecuniary allowance now averts.' By the same token, he did not think it would be wise to allow the children to feel too comfortable or to mollycoddle them in any way. The food and clothing should be of the coarsest kind and nothing, other than moral and religious instruction, 'should be upon a liberal scale'. Courtenay would give the state extensive discretionary powers. It would be entitled to enforce separation of children from parents, who were deemed unfit to raise their children, and to claim the services of a child for a specified period in compensation for the cost of assuming responsibility for its welfare. While this requirement for children to work for the state might be interpreted by some critics of the system as a form of slavery, it would be simply, he explained, a 'system of apprenticeship, of a peculiar description, and commencing at a very early age'.[19]

Where Courtenay particularly disagreed with the committee was in the provision of relief for able-bodied paupers. Most of those who defended the Poor Laws did so on the grounds that the sick, the elderly and the orphaned child had a right to protection from the state. They refused, however, to accept that the same right should be extended to the able-bodied. Turning the argument around, Courtenay declared that no individual 'has a stronger claim upon the public than he who without any fault of his own ... finds himself without the means of obtaining ... the food which he is able and willing to earn by labour'.[20] To penalize unemployed labourers was to hold them responsible, he believed, for the vicissitudes of trade and commerce.[21] For Courtenay, neither marital status, age nor family size should determine whether or not individuals qualified for relief; rather, such decisions should be based on a person's conduct and character, and the source of his or her distress. The only reason why a single, unemployed man should be barred from receiving assistance was that he had proved himself unworthy of it. 'We must be governed in the administration of our relief by the previous habits and conduct of the Man; thus attempting to avoid the waste of public money upon undeserving objects.'[22] In line with many early nineteenth-century paternalists, Courtenay believed that one of the chief functions of the state was to provide work for the unemployed, particularly during periods of extreme privation. While the expense of large-scale public works should be divided between national and local authorities, the responsibility for, and organization of, such measures ought to rest with the government.[23]

On 9 May 1817, Lord Liverpool, dissatisfied with the Commons' handling of the Poor Laws issue, proposed that the Lords undertake their own investigation. Again, it was concern about interfering with a system that had become 'intermixed with the habits and prejudices of the people' which accounted for the Prime Minister's reservations on the issue.[24] He realized, moreover, that Malthusian dogmas and barely disguised contempt for an established institution of the state would most likely discourage many parliamentarians from accepting even minor reforms. The Lords' Report on the Poor Laws acknowledged many of the criticisms detailed in the Commons' inquiry but its tone was more measured and its consideration of the poor less judgemental. On the question of increasing costs, the Lords argued that the increase had not been that significant, particularly given the extent of the distress in recent years.[25] Most of their criticism concerned the administration of the system, especially the extensive use of roundsmen in agricultural districts and the practice of topping up insufficient wages. For the same reason as Malthus, the Lords were opposed to any extension or equalization of poor rate assessments:

> Nothing can tend to keep the present system of the Poor's Rates within reasonable bounds, but that the assessment should continue to be levied upon those who are immediately interested in the disbursement; and who, from personal knowledge of the character and situation of the individuals, are best enabled to judge of the

justice of their claims and the extent of their wants, in cases of application for relief.[26]

This sort of thinking chimed with the traditional, face-to-face concept of social relations.

One of the areas in which the Lords and the Commons were in agreement was in the formalization of parochial management of poor relief through the appointment of vestries and the substitution of permanent, salaried officials for annually elected overseers. The Lords' committee was in favour of plural voting at vestry meetings for those who contributed the largest proportion of the poor rates. It also approved of parishes being given the authority to acquire land for employment-creation schemes. Fundamentally, therefore, the Lords sought to reinforce the community-based structure of the system. At the same time, however, they recognized that there was a need for improved scrutiny in the general management of the poor. To that end, the report suggested that the permanent officials be made responsible for lodging periodical returns with county magistrates on the state of the poor in their districts.[27] These administrative reforms were incorporated into the Vestry Acts of 1818 and 1819.

When Bourne tabled his Poor Laws amendment and parish vestries bills at the beginning of March 1818, he reassured the House that he did not wish to alter the system only to improve its administration.[28] The Parish Vestry Act of 1818 and the Select Vestry Act of 1819 marked the first phase of administrative reform of the Poor Laws in this period. Both Acts reaffirmed the parish's responsibility for protecting the poor. Their primary objective was to increase the influence of major landholders in the management and distribution of poor relief at the expense of magistrates and overseers. Much of the criticism levelled against the poor relief system concerned misman-agement. The responsibility for distributing and managing parish funds was often left to the discretion of overseers, some of whom were unwilling appointees and were considered by critics of the system to be men of inferior character.[29] This 'important duty', observed one pamphleteer, 'had devolved on persons ill calculated from want of education, information and knowledge, to fill the offices thrown upon them'.[30] In other words, it was a duty of care which should fall to men of substance and education.

The first Vestry Act introduced the principle of plural voting rights, endorsed by the Lords' committee. Bourne wanted to encourage 'the wealthier and the more respectable classes' back to vestry meetings, which were said to have become increasingly rowdy and disorganized.[31] The proposal appealed to members who felt that the upper classes ought to be more actively involved in the management of parochial relief. In Curwen's experience of parish meetings, the lower classes were always

> ready to be guided by the example of those above them, to adopt any reasonable proposition. The evil now complained of grew out of the absence of those who ought to take the lead on such occasions.[32]

The second Vestry Act also reinforced the influence and authority of the principal ratepayers. It enabled parishes to establish select (as opposed to open) vestries which would be responsible for supervising the collection and distribution of relief. These bodies of between five and 20 members would comprise the major ratepayers, together with local ministers or other representatives of the church and the overseers of the poor. The new legislation gave parishes the authority to purchase or appropriate land of up to 20 acres for community employment schemes and to appoint salaried overseers to carry out the instructions of the select vestry. Indicative of the weight of authoritarian-paternalist views among the ruling classes, the new Act incorporated the principle of discrimination in which a distinction was to be made between the 'deserving' and the 'idle, extravagant, or profligate poor'.[33] These discriminatory powers, explained Bourne, would enable parishes to regulate the amount and type of assistance 'by the character and habits of those to whom it was granted'.[34] At the same time, the Act curtailed the discretionary powers granted to magistrates in 1796. Paupers could no longer directly appeal to magistrates for relief. Such entreaties could only be made after an application had been rejected by the select vestry.[35] Parochial authorities were more competent, it was felt, to judge the needs of their parishioners and merits of an application than magistrates who might not be conversant with local circumstances.[36]

Bourne's proposal for dispensing with the allowance system was not so well received. This was the scheme favoured by Courtenay in which parishes would be empowered to institutionalize children whose parents were unable to support them. Initially, this measure was incorporated into Bourne's Poor Laws amendment bill introduced at the same time as his parish vestries bill in early March 1818. Several members questioned the propriety of the clause. Frederick Douglas declared that it was both impolitic and cruel.[37] It was eventually thrown out by the Lords. The Marquis of Lansdowne feared that it was calculated 'to weaken those social feelings on which the very strength and consistency of society depended'.[38] Bourne was not yet ready, however, to relinquish the scheme, and in March of the following year introduced it as a separate measure. Rather than give parents 'a relief which was often squandered and not applied to the benefit' of their offspring, provision would be made for placing children in work and providing them with sustenance. The bill also included a provision for dispensing with relief for able-bodied labourers. In order for wages to find their own level, explained Bourne, all 'artificial' impediments had to be removed. With much faith in modern economic doctrine, therefore, he hoped that the measure 'would point out the necessity of granting [labourers] more adequate wages'.[39]

This time, a more thorough examination of the issue highlighted the polarity between the authoritarian and the humanitarian strands of paternalist thought. Typically, those of the former perspective focused on the value of reforming the character of the poor and of instilling in them industrious habits. The latter stressed the importance of community relations and familial ties. John Mansfield, the newly elected member for Leicestershire, numbered among the humanitarian paternalists. A magistrate of long experience, he was highly critical of members' preoccupation with the interests of landholders. In addition to the financial burden of the Poor Laws, it was incumbent on them to consider 'how they might alleviate the misery and alleviate the condition of the poor'.[40] From his own experience, he did not expect Bourne's scheme to work, particularly given the paltriness of most labourers' wages. What would become of these individuals, if an Act of parliament prohibited magistrates from granting them relief from the poor rates?[41] George Philips (Steyning) objected to giving magistrates the authority forcibly to remove children from their parents. Like Lansdowne, he thought that it would destroy 'those filial and parental feelings which were the great bond of union in society'.[42] Similarly, it was the insensitivity of the proposal and the possibility of it undermining social relations, which appalled Lord Milton (Yorkshire). During the war, he reminded his parliamentary colleagues,

> the poor had displayed more attachment to the higher orders than had ever been known before, were these now to be rewarded with this bill, and to be told that, after all the exertions they had made, it was the pleasure of the higher orders to break through the long

established system, and determine that provision should no longer be made for them from the poor rates, on which they had been taught to depend.

On the other side of the debate, Thomas Brand (Hertfordshire) spoke of the social benefits. The 'poor would be educated in principles of morality and religion, and apprenticed out to trades'. This would be of more value to society he suggested than allowing them 'to grow up in sloth and ignorance'. Courtenay of course welcomed the measure, observing that it would 'save a poor child from starving'. Notwithstanding an uneasy alliance between the humanitarian pater-nalists and the Malthusian political economists, the supporters of the bill outnumbered its opponents and Curwen's motion to forestall the second reading for six months was defeated by 25 votes.[43]

The opponents of the measure continued to resist it. A motion to postpone the third reading was moved by Francis Primrose, a repre-sentative of one of the Scottish counties. He objected to it on the grounds that it would unfairly penalize honest and industrious parents. 'It would enable the idle and ill-disposed labourer to have his children provided for by the parish, while those persons, whose parental affection induced them to keep their children at home, were to be deprived of parochial assistance and left to struggle as they could to support their families.' Peter Moore, the long-serving member for Coventry, seconded the motion. He remarked upon the injustice of depriving the labourers of 'a share of the poor-rates'. In the district which he represented, many labourers worked 16 hours a day, yet they did not earn enough to support a bare subsistence. Milton and Philips reiterated concerns about the social effects of the measure. They were joined by Sir Robert Wilson, who 'was wholly averse to the principle of taking away children from their parents and thus extinguishing all the natural affections of life', and by Sir James Mackintosh for whom the scheme 'appeared to be too much like that Spartan system of education, by which the mind was moulded into shape by rule'. This, for some supporters of the bill, was of course precisely the intention. In the opinion of Colonel Matthew Wood (London), the best means of improving the morals and conditions of the lower orders was to give their children instruction. Sir John Saunders Seabright, who shared representation of Hertford with Brand, likewise extolled the merits of social conditioning. The children would be taken from 'the profligacy and idleness which they might see at home' and given an education of which they would otherwise be deprived. The supporters of the bill prevailed once more. The motion for postponing it was defeated by a margin of 23 votes.[44]

The bill was swiftly dealt with in the House of Lords. Speaking for the humanitarian paternalists, Lansdowne reiterated concerns about the measure's likely impact on familial and community relations. It would 'destroy those ties of affection which knit together the families of the poor' and thus undermine the social relations upon which 'the well-being of society mainly depended'. The Earl of Harrowby spoke for the authoritarian paternalist. It 'was of the utmost consequence', he argued, 'that the children of profligate parents, who had nothing before their eyes but continuat [*sic*] scenes of vice and immorality, should be removed from the corruption of such an example, for the purpose of having that education given to them which might render them useful members of society'. After a few short exchanges, the debate was terminated and the bill summarily dismissed by the decisive intervention of the Prime Minister, who felt that it would be imprudent for them to risk experimenting with a measure which seemed to be of 'doubtful utility'.[45]

Two years later, the issue was revived by James Scarlett, a Whig and member for Peterborough. His highly contentious bill proposed changes which questioned the poor's fundamental right to relief. Similar to those of Curwen, Scarlett's ideas were an odd mixture. He was strongly influenced by Malthusian and *laissez-faire* principles, yet lamented the decline of paternalism and deference. The worst effect of the poor relief system, was that it had

> dissolved between the poor and the rich those ties which had formerly bound together the different orders of society; there was no longer gratitude on the one hand, or real charity on the other; the poor received without thanks what they were entitled to receive, and the rich gave without compassion what they were compelled to bestow.

In line with the extremist populationist, Scarlett feared that the system of parochial relief would eventually 'absorb the whole property of the country'. A way to prevent that, he believed, was to place an upper limit on poor relief expenditure. He would also preclude single, able-bodied persons from receiving parish assistance.[46] In 1704, Daniel Defoe was able to declare with a clear conscience, given that there was more 'labour than hands to perform it', that 'no man in England, of sound limbs and senses, can be poor merely for want of work'.[47] Similarly, Scarlett wanted to deny relief to those who 'merely grounded their claim upon being unable to obtain work'.[48] At the beginning of the nineteenth century, however, there was a shortage of work not labourers, and petitions to that effect were soon making their way to parliament.[49] Scarlett wanted to place systematic relief on a new footing, substituting the economic-rationalist imperatives of the new society for the paternal, social priorities of the old. Under his system, financial considerations would prevail over the needs or rights of the poor.

Heading the opposition to Scarlett's proposal, Wilson insisted that the poor had the same right to a subsistence 'as every gentleman had to his estate'.[50] He blamed the increasing cost of poor relief and the problems of unemployment on protectionist policies, high taxation and inflated prices, suggesting, in other words, that the poor were victims of circumstances which were beyond their control. If they were unable to find employment, 'surely', he declared, 'they had a right to look for the means of existence, to those who had the power of affording them those means'. From references to the 'artificial state' of the economy, it is evident that Wilson upheld rationalistic, *laissez-faire* principles to some extent. But, in the context of social issues and social relations, his views also chimed with Tory paternalists' ideas about interdependent social relations and the harmony and balance of interests. At the same time, and again like many conservative paternalists of this period, he combined a sympathetic regard for the poor with a pragmatic awareness of the need to maintain order and stability.

Frankland Lewis, one of the main architects of the 1817 Poor Law Report, took exception to Wilson's inference that poor relief was an unassailable right. The nation's governors were entitled, he believed, to amend that or any other law, 'according to the demand of the time, or their altered view of the circumstances of the case'. In any case, property rights were paramount. The integrity of the constitution rested on 'the security which it gave to all persons in the enjoyment of whatever property they had honestly come by'. These arguments drew some angry responses. To many of those who challenged Lewis's claim, the rights of the poor were as unequivocal as those of the rich. 'The basis of the constitution', observed Milton, 'was the protection of rights; and the rights of the poor ought to be protected as well as those of the rich.' For Hudson Gurney (Newtown), the 'right of the poor to reasonable support was as old as the law of England'. This bill, he added, 'went to the reversal of the law of the land, the laws of nature, and the law of God'. Charles Palmer (Bath) likewise regarded the Poor

Laws as 'the chartered rights of the poor, and hoped the House would pause before it consented to touch them'.[51] In the face of so much opposition, particularly from Wilson, who had 'got together a great mass of legal matter' with which to challenge the bill, Scarlett was forced to withdraw it.[52]

The tone of the Poor Laws debate had altered considerably since the inquiry of 1817. Members were not only prepared strenuously to defend the Poor Laws, they were more ready to criticize and reject Malthusianism. Wilson referred to Scarlett's 'anti-matrimonial and anti-population scheme'.[53] Gurney spoke of this 'attempt to bring the detestable system of ... Malthus to bear upon the legislation of the country'.[54] There was also more scepticism about whether the Poor Laws had in fact contributed to the growth of the population. Malthusian fears and 'gloomy predictions' were regarded by some members as grossly exaggerated.[55] Like Sadler, they upheld the more optimistic, mercantilist, idea of population in which the wealth and prosperity of a country was determined by the number and productiveness of its people.[56] Undoubtedly, the arguments of the immediate postwar years in favour of the gradual abolition of the Poor Laws had lost much ground. There were, in addition, repeated calls for the Poor Laws to be extended to Ireland. These became more strident in the late 1820s when Catholic emancipation, coupled with growing discontent, forced members to reconsider their position on Ireland. The criticism of Malthusianism and the extreme *laissez-faire* perspective coincided with *Blackwood's* and the conservative paternalists' reaction, in the mid-1820s, to the popularization of Ricardian economics. The extent to which this helped to rekindle paternalist social thought was evident in parliament's response to the proposal introduced by Robert Slaney (Shrewsbury) in 1830. An ardent Malthusian, Slaney reintroduced Bourne's measure for institutionalized relief of children whose parents were unable to support them.[57] This time the proposal never got to the Lords. The majority of the members who spoke on the issue rejected it as thoroughly abhorrent and inhumane. Again, there was great concern about its social implications and impact upon familial and community relations. Sir Thomas Baring, the long-serving Whig member for Wycombe, was determined to thwart the proposal. 'Good God!', he exclaimed, 'was it not enough, that these people were poor? must the legislature also deprive them of their children'? His response and the size of the vote against Slaney's proposal were indicative of the more sympathetic mood of the House. Nine members voted for the clause and 82 against it.[58]

II

Paternalist-inspired argument was not always successful, however. On the issue of wage regulation, which the political economists' viewed as an economic not a social issue, *laissez-faire* arguments prevailed. The subsidy of labourers' wages was a feature of the Poor Laws over which there seemed to be almost interminable debate. For some members the answer lay in simply prohibiting the practice.[59] The issue was examined in 1824 by the Select Committee on Labourers' Wages and in 1828 by yet another committee on the Poor Laws, which Slaney had initiated specifically to inquire into that aspect of the system.[60] Like most such investigations of that period, both committees were strongly influenced by Malthusian pessimism. The poor relief system had not only contributed to the growth of the pauper population, but tended, it was felt, to degrade the character of the poor. Much of their criticism, however, was reserved for those who administered the system. Mainly, this concentrated on the liberality with which, it was thought, magistrates exercised their discretionary powers, particularly where parishes had yet to establish a select vestry or appoint a permanent overseer. Notwithstanding these criticisms, the 1824 committee was somewhat cautious. Beyond urging parishes to make use of the vestry system and to discriminate more carefully between the 'deserving' and 'undeserving' poor, it was not prepared to make any specific recommendations let alone propose a radical alteration of the existing system. Moreover, 'much might be done', it was felt, 'by the vigilant and enlightened attention of the Magistrates'.[61] The 1828 committee adopted a firmer line. If the abuses of the system were to be prevented, then a more positive initiative was required than reliance on magisterial regulation. To that end, the report recommended that the practice of giving allowances to labourers, whether on account of themselves or their families, 'be declared unlawful'.[62]

In recommending abolition of the allowance system, the 1828 committee insisted, in accordance with *laissez-faire* logic, that the policy would operate in the labourers' interest in the long term. On both sides of the debate, it was recognized that farmers were happy to perpetuate a system which provided them with cheap labour, subsidized by ratepayers. Under the proposed scheme, families deprived of allowances would be forced to subsist wholly on poor relief, with the able-boded receiving assistance through parish work schemes. These labourers would thus be removed from the employment market. The committee was confident that the shortage occasioned by their removal would see the wages of the remainder rise, 'until they reached that point which it would answer to the masters to pay'. The report acknowledged, however, that the 'success of such a measure would depend in many cases on the adoption of a well-regulated system of workhouse industry, where a full measure of labour may be constantly exacted, proportioned to the ability of each individual'.[63] In other words, the framers of the 1828 report were prepared to make parishes responsible, albeit temporarily, for organizing large-scale work schemes in order to force farmers to pay adequate wages. The simplest and least costly solution would have been to establish a minimum wage. However, that idea was anathema to the advocates of the new free market doctrine.

It was during this period that the Acts regulating the Spitalfields silk industry were repealed. In the spirit of the paternal industrial code of the Tudor era, these statutes, enacted during the late war, empowered magistrates to determine rates of pay for journeymen silk-weavers residing in the Spitalfields district.[64] The political economists and free traders objected to the Acts' sanctioning of statutory regulation and intervention between masters and servants. David Ricardo, dismayed that such legislation was still in force in 1823, thought it was 'improper' for wages to be 'artificially kept up by the interference of a magistrate'. Alderman Thompson 'bore testimony to the pernicious operation of the law' and Lord Milton 'rejoiced in any prospect of getting rid of the obnoxious statutes'. The President of the Board of Trade, William Huskisson, agreed that the Acts should be repealed. His liberal-Tory colleague, Thomas Wallace, considered them 'a disgrace to the Statute-book'. To members on the other side of the debate, the political economists were taking a too doctrinaire view of the issue. Thomas Fowell Buxton (Weymouth) presented a petition signed by 11,000 journeymen weavers. It was 'rather hard to say to these poor people', he observed, 'that they should lose their bread by the principles of political economy'. Edward Ellice (Coventry) drew attention to the arbitrary nature of liberal-Tory arguments. He agreed that it was 'an unwise principle to regulate the price of labour', but parliament had seen fit to regulate 'the price of bread and other articles; and if one such regulation was to be done away with so ought all'. His motion for a select committee on the issue was defeated by eight votes and the Lord Mayor's motion to postpone the third reading of the bill failed by 13 votes.[65]

The Spitalfields Acts had been mentioned briefly by an inquiry of the Lords into the silk and wine trade, which reported in June 1821. In a highly critical assessment of the impact of the regulations on the industry, the report noted that manufacturers were obliged to pay unskilled workers the same rates as skilled workers and that they were discouraged from investing in new machinery. Unable to give work to weavers at a reduced rate, when trade was slack employers were obliged to discharge them. Because the other silk manufacturing centres were not subject to these regulations, the Spitalfields manufacturers were severely disadvantaged. Unless the law was modified, the industry would be either ruined or driven out of London, concluded the report. It conceded, however, that William Hale's evidence in favour of retaining the regulations included some important considerations, particularly in relation to their effect in checking the poor rates.[66] A major silk manufacturer in Spitalfields, Hale had published a spirited defence of the Acts.[67] It was because the weavers of Spitalfields were given a 'just price' for their labour, he believed, that they were able to maintain their families without resorting to parish relief.[68] Also, too much had been made, he felt, of the magistrates' role in settling wage rates. The usual practice was for these to be settled by manufacturers in consultation with journeymen weavers. If either party felt the price was unfair, then a magistrate would be called upon to arbitrate, but that was rare. There had only been two such incidents. For Hale, the most important function of the regulations was in preventing masters from underselling their neighbours and from gaining 'inequitable' profits at the expense of 'their helpless workmen'.[69] There was a time when manufacturers could be relied on to treat their workers fairly. They 'were bound *in honour* to pay their men' according to an agreed schedule of prices. But this system of self-regulation required the co-operation of all the manufacturers. Once the emergence of a more aggressively competitive market began to dictate employer/employee relations, self-regulation gave way to avariciousness and self-interest. 'One oppression', wrote Hale 'succeeded another, till the hard-working men found it impossible to live by their labour; they grew desperate; and frantic with rage, they destroyed the property of their employers. The district became the scene of the greatest tumult.' Above all, the Spitalfields Acts had helped to restore order and revive a spirit of co-operation and harmony. Since the passing of these Acts, he concluded, 'all the existing gradations in society are highly respected, the laws are obeyed, good order prevails, our days are well occupied, and our nights are secure.'[70]

   Despite their own committee's unfavourable assessment of the Spitalfields Acts, the Lords were reluctant to approve their repeal.

Ellenborough reiterated the argument raised by opponents of the bill in the Commons that there was no sound practical reason for repealing the Acts. He felt that they were being asked to interfere with an industry, which was experiencing a period of prosperity, 'merely to gratify the theoretical views of political economists'. He also reiterated Hale's argument that the regulations were 'most efficient in preserving peace, and a good understanding between masters and journeymen'.[71] Similar sentiments were expressed by the Earl of Harrowby, who was keen to preserve the domestic character of the industry. If the Acts were repealed, then 'thousands of weavers who now lived with their families would be taken away from them, and stowed into enormous buildings, where they would be exposed to every evil, and where their excellent moral habits would be destroyed, while half a dozen great manufacturers would amass large fortunes'.[72] The Lords did not reject the entire bill. They agreed to repeal that part of the legislation which prevented manufacturers from transferring capital to other districts, but elected to retain the regulation which empowered magistrates to determine journeymen's rates of pay.[73] For the opponents of repeal, this proved to be a short reprieve, however. The following year the measure was reintroduced and this time with barely any resistance the Lords gave it their assent. The government had, in the meantime, set in train its programme of trade liberalization, which included a significant easing of the restrictions on the importation of silk. Having accepted the economists' argument for discontinuing the protection of the industry as a whole, the Lords would have had some difficulty in justifying a contrary policy for its Spitalfields branch.[74]

Notwithstanding periods of severe depression, parliament continued to resist calls for a minimum wage. In 1827, William Smith was entrusted with two petitions from his Norwich electorate. One, containing more than 10,000 signatures, came from weavers and the other from a group of master manufacturers. The petitioners complained about the appallingly low wages in Norwich and called on parliament to devise some legislative mechanism for settling pay disputes. Despite the master-manufacturers' willingness to participate in the experiment, few parliamentarians were prepared to revert to the old paternalist principle of statutory regulation. The following year, the Norwich weavers again lobbied for the appointment of a committee, comprised of masters and workmen, for 'fixing an established rate of wages'. John Berkeley Monck (Reading) was one of the few members willing to support the petition. It was the 'duty of

Parliament', he believed, 'to interfere in all cases of distress and oppression'.[75] Five years before this, under the influence of Malthusianism, Monck had numbered among the Poor Law abolitionists. He had since acquired a less extreme, essentially proto-Keynesian, view of social and economic issues, which was out of step with the prevailing *laissez-faire*, non-interventionist doctrine.[76] He not only defended the principle of a minimum wage, but argued that the prosperity of the labouring community was directly linked to the prosperity of the nation as a whole. Thus it was in parliament's interest to ensure that the masses enjoyed 'the highest standard of existence', which could only be achieved through high wages. 'Where wages were high', declared Monck, 'the revenue would be great, and the people more moral and happy.'[77] While these ideas echoed the 'Keynesian' position adopted by the Tory paternalists, Monck's view that the landed interest was shown too much favour and his demand for repeal of the 'obnoxious' Corn Laws clearly put him at odds with traditional Tory thinking on these issues.[78]

III

Proposals for dealing with distress and unemployment were broadly divided between those that emphasized the role of government and argued for public works or publicly funded community projects, and those that highlighted the responsibilities of individual landholders. Community-based schemes involving spade husbandry and the cultivation of waste land were popular. A series of such proposals were introduced into parliament between 1819 and 1821. The civil unrest which culminated in the Peterloo débâcle of 1819 encouraged discussion of the state's social responsibilities. Many members felt that the government's repressive measures should be accompanied by some positive initiatives for alleviating widespread distress, the underlying cause of unrest in manufacturing districts.[79] During this period, Robert Owen's schemes for employment of the poor and improvement of social conditions began to claim some attention. The necessity for government regulation and centralized planning was central to Owen's proto-socialist idea of the state. In a report submitted to the 1817 Committee on the Poor Laws, he explained that his plan for managing the poor and alleviating poverty would be 'much better directed nationally than privately'.[80] He joined with those who believed that the state's paramount responsibility was to provide work for its people. It was not make-work schemes or public works that he had in mind, but 'perpetual employment ... of real national utility, in which all who apply may be immediately occupied'.[81] Owen published numerous pamphlets outlining his visionary scheme for co-operative, self-sufficient communities. The most detailed account of this scheme appeared in his *Report to the County of Lanark* (1820), which was commissioned by a group of magistrates, lords and other influential individuals concerned about unemployment and the prevalence of distress in Lanarkshire.[82] Like the conservative paternalist, Owen believed that one of the fundamental errors of modern society was in 'separating the workman from his food, and making his existence depend upon the labour and uncertain supplies of others'. He wanted to restore agriculture as the primary occupation of the labouring people with manufacture serving as 'an appendage'. His communities would be 'associations of the cultivators of the soil'.[83] To that end, his plan involved a return to the labour-intensive system of spade husbandry, which was considered by some to be a more effective utilization of human and material resources than modern methods. There was said to be scientific proof that it produced higher and better yields than plough cultivation.[84]

In December 1819, Sir William De Crespigny (Southampton) moved for the appointment of a select committee to examine the feasibility of parishes setting up co-operative communities similar to the one at New Lanark. In addition to providing employment, the scheme's emphasis on improving the character of the poor clearly appealed to De Crespigny's authoritarian-paternalist frame of mind. From the age of two, the children of New Lanark 'were instructed in those principles', he explained, 'which were calculated to make them useful and excellent members of society'. Lord Archibald Hamilton, the seconder of the motion, was impressed by the extent to which Owen's paternalistic methods had succeeded in encouraging a community of feeling among the inhabitants of New Lanark. Most members, however, were either sceptical of the scheme or suspicious of Owen's spiritual beliefs, and the motion was defeated by a huge margin of 123 votes.[85] In 1821, another Owenite, John Maxwell (Renfrewshire), proposed the appointment of a parliamentary commission to visit New Lanark and determine whether co-operative schemes would help alleviate distress in agricultural districts. The House again refused to give its consent. The scheme's critics regarded it as too authoritarian. Joseph Hume feared that it would enervate the people's spirit and sense of independence. Gurney felt that it would 'destroy all individuality'. George Canning, the liberal-Tory President of the Board of Control, had been behind some far-reaching economic reforms, but this scheme clearly struck him as too visionary. 'It was a known principle which connected tenants with landlords, and workmen with manufacturers. But on what principle thousands of persons could be congregated together in Mr. Owen's establishments, he could not conceive.'[86]

In May 1820, Earl Stanhope presented the Lords with a proposal for employment of the poor in the cultivation of waste land. A man of old world protectionist, paternalist, Tory principles, there was no suggestion of social control, co-operative communities or any 'new view' of society in his proposal. Rather, he wanted to revive the old yeoman class – 'that order of men, which once formed the happiness and strength' of the country – by restoring their common rights and access to waste land; thereby enabling them to 'secure an independent subsistence'. Under Stanhope's scheme, waste land would be divided into areas large enough for the subsistence of individual families, but not for commercial purposes. As well as encouraging a sense of independence, Stanhope wanted to instil a feeling of ownership and 'an interest in the soil'. Labourers would be given the materials for constructing cottages, which they would then rent from the parish. Stanhope believed this scheme would not only diminish the poor rates, but restore a balance between the supply of labour and its demand. By enabling labourers to 'secure their subsistence by labouring for themselves instead of labouring for others; and by diminishing the number of the labourers, you would proportionally increase the demand and the wages of labour'. From Stanhope's old world perspective, most of the social and economic problems affecting the poor were due to mechanization. The increase of the population, and subsequently of distress, he attributed to the spread of the manufacturing system. 'The temptation of high wages, and consequently of idleness had attracted large numbers of persons to manufacturing employments, and afforded great encouragement to marriage.' The 'first victim' of increased mechanization had been the rural worker, 'whose domestic industry has been destroyed by it'. Thus, in addition to promoting spade husbandry, Stanhope wanted government to regulate and restrict the use of labour-saving machinery.[87] His ideas were too reactionary to be taken seriously. But they illustrate the extent to which old world, protectionist, paternalist ideas still flourished among the country's most highly placed political figures.

Finally, it is worth examining Slaney's ideas for alleviating poverty and improving the condition of the poor. They represented the views of an ardent Malthusian and proponent of *laissez-faire* principles, yet were strongly influenced by the same old world paternalism which governed Stanhope's thinking. Slaney's ideas were also representative of agrarian paternalists, like Cobbett, who emphasized the responsibilities of individual landholders and community leaders. Slaney's upper classes were disinterested, public-spirited individuals whose role was to guide and instruct the poor, by example as well as directly. Through a judicious 'direction of their expenditure', explained Slaney, they 'can exercise a good or evil influence on those around them; they are not only the makers of the law, but the manners of the country'.[88] The objective was to encourage the poor to help themselves; 'to incite, but not to supersede their exertions; to hold out to them a friendly hand, rather to beckon them forward and direct their course than to bear their weight'. A good landlord attended to roads and footpaths, provided tenants with decent gardens and organized improvements to their lodgings. In addition, he gave special consideration to the more enterprizing and industrious tenants on his estate.[89] Mixing notions of property with those of responsibility, a 'rich man should be as proud of the peasantry as of the trees on his estate,' declared Slaney. As a Malthusianist, Slaney considered improvements to existing cottages to be more desirable than the erection of new ones. But if a landlord were to invest money in draining a marsh, clearing woodland or found some other means of augmenting the country's resources, he 'will have the high gratification of calling into existence an additional number of human beings, for whose subsistence in useful and permanent occupation, he has already, by his intelligence and forethought created a provision, without lessening the means of any other person'.[90] To strengthen the bonds between the upper and lower classes, Slaney advised landlords to engage in some 'condescending benevolence' and spend a portion of their 'superfluous income' on annual festivals for their tenants and workers.[91] The landlord might also favour his tenants with a few days' hare coursing and it would be an honour if, instead of sending his gamekeeper, he accompanied them himself. The people, Slaney assured his readers, 'for the sake of mixing with their superiors on these occasion ... will redouble their industry'.[92] In Slaney's ideal world, the rich would guide the poor and teach them to subsist by their own efforts, and the poor would be suitably appreciative and deferential. 'By these means, that respect towards superiors which the manufacturing system and other causes have so much diminished, would be preserved, and education and rank would have their due weight.' In addition to private initiatives for elevating the social condition of the poor,

Slaney strongly approved of government initiatives for such things as savings banks, public libraries and schools, and the provision of public walks and parks, which would encourage exercises and entice the poor away from 'country wakes and ale houses'.[93] Inspired by a combination of self-help and paternalist ideas, Slaney's views highlighted the ambiguity – the conflation of modern *laissez-faire* principles and old world paternalist idealism – which characterized parliamentarians' responses to social questions in this period.

IV

It was in the area of child labour where arguments for legislative regulation proved most persuasive, even to the most ardent non-interventionists. In June 1817, Lord Milton tabled a petition to abolish the use of 'climbing boys' in sweeping chimneys. His intention was to bring the issue to parliament's notice in the hope that some measure might be introduced in the next session. However, the House was so warm in its approval of the petition that Milton decided to propose its referral to a select committee immediately.[94] This committee was chaired by Henry Grey Bennet, MP for Shrewsbury and an active member of the Society for Superseding the Necessity of Climbing Boys. One of several organization formed after the plight of these children was first brought to public notice in the 1770s, this society was founded in February 1803.[95] Its chief executives included William Wilberforce, Colonel Matthew Wood, Sir Thomas Baring, the Duke of Bedford, the Bishop of Durham, who was President, and several other members of parliament. Bennet, Peter Drummond Burrell, Sir Francis Burdett and William Wigram, were on the society's committee and a number of Lords and MPs appeared on its list of subscribers.[96] With the help of the society, the Commons inquiry took less than three weeks to complete. The society's claims of neglect, undue hardship and cruel treatment were all strongly supported.

Under the 1788 Act, it was illegal for master chimney sweepers to employ children under the age of eight. However, because of the trade's requirement for diminutive children, this age restriction was largely ignored. Among the worst offenders were masters who employed their own children and those, yet to establish themselves in the trade, who picked up boys where they could, wandering from place to place in search of work. Also, some parents were either unscrupulous or desperate enough to lie about the ages of their children. Concluding that it would be futile to expect any notice to be taken of additional and more stringent regulations, the committee recommended that the use of climbing boys be abolished altogether and that the minimum age be raised from eight to 14, by which time most children had outgrown their usefulness as chimney climbers. Notwithstanding the objections of some master chimney sweepers, the committee accepted the abolitionists' claims that, pending a few alterations to exceptionally narrow flues and those with double-bends, the device patented by Smart, which consisted of a brush attached to a series of rods or to a weight and pulley, would be able to sweep all chimneys as efficiently as climbing boys.[97]

Encouraged by public interest in the issue, in early February 1818, Bennet introduced a bill to amend the 1788 Act in accordance with the committee's recommendations.[98] The age restriction would take effect immediately, but the actual prohibition of climbing boys would be delayed for 12 months.[99] Bennett had no difficulty getting his proposal through the Commons. The only dissenting view was Milton's. He had begun to doubt whether direct intervention was the most appropriate course. As some chimneys could be swept using only climbing boys, he felt that Bennett was moving too quickly on the issue. As a compromise, he proposed the introduction of a heavy tax on the use of climbing boys. The question of abolition would then take care of itself. Bennet and Edward John Littleton (Staffordshire) pointed out that the majority of chimneys requiring alteration belonged to those who could afford the modifications. Milton's suggestion would thus 'have the effect', observed Bennet, 'of sacrificing the children of the poor in order to preserve the chimneys of the rich'. Littleton suspected that Milton had changed his position in deference to the Lords' concerns about the issue.[100]

The Lords were unable to reach agreement on the bill. On the second reading, they decided to refer it to another committee. Lord Holland, the Bishop of Chester and Earl Grosvenor, who was one of the vice-presidents of the Society for Superseding Climbing Boys, were strongly in favour of the bill. But the Earl of Lauderdale questioned whether there was sufficient evidence to prove that all chimneys could be swept by mechanical means.[101] The Lords' committee was chaired by Lord Auckland, another supporter of the society. On practically every aspect of the issue there was unequivocal agreement between the two reports, which taken together were a clear indictment of the trade. The Lords' report confirmed that conditions varied considerably between the established or 'more respectable' class of master and the itinerant and smaller operators, among whom were to be found the worst cases of mistreatment and neglect. An oversupply of journeymen made it difficult for new entrants to secure work. Their condition was generally no better than that of their charges. They 'pick up boys as they can', explained the report, 'and are but little scrupulous in their means of obtaining them'. In those circumstances, little or no attention was given to the children's health and welfare. Often lodged in cellars where the soot was stored, they suffered from poor hygiene, lack of decent food and inadequate clothing. In addition to the harsh nature of their employment, they were frequently subjected to beatings and cruel treatment. Their masters, being 'too poor to allow them to become gradually and properly inured to climbing', frequently had to resort to cruel tactics to force them to work. The report also confirmed that the minimum age regulation was generally ignored, particularly by masters who employed their own children.[102] There were strong grounds for legislative intervention but, given the fire risk and uncertainty about the effectiveness of the existing devices, it was decided that more information was required before any determination could be made on the feasibility of abolishing climbing boys altogether. In the meantime, the Surveyor-General of the Board of Works, Colonel Stephenson, was ordered by the committee to undertake a large-scale experiment to determine the effectiveness of the various chimney-sweeping devices already in operation.[103] His report was made available in early February 1819. Out of 1,000 flues, 910 had been swept successfully and 80 adequately. Ten of the flues containing inaccessible horizontal sections could only be partially swept. Stephenson conceded, given the imperfect results of his experiment, that 'climbing boys cannot be at present totally dispensed with'.[104] He did not rule out their eventual abolition, however, and a week later Bennet introduced another bill. The only difference between it and the former bill was that full abolition of climbing boys was to be postponed for two years instead of one year.[105]

Bennet's second bill did not have quite such an easy passage. Several members had since acquired some strong reservations about the efficiency of mechanical sweeping and the costs involved in altering 'some hundred thousands of chimneys'. Also, given that many of the children to be deprived of this employment were pauper apprentices, it was felt that the measure would place unwelcome additional pressure upon parish poor rates.[106] For Thomas Denman, member for Wareham and a strict non-interventionist, 'the good sense of the public was sufficient to correct the evil without loading the statute book with another penal law, every penal law being in his opinion a great evil'.[107] Most of the speakers on behalf of the bill were connected with the society. In Brougham's opinion, as these children were not free agents, the legislature was bound to protect them. 'If the parties to be protected had been of an age sufficient to protect themselves, he thought the principle of interference would not only be wrong, but criminal, be the nature of their employment ever so unwholesome or severe. But in the present case, as the boys were not *sui juris*, master of their own acts, he hoped the House would interfere and fix some regulation by which relief would be afforded them'.[108]

The measure was again strongly resisted in the Lords. The bill scraped through the second reading but was rejected on the third.[109] Attacking the measure from both a non-interventionist and a pragmatic standpoint, Lauderdale questioned the propriety of legislation presuming to determine a code of moral conduct. Reforms of this kind should be left 'entirely to the moral feeling of, perhaps, the most moral people, on the whole face of the earth'. Given Stephenson's report and the fact that the experiment had been only partially successful, the danger of fire was too high, he believed, to risk abolishing climbing boys. In the face of this twin assault, Grosvenor's suggestion that abolition should proceed immediately did not assist the reformers' case. With the assistance of Lord Melville who was likewise concerned about safety, Lauderdale moved for a postponement of the third reading and the bill was defeated by a comfortable majority of 17 votes.[110]

Bennet refused to admit complete defeat, however, and a few weeks later he introduced another bill. He had given up the idea of abolishing climbing boys. He now proposed that the minimum age be raised from eight to ten and the number of apprentices allowed to each master be reduced from six to four. The bill also sought to prohibit hawking or 'crying the streets for employment'. It was customary for journeymen at the end of a day's work to enlist the services of their masters' apprentices and seek work on their own account.[111] Bennet's proposal was in line with a series of recommendations which had been submitted to both committees by an association of master chimney sweepers, who were opposed to the abolition of climbing boys, but accepted the need for 'such laws as will ensure to the children employed in this necessitous business, a mild and humane treatment'.[112] The Lords remained intransigent on the issue, however. Lauderdale reiterated that it was improper for the legislature to 'lay down rules of humanity'. The Chancellor, Lord Eldon, disapproved of the selective nature of the bill, and his suggestion that a general measure encompassing several trades was preferable to one which specified rules for a single trade effectively sealed the bill's fate.[113] While there appeared to be genuine concern about the fire risk involved in dispensing with climbing boys, the Lords' total rejection of Bennet's modified proposals suggests that fundamentally the issue was about the propriety of government regulation and control.[114]

These attempts to reform the chimney sweeping trade coincided with a revival of the factory regulation issue. At the beginning of April 1816, Sir Robert Peel secured the appointment of a select committee to inquire into the state of children in manufactories. He accepted that some masters treated their young hands with humanity, but too often 'the love of gain' outweighed all other considerations. Children as young as six were 'torn from their beds', he exclaimed, and forced to work up to 16 hours a day. Anticipating strong objections from non-interventionists, Peel spoke of parliament's paternal and consti-tutional obligation to protect 'helpless children'.[115] Peel had already tested the House's views on this issue. The previous year, he had intro-duced a bill initiated by Robert Owen. Owen had persuaded a number of parliamentarians of the need for an improved system of regulation in factories for the sake of the children's health and welfare. Peel was recommended as the ideal person to take charge of the issue in the House of Commons. He was an experienced cotton manufacturer and had instigated the proceedings which led to the passage of the 1802 Factory Apprentices Act.[116] Reliant on running water, the first cotton mills were often situated in remote country areas where labour was in short supply. The majority of children who worked in the water-powered mills were pauper apprentices supplied to the manufacturers by metropolitan poorhouses. With the advent of steam power, the new mills were located in towns where there was an abundance of cheap child labour. As these were 'free' not apprenticed children, there was no legislative requirement for urban-based manufacturers to assume the role of guardian or protector. The object of Owen's proposal was to extend protection to all children employed in all textile mills and factories, whether apprenticed or not. The minimum age requirement for children entering factories would be ten years and the under 18s would be restricted to a $12^1/_2$ hour day, with $2^1/_2$ hours to be set aside for meals and schooling. The bill also included a provi-sion for paid inspectors. Peel proceeded with some caution, however. Aware that there was insufficient time to pursue the matter that session, he introduced the bill as a preliminary step to gauge parlia-ment's and the public's reaction.[117]

The 1816 select committee chaired by Peel carried out a lengthy investigation, which continued from 25 April to 18 June, but its evidence was inconclusive and there was insufficient time before the close of that parliamentary session for the committee to produce a report or summary of its investigation. The estimates of the hours worked each day by factory operatives ranged from 12 to 16.[118] The majority of the manufacturers interviewed by the committee claimed that the children's health was not adversely affected by their work. Their evidence was countered by the testimonies of a number of medical authorities but, with little or no experience of factory conditions, these witnesses generally spoke in hypothetical terms.[119] On 19 February 1818, 18 months after the inquiry, Peel introduced his second factory bill. This contained few traces of Owenism. The education clause had been quietly laid to rest and the manufacturers had been given some concessions. Far more limited in scope than the previous bill, it was confined to the cotton industry. Peel proposed a minimum age of nine years and a working day of $11^1/_2$ hours for children under 16, with $1^1/_2$ hours for meals and recreation. He also sought the abolition of night work in factories.[120]

The opponents of the measures focused upon the propriety of the legislature interfering with 'free labour'. Parliamentarians who had supported intervention on behalf of chimney sweepers opposed this measure on the grounds that the legislature was only bound to protect apprenticed children. Even if these children were not in a position to bargain with employers, their parents were.[121] Children who had no free will of their own could hardly be called 'free labourers', exclaimed Peel in reply. 'They were either under the control of a master or a parent.'[122] In rejecting claims of hardship and mistreatment, the representatives of the manufacturing interests insisted that there was no need for any regulation and they objected to the selectiveness of the bill. If children employed in cotton factories were to be regulated, then there was no reason why all children in every area of manufacturing should not be similarly protected.[123] This line of argument highlighted two fundamental questions left unresolved by the 1816 committee: Was factory work harmful to the health and welfare of the children? And, even if it was accepted that the conditions were as bad and the hours of labour as long as had been suggested, were these any worse than other manufacturing occupations? As Edward Stanley (Lancashire) observed, working people were 'exposed to the vicissitudes of excessive heat and cold, to damps of every kind, and to every species of bodily infirmity, in the coal and lead mines, and yet nobody ever called for such legislative enactments in the management of those concerns'.[124] A number of members objected to the authoritarian implications of the measure. To Curwen, it implied that 'the poorer orders were not fit to be trusted with the management of their own children'.[125] He also joined with Stanley and Sir James Graham (Hull) in cautioning the House against a measure which could set a dangerous precedent. With barely concealed contempt, Graham referred to a petition from cotton-spinning workers in Stockport, which claimed that 'workmen were over-laboured, over-heated, and subject to oppressive inconveniences'. They were 'a set of idle, discontented, discarded and good-for-nothing workmen, who conceived that they did too much, when in employment, for the wages which they received'. If the bill was allowed to pass, within a year they would be clamouring for a further reduction of hours. Before long workers in every trade would be pressing for similar concessions, added Curwen.[126] Clearly, these members were not only opposed to legislative intervention, they were also apprehensive about workers having the freedom to bargain for themselves. They certainly objected to workers using the issue to plead their own case.

Ironically, it was the support of two of the most high-profile advocates of *laissez-faire* policies, namely Robert Peel and Frederick Robinson, which strengthened Sir Robert Peel's hand and secured passage of the bill in the House of Commons. Like his father, Peel could speak with some authority on the rigorous and inflexible nature of factory management. The hours of labour for all employees were determined by the proprietor or manager of the mill. The child either worked the 'ordinary number of hours or not at all'.[127] Moreover, the regulation of trade and commerce was hardly unprecedented. He could point to numerous instances in which the legislature had intervened to resolve 'particular evils without prejudice to general principles'. Fundamentally, he believed that the children employed in the cotton trade should be treated as a special case. In some establishment, 'more than 1,000 children were kept at work 12, 14, and sometimes 15 hours a day'. There was no discrimination 'between the child of the tenderest age and the most grown, or between the imbecile and the strong'. In those circumstances, it was 'incumbent upon the legislature to see that such a system of over-working was not applied to the infant race, as paralysed their future exertions, and deprived them of all fair and useful recreation'.[128] As President of the Board of Trade, Robinson felt that the 'less the legislature interfered in regulating matters of trade and commerce, the better it would be for the country, but he did not rule it out categorically and after listening to arguments on both sides of the debate had come to the conclusion that 'a case had been made out to justify interference'.[129] In a division organized by Stanley, 26 members voted against the bill and 91 endorsed it.

The bill was held up in the Lords for a year. Once again, Lauderdale was prominent in leading the opposition. On the grounds that the bill was based upon inconsistent information taken by a select committee some two years' before, he successfully pressed for another committee of inquiry. This committee was chaired by Kenyon, who was strongly in favour of the bill. Between 22 May and 1 June 1818, testimonies were heard from a large number of physicians, whose evidence was generally less damaging and less speculative than that of the medical witnesses who appeared before the 1816 select committee. With the help of the Manchester Cotton Spinners' Committee, many of these witnesses had gained direct access to cotton factories and some had carried out independent investigations.[130] The credibility of their statements was thus reinforced by the fact that they were based on direct observations of factory environments. At the beginning of June, Kenyon asked parliament to postpone the committee until the next parliamentary session as there was insufficient time for it to complete its inquiries in the current session. Lauderdale was ready to claim a victory for the manufacturing interest, declaring that the 'evidence already presented to the House against the bill, was to an extent far beyond his own calculations'.[131] In early February 1819, Kenyon moved for reappointment of the committee. Having since carried out some inquiries of their own, both Kenyon and the Bishop of Chester were determined to pursue the matter. Lauderdale was equally determined to resist it and moved an amendment for the bill to include 'silk, hardware, and other manufactures'. He was joined by Grosvenor and the Earl of Rosslyn, who pointed out that reduced hours meant reduced wages. In acknowledging that he had given his support to the bills for regulating chimney sweeps, Grosvenor insisted that there was no analogy 'between the situation of an apprentice, as regulated by law, and that of a free labourer, under no restriction but that of his own will'. Eldon reiterated objections to measures which singled out particular trades or occupations and argued for a 'general law ... for the regulation of manufacturers of all kind'. This proposal was a pretext, of course, for derailing the bill, but his point about the humanitarians' selectiveness was pertinent. In a provincial newspaper he had read 'a feeling description of the hardships to which climbing-boys were subjected'. Yet, no pity 'was expressed for boys compelled to descend into coal-pits at three or four o'clock in the morning'.[132] These arguments made no impression, however, on Liverpool, who again sided with the humanitarians. With much exasperation, he dismissed concerns about the implications of the measure for the principle of non-intervention. It 'would not introduce any new principle into their statute-book' and it was 'preposterous', he exclaimed, 'to talk of these poor children as free agents'. Lauderdale's motion was defeated by 13 votes. The committee sat through most of March and for the first time evidence was heard from the factory operatives themselves. Their statements, describing mistreatment, long hours and the prevalence of poor health among the operatives, countered the favourable evidence taken the previous year.[133] On 14 June, with barely any comment, the Lords endorsed Peel's bill, with 27 votes in favour and six against.

It was another six years before the issue came before parliament again. In the meantime, the *laissez-faire* philosophy had become more entrenched, particularly among liberal-Tories, whose programme of trade liberalization was by then in full swing. In May 1825, a bill to amend the 1819 Act was introduced by John Cam Hobhouse, a Whig and member for Westminster. In addition to some fairly innocuous amendments to improve enforcement of the Act, it contained a provision to reduce the working hours of children under 16 from 12 to 11. Robert Peel Jr, who had since been appointed Home Secretary, was highly circumspect, particularly after several members spoke of extending the 1819 Act to incorporate flax and woollen mills. He warned the House not to 'carry this sort of legislation too far'. In 1819, Peel had expressed regret that children in factories were required to work 12 or more hours a day. Now he 'doubted the policy of limiting the number of hours for labouring'. He did not, however, object to that part of the proposal which gave magistrates additional powers to deal with manufacturers who ignored the existing regulations as this rendered the 1819 act more effective. Huskisson adopted a similar line of argument. He 'would not give up one point of his opinion as to the impolicy of attempting to regulate free labour; but, as parliament had thought it right to interfere with respect to the cotton-mill, certainly the more fully the provision of a former bill were carried into operation the better.' Against this opposition, Hobhouse was obliged to drop the offending clause.[134]

From this survey of social debate in the parliaments of the postwar and pre-reform period, we can see the tension and interplay between two apparently conflicting social outlooks: the first governed by individualistic and *laissez-faire* principles, the second by aristocratic and paternalistic notions of social responsibility and community-based values. Notwithstanding the weight of *laissez-faire* opinion in the 1820s, we can see that old world, paternalist views continued to influence parliamentarians' responses to social issues. This was particular evident in responses to Malthusian-inspired arguments for abolishing or radically altering the system of compulsory relief. The humanitarian and conservative paternalists were not sufficiently united, however, to succeed on every issue, and in some cases either the authoritarian or the *laissez-faire* argument prevailed. The non-interventionists and political economists usually did better in areas where the economic and financial aspects of an issue were more prominent than its social dimensions, such as in the case of wage regulation. In some respects, the influence of utilitarian liberal thinking came about because there was no predominant strand of paternalist thought at this time and the authoritarian-paternalist ideas, characteristic of Owen's 'new view' of society, were often the basis of parliamentarians' perceptions of, or solutions to, the social problems of their day.

In addition to the lack of unity, paternalists in this period did not speak explicitly of the paternal responsibilities of parliament or of the notion of a paternal government, although the institutionalization of paternalism was implicit in many of the arguments for statutory regulation. This contrasts with the early Victorian period where the phrase 'paternal government', we learn from David Roberts, 'enjoyed considerable popularity in the Parliaments and press of the 1840s'.[135] It was not until after Sadler entered parliament in 1829 that Tory advocates of protectionism began to focus on the social responsibilities of the state. This association of old world Toryism with state interventionism or state paternalism was to some extent, a product of the political tensions created by the popularization of the *laissez-faire* doctrine in the 1820s. In other words, the free-traders' increasing resistance to government intervention and regulation prompted the Tory advocates of protectionism to give more consideration to statutory regulation as a solution to social as well as to economic. None the less, it was a perceptible and crucial shift in perspective which coincided with Sadler's rise to fame as parliament's leading spokesman for Tory paternalism. Sadler was in fact first among the Tory paternalists to speak in parliament of paternalist social values explicitly in the context of parliament and government.

4
The 'Sadlerian School': a Defence of Protectionist, Paternalist Ideals

> The Session which has just concluded, if remarkable for the fall of one public character, is not less so for the rise of another. Let the friends of the Constitution remember, for their comfort, that they are indebted to the desertion of Peel, for the accession of Sadler.
>
> *Blackwood's Edinburgh Magazine*, 29 August 1829[1]

Sadler's parliamentary career began in 1829 and ended with the passing of the first Reform Act in 1832. Under the patronage of the ultra-Tory Duke of Newcastle, he was elected to Newark in 1829 and 1830 and to Aldborough in 1831. In that short period of time, he rapidly emerged as one of the leading (and for some *the* leading) high-Tory paternalist in the House of Commons. By 1830, his brand of Tory paternalism was distinct enough for contemporaries to speak of 'the Sadlerian School', and to identify protectionism and state interventionism as key characteristics. The notion of state responsibility became increasingly important to Sadler's paternal social outlook after he entered parliament. Three phases can be discerned in the evolution of his thinking during that period, which advanced from a vague, intuitive and essentially old-fashioned belief in the value of hierarchical responsibility and protection when he first entered parliament, to a growing awareness of the responsibilities of government in his advocacy of compulsory relief for Ireland and state assistance for agricultural labourers, and culminated in a positively interventionist idea of the state in his campaign for a regulated factory system.

We begin with an examination of the first phase of Sadler's career, which was, as was most of his career, marked by considerable controversy. It was launched with his crucial speech attacking the Catholic

Relief Bill. This secured his affiliation with the ultra-Tory faction in Parliament, but it soon became apparent that this association was not only about safeguarding the Protestant purity of the constitution, it was also about protecting the national interest which involved, above all, defending the rights of the poor and the vulnerable. Accordingly, his criticism of the Tory government's reformist policies was continued in the debates on the silk trade, a focal point of the conflict in the 1820s between protectionism and free trade. He sided with those who held that the government's free trade programme was largely to blame for the decline of the silk industry and indeed of the entire economy. This was followed by a dispute with Sir Wilmot Horton over his proposals for government-funded emigration for Ireland's 'redundant population'. After the drubbing his pet project had received in *Ireland; its Evils and their Remedies*, it was not surprising that Horton was ripe for a quarrel with Sadler. From the outset of his career, Sadler thus faced strong criticism and opposition, even derision, but with a powerful sense of his own destiny and a preparedness to defy the political economists, it was not long before he gained confidence and earned respect as a man of great piety and benevolence, genuinely concerned about the well-being of the labouring poor and a staunch defender of high-Tory principles.

I

Newcastle wrote to Sadler towards the end of February 1829 and asked him to consider contesting Newark in a forthcoming by-election. Because Newcastle 'would not allow any one connected with him if possible to vote in favour of' Catholic emancipation, the sitting member and Lieutenant-General of the Ordnance, Sir William Henry Clinton, had been obliged to vacate the seat.[2] Newcastle warned Sadler that there might be some opposition at Newark. As a substantial land and property holder in the district, he had considerable political influence but, strictly speaking, it was not a closed borough. Sadler was agitated about the prospect of confronting Newcastle's opponents, but after hasty consultation with friends and relatives he agreed to accept the offer. He immediately set off for Newark accompanied by Samuel Fenton, his relative and confidant.[3] It was only three weeks since Sadler had admitted to Fenton that he was having some difficulty completing his work on population and that it was beginning to undermine his health. In fact, he feared that the strain might prove fatal and was, as a consequence, torn between 'his public duty & his obligation to his family'.[4] Newcastle's offer was perhaps fortuitous in enabling Sadler to resolve his dilemma in favour of the public interest.

Sadler and Fenton arrived at Newark on 22 February 1829 and on the following day began canvassing the electorate. Sadler adjusted to his new role with relative ease. 'I suppose there had not been such a canvasser', wrote Fenton, 'he won every heart, talked politics to the men, flattered the women, noticed the children, condoled with the widows and out of 300 calls had not half a doz[en] refusals'. By the week's end, Sadler's team was confident that he would win the election. 'All the people', wrote Fenton, 'say he has won all the hearts in Newark.'[5] Sadler's Whig opponent, Thomas Wilde, arrived at Newark on Saturday, escorted into town by a large crowd of supporters. The poll opened on Monday, 2 March and closed at midday the following Friday. By Thursday evening, it was clear that Sadler had won the ballot, but the presence of a large number of intoxicated people in the town persuaded the electoral authorities that it would be prudent to keep the poll open until the next morning.[6] The final count was 587 votes to Wilde and 801 to Sadler, giving the Tories a comfortable margin of 214.

Sadler and Fenton continued their journey south. They arrived in London on the evening of 7 March. The next day, Sadler had his first meeting with Newcastle. Fenton was impressed by the Duke's fine appearance and prepossessing manner. He 'was most cordial' towards Sadler, 'shook him by the hand two or three times & remained above 3 hours conversing on various subjects'. Sadler had not expected his patron to be quite so amiable. He 'never dictated any thing, but entirely left him to pursue his own course of policy'.[7] Sadler spent the next week or so adjusting to his new role. He planned his first speech for 17 March when the Catholic Relief Bill was scheduled for its second reading. He was understandably apprehensive and for several days prior to the debate was almost constantly occupied in refining and rehearsing his address.[8] When the day arrived for Sadler to give his speech, Fenton went with him to the House and obtained a front seat in the public gallery. They arrived just before 4 pm and by the time debate began, both the House and gallery were full to capacity. Sadler had a daunting task before him. 'During the even[ing] he was in & and out several times', wrote Fenton,

& was I dare say very naturally a good deal agitated. The debate on the question commenced at 8 o'clock. Mr. Benson opened it, then

S[ir] E. Knatchbull spoke in opposition, Mr. Goulburn on the other side & then Mr. Bankes, after whom Mr. S[adler] rose & the House called loudly for him but the speaker decided in favour of Lord Castlereagh who made an exceedingly dull speech; after which Mr. S[adler] rose again with exceedingly loud cheering. He began diffidently and warmed as he went on & kept up the undivided attention of the House for 1 hour & 10 minutes. I suppose he told them such home truths as they had never heard before for many a year. Several times the Whigs showed much disapprobation but he maintained his ground and would have attention to what he said. Mr. Wilson said he was a master of the House. Many times during his speech there was much cheering and at the close of it [there was] loud and continued applause for several minutes. No one was attended to afterwards.[9]

While it was customary for the House of Commons to receive maiden speeches with much good-natured cheering and applause, Sadler evidently made a good impression; his defence of the Protestant constitution gave the Tory 'Church and King' party a much needed boost of confidence. Sir George Hill said it was 'the best speech that had been made for several sessions on the subject'. Lord Eldon 'had never known any one make such an impression in the whole of his parliamentary career'.[10] In a letter to Lord Lonsdale, the speech 'displayed great force, power, and energy of mind', wrote Viscount Lowther.[11] 'Sadler has answered my expectations', enthused Southey,

> and yet they were very high. You will give me credit for a good forefeeling in such things when I tell you that without knowing whether he were qualified, or, if so, willing to sit, I had fixed upon him as the fittest person to succeed Inglis at Ripon, and talked with Wordsworth about it, and had resolved to write to Inglis, in case he should succeed at Oxford. My opinion was formed from his book, and from a speech of his at the Leeds Pitt Club. No doubt great efforts will be made to put him down, but he is a strong man, and having right on his side in all things (which is the Constables staff) will make his strength felt. I hope and trust to see him the first man in the H. Commons.[12]

Sir Robert Inglis visited Sadler to congratulate him on his performance, and spoke of Southey's letter and political manoeuvring on his behalf. By the end of the week, wrote Fenton, Sadler's speech had 'produced a complete excitement through England'. It was published by several different printing firms in London and more than half a million copies were sold.[13] Sadler had thus become the 'rising hope', to borrow the phrase coined by Lord Macaulay in reference to another celebrated representative of Newark, 'of those stern and unbending Tories'.[14]

The election following George IV's death was held in August 1830. Wilde again contested the seat and succeeded in narrowing the margin between himself and Sadler, but the borough was retained in the Tory interest, with Henry Willoughby, a long-serving Member for Newark, at the head of the poll.[15] It had been an arduous campaign for Sadler who was not, according to Edward Tallents, Newcastle's political agent, 'fitted to harangue a multitude'.[16] He had been subjected to considerable abuse and hostility from Wilde's supporters.[17] At a time when the parliamentary reform movement was regaining momentum, many of the townsfolk of Newark regarded Newcastle's interference as intolerable. For his part, Newcastle believed that he had an unequivocal 'right to do what he pleased with his own', and when the election was over instructed Tallents to serve eviction notices on those tenants who voted for the Whig candidate. Tallents anticipated serving between 20 and 30 notices.[18] Similar instructions had been issued following the 1829 by-election. In March 1830, a petition to parliament from the Newark electorate censured Newcastle for his unfair treatment of those tenants who had opposed Sadler in the by-election. The petitioners pointed out that as a lessee of the Crown he had seriously abused his privileges. This placed Sadler in the embarrassing situation of having to defend his patron's actions.[19] Attempting to side-step the issue, the 'few ejectments that had been made might be accounted for', he explained,

> without looking to political motives, and might be easily defended, but he did not think that it was in Parliament, one of the first duties of which was to preserve inviolate the right of property, that he ought to justify that noble person, for exercising a right as he pleased, which was unquestioned in the meanest subject of the land.

Sadler also endeavoured to defend himself against the aspersion that he was in parliament to serve Newcastle's interests. 'That noble person, contrary to what had been said concerning dictation, had left him as a Representative of the people, to promote and secure their interests, according to his own judgment.' As John Cam Hobhouse was quick to point out, this was virtually an admission that he had in fact obtained his seat from a peer. Ultimately, the question was decided by Robert Peel, who declared that the land and tenements which Newcastle leased from the Crown 'could not be distinguished from his other property, and it was no breach of the privilege of that House for him to use the influence which that property gave him'. With regard to the charge of borough mongering, there was no proof, observed Peel, that Newcastle's tenants had been 'dispossessed because they had refused to vote for their landlord'. Moreover, interference by parliament in such instances would set a 'dangerous precedent'. Peel's liberality in matters of trade and finance did not prevent him from defending the rights and privileges of property in a thoroughly Tory manner. 'He thought that property, whatever might be the nature or extent of the constitutional part of the question, ought to have a due influence in the State, whether the possessor was a Peer or a Commoner.'[20]

Parliament reopened in October 1830 and in November the rift in the Tory Party came to a head. Still smarting from the betrayal over Catholic emancipation, the Ultras voted with the Whigs against the Wellington administration. The Tories promptly resigned and Lord Grey formed the first Whig, or predominantly Whig, ministry since 1807. The first parliamentary session for 1831 was dominated by the reform issue with the Ultras gradually distancing themselves from the Whigs. The debates reached a climax in April when the government's insistence upon an unreserved endorsement of its revised reform bill precipitated the dissolution of parliament. Sadler seconded Isaac Gascoyne's crucial motion, which defeated the government's bill by eight votes.[21] Sadler emphasized the distinction between delegatory and virtual or disinterested representation and endorsed the dictum that 'All men have an equal right to representation, but all men have not a right to be equally represented.' Above all, he was anxious about the impact of the proposed measure upon country electorates, insisting that the interests of towns and populous districts would predominate and that the influence arising from ancient privileges, vested interests and the rights of property would cease to be effective.[22] Sadler's involvement in these debates and the ill-feeling which continued to prevail among some of the townsfolk in Newark over Newcastle's political interference, raised doubts about his chances of winning a third contest against Wilde.[23] Anxious to keep such an indefatigable champion of high-Tory principles in parliament,

Newcastle offered Sadler the seat of Aldborough, an electorate in which he commanded enough political influence to guarantee Sadler's return.

By the time of the resumption of parliament in June, the Wellingtonian and ultra-Tories had arrived at an uneasy truce. In a letter to his son, Ferrebee, Sadler described the 'grand party of the opposition'. It was a 'party of reconciliation of all the tories.... The Duke of Newcastle & Sir Robt. Peel were reconciled. The Duke of Wellington was expected, but was absent from severe indisposition,' added Sadler. After cheerfully describing the pomp and pageantry of the gathering, he assumed a more solemn and candid tone in contemplating the motives which had prompted the Duke and his friends to invite someone of his inferior rank and wealth to such an occasion. I have no entitlement to the distinction, wrote Sadler, beyond 'its being supposed that I am true to my principles & have employed my abilities be they what they may in furthering them; that was the consideration that moved the Duke of Newcastle to promote me to a seat, but if the consideration is destroyed neither he, nor any one will have it in his favour to continue those distinctions, many years.'[24] Of course, it was not just Sadler's position on constitutional issues that accounted for his close political alliance with the Ultras; it was also his advocacy of protectionist policies.

II

By the late 1820s, the state of the silk industry was an issue that had become pivotal to the controversy between protectionists and free traders. A thorough review of foreign trade and commercial policy was undertaken in the first half of the 1820s. Ostensibly, the London merchants' petition, tabled by the Whig and merchant banker, Alexander Baring, in May 1820, provided a trigger for this review, but the Prime Minister and members of his Cabinet concerned with commercial policy hardly needed any encouragement. They 'were at that time far more sincere and resolute Free Traders than the merchants of London'.[25] Largely the work of Thomas Tooke, David Ricardo's friend and fellow political economist, the petition called for a complete review of trade policy and an easing of restrictions on foreign imports. The issues raised in the petition were subsequently examined by a series of select committees of both the Lords and the Commons. These were generally in favour of a move towards a more liberal trade policy, and from 1822 an extensive overhaul of the country's commercial system was carried out under the auspices of the ministers of the Board of Trade, Frederick Robinson, Thomas Wallace and William Huskisson.

The Marquis of Lansdowne, a leading proponent of free trade in the House of Lords, headed an inquiry into the silk industry, which reported in June 1821. Aware that a reduction or abolition of import duties 'would cause immediate hardship' for domestic manufacturers of silk, he suggested, prior to the committee's appointment, that parliament set aside a sum of money for those workers who would be adversely affected by any change of policy.[26] The report did not propose any safeguards of that nature but cautioned against the adoption of any rash measures, noting that an industry which had 'so long enjoyed an exclusive protection' was ill-equipped to withstand a sudden change of policy. The committee recommended a small reduction of the duty on raw silk and a gradual reduction of the duties on organzine.[27]

In 1824, Huskisson succeeded in getting parliament to approve a reduction of the duties on raw and thrown silk. It also resolved, amid much opposition from silk weavers and manufacturers and opponents of free trade, to allow the importation of foreign-wrought silks on payment of an *ad valorem* duty of 30 per cent.[28] Effective from July 1826, this ended the embargo on foreign-manufactured silks, which had been in force since the late seventeenth century.

By the late 1820s, the silk industry was in a serious slump, and even the custodian of the London Merchants' petition, Alexander Baring, had begun to doubt whether free trade was necessarily the best policy. 'Perhaps', he mused, 'too much was done, and an impetus given to our commerce which ended in the throwing of it into a state of greater depression.'[29] The weavers and silk workers of Spitalfields and Macclesfield took to the streets in protest and parliament's tables were loaded with petitions, mainly from throwsters seeking an urgent inquiry into the state of the industry.[30] The free traders in parliament resisted these demands, believing that such an investigation would be simply a pretext for the restoration of protectionist policies. The President and Vice-President of the Board of Trade, William Vesey Fitzgerald and Thomas Peregrine Courtenay, made it clear that they had no intention of backing away from the *laissez-faire* policies initiated by their predecessors.

The extent of the government's commitment to free trade was of grave concern to the Tory paternalists. This system, exclaimed David Robinson, 'is to make trade *free in everything* – in corn as well as manufactures'.[31] The author of a number of articles in *Blackwood's* on free trade and the silk industry, Robinson's views were indicative of his Tory colleagues' growing sense of disquiet. 'We who look, not at men, but at principles and institutions', he wrote, 'and who have a mortal dislike to sweeping alterations in either, may be pardoned if we examine the change which our commercial system is undergoing, instead of joining in the laudations which are heaped upon it from all quarters.'[32] A carefully considered, case-by-case, assessment of each industry would be more sensible, urged Robinson, than these sweeping measures of reform.[33] He had no objections to the opening of any industry that was in a position to withstand foreign competition, 'but the opening of one that can be undersold [was] another matter'.[34] In the case of the silk industry, the lifting of restrictions had given the French manufacturer a considerable advantage over his British counterpart.[35] 'There are few things in the New Political Economy that have a greater effect in causing us to detest it', he declared, 'than the ferocious levity with which it sports with the fortunes and bread of the community.' Not only were the new policies founded upon erroneous principles, they were 'totally uncalled for by public necessity', and nothing, he added, 'but imperious necessity, could justify the government' engaging in such 'experiments'. The suggestion that the government were acting slavishly, in accordance with the 'commands of Political Economy', was a particularly sensitive one for the ministers of the Board of Trade, who repeatedly denied the charge.[36]

On 13 April 1829, a motion for an inquiry into the causes of distress in the silk industry was introduced by Thomas Bilcliffe Fyler, MP for Coventry, a major silk manufacturing centre. Fyler blamed Huskisson's free trade 'experiments' for the industry's depressed state.[37] The concept of free trade was good in theory, but it was not practical, he believed, in the current economic climate. Given the high levels of taxation and on-going protection in the rural sector, he doubted whether there could not be 'a free trade of manufactures while, in every other respect, there was a system of monopoly'.[38] Seconding the motion, George Richard Robinson, questioned the value of reciprocal agreements with foreign states. These were regarded by political economists as fundamental to the success of the free trade system. In spite of their assurances, there was no guarantee, observed Robinson, that once England lifted its trade barriers other nations would be encouraged to follow her lead. Indeed, many of the countries with whom England traded continued 'their almost prohibitory system against' her.[39]

The motion for the inquiry was strongly resisted by the ministers of the Board of Trade. It had been put forward, Fitzgerald believed, not to determine the causes of distress in the silk trade but to discredit the government's entire commercial policy, and it was unfortunate that people in the industry had been led into thinking that a departure from the system of protection had 'caused their distress and that a return to it would remove the cause'. Fitzgerald had few doubts as to the real cause of the slump in the industry. Since duties were first lowered in 1824 there had been a huge increase, he explained, in the importation of raw and thrown silk. This occurred prior to the lifting of the prohibition on foreign-wrought silks, which had been delayed for two years in order to give domestic manufacturers an opportunity to fortify their businesses against overseas competition. Instead of making such preparations, however, the manufacturers had taken advantage of the cheaper raw product and embarked upon a 'self-destructive' programme of expansion. The subsequent increase in the number of silk-looms had boosted output to such an extent that the industry was now suffering from the effects of a saturated market. These were causes, concluded Fitzgerald, 'over which neither the government nor the parliament has had control'. Of course, the Board of Trade could be accused of having created the circumstances which had led to this over-extension of the industry. Anticipating such an accusation, Fitzgerald pointed out that the problem pre-dated the government's commercial reforms. Prior to 1824, 'the silk manufacturer had begun to extend his establishments, not from any wholesome impetus of trade', he explained, 'but on account of those impolitic laws which have been since repealed, but which found advocates to the last day of their existence.' In fact, the minister did not believe free trade had been given an adequate trial. Somewhat defiantly, therefore, he informed the House of the Board of Trade's intention to press for a further reduction of the import duties on both thrown and manufactured silks.[40]

For several days prior to the debate, Sadler spent many hours diligently studying pamphlets on the silk issue. Deputations from both the weavers and the merchants had already solicited his support.[41] On the first day of the debate, he spoke briefly about the principles underpinning the government's policy, reserving judgement on the details of the bill for a later stage. Replete with heartfelt sentiments about the desperate situation of the silk weavers and the 'victims of the free trade system', his statement was not calculated to endear him to the Tory ministry. His suggestion that the government was sporting with the fortunes of the people, risking their livelihoods for the sake of an experiment, provoked some angry replies. The silk industry, which had been 'so long nourished and protected' under the old system, was forced to accommodate and adapt itself to a new system based upon a contrary set of principles. 'It should not be forgotten', observed Sadler, that this 'great manufacture', which has

> grown to so high a state, and spread its branches so wide amongst us, was yet an exotic, and still retained all the delicacy as well as the beauty of one. Your state horticulturalists have removed it from the sheltered spot where it long flourished, to a less congenial scene; and it already fades and droops: let them persevere and it dies.[42]

The claim that tariff reform reduced the cost of silks and thus bene-fited the consumers was fundamental to the argument for free trade. Against that Sadler posited the principle of redistribution. The high price of quality silk should be set against the amount of labour involved in its production. Thus, 'it was the means', he explained, 'of distributing the means of the wealthy amongst the lower and labour-ing classes of the community.'

> It would be no national benefit, though my lady wore her robe at half the cost, or even her servant dressed in silks instead of cotton, if that cheapness left the home-manufacturer and his family naked, and robbed his board of its daily bread.[43]

Sadler's contribution to the debate provoked testy responses from members on both sides of the House. Huskisson had difficulty masking his exasperation at Sadler's vague and highly rhetorical claims. Will the member for Newark, he exclaimed, 'tell me what object he wishes to see accomplished, what evils remedied, which the present system fails to accomplish or fails to remedy? What would he permit or what would he restrict, in our commercial system, that is not now permitted or restricted?' Irritated by the suggestion that silks 'constituted not an article of necessity, but one of distinction', he accused Sadler of being conceited enough to 'think it a duty to forbid the lower classes, from indulging in those luxuries which he would reserve for the higher'.[44] Sadler was also upbraided for his unparlia-mentary language. It 'was very easy to declaim for years, and yet not to come to any decided conclusions', observed Joseph Hume, 'if the parties arguing did not understand the express meaning of the position advanced, and the phrases used.' As to what, he continued, Sadler meant 'by some of his statements ... he was perfectly at a loss to conjecture'.[45] Robert Cutlar Fergusson dismissed Sadler as 'that advocate of exclusion, civil, religious, and commercial'. In a long speech defending the principles of free trade, Charles Poulett Thompson suggested that the member for Newark, 'besides making use of mere declamation, and warning the House of the danger of adopting the measures proposed by government, ought also to produce arguments to bear him out in his statements'. Notwithstanding his contempt for Sadler and the opponents of free trade in general, Thompson assured the government's critics that what counted was 'not the principle of free trade, but the approximation of that principle'.[46]

For those members who joined Sadler in supporting Fyler's motion, it was the duties and obligations of government that were at issue. They spoke of the silk workers' just claims and right to protection. In Edward Davenport's opinion, unless something was done for these 'poor, industrious, well-behaved, well-conducted people', who 'looked to parliament for redress', the industry was doomed to perish.[47] Thomas Fowell Buxton felt that the debate had become paralysed by the free trade question. His 'motive for wishing for investigation [was] not any positive desire to return to the principle of restriction, but that justice may be done'.[48] Henry Bankes, a Tory of the old school, agreed with Sadler that modern theories could not be applied successfully 'to the complicated condition of an old commercial community. It might do in a new country', added Bankes, 'or in a small and isolated state; but it could never be practicable in an old community, with engagements and connexions wrought into the long-established systems of other countries.'[49] While not advocating a return to the old policy of prohibition and restriction, he thought 'it was utterly incompatible with the state of trade in this country to expect that the free system could be generally acted upon'. It behoved ministers to steer a 'medium course ... avoiding alike new theories and obstinate prejudices'.[50] Robert Waithman, an avowed opponent of *laissez-faire* principles, commented on the failure of reciprocal arrangements and the fact that France benefited from the massive imbalance of trade between the two countries. He likewise felt that the issue had become bogged down in discussion about 'the policy or impolicy of free trade'. It was the 'duty of the House closely to investigate all the circumstances, and allow the matter to undergo a serious inquiry'. He had no qualms about defending prohibition 'if it were found that prohibition was necessary'.

We must yield to circumstances; and particularly when the principle of yielding was founded in justice, as he thought it was; for the government and the legislature were bound to protect our people and workmen.

Similarly, Charles Western believed that it was 'the positive duty of the House to appoint a committee to inquire into the universal distress which at present pervaded' the industry. In his concluding statement to the House, Fyler attempted to salvage the debate and clarify his position. He did not seek a restoration of the old system: he sought the appointment of a select committee.[51] This proved to be of no avail, however, as the motion failed by a huge margin of 118 votes, with 31 voting in favour of a committee and 149 against. The ministers of the Board of Trade could now proceed with their silk trade bill.

The government's silk bill was deferred until after the Easter break.[52] On 1 May, when the House was scheduled to resolve itself into a committee on the bill, Fyler and Robinson moved for a six-month postponement. Leading the defence, Sir Henry Parnell endeavoured to clarify the government's position on free trade. He elaborated on the argument, touched on by Thompson, that these measures represented a move towards freer trade but not necessarily an acceptance of the extreme *laissez-faire* position. 'The whole of the alterations, which have been made in our laws concerning trade and manufactures, are no more', he explained, 'than a very slight modification of the old system, and merely the first step towards a freer system.' For the benefit of those who distrusted the government's free trade policies, Parnell outlined some of the areas where trade and manufacture were still subject to extensive legislative regulation and restriction. In reference to the suggestion that commercial policies were dictated by abstract economic theories, he insisted that these were the work of practical men, not of theorists. Lastly, Parnell questioned the paternalists' assumption that 'all commercial prosperity and distress depend wholly on government and legislation'.[53]

Stung by the taunts of his parliamentary colleagues, Sadler had spent the recess 'almost wholly employed in preparing' his speech.[54] To those who had accused him of being vague in his understanding of the free trade system and declamatory in warning of its evils, he pointed out that they had themselves acknowledged that it was a theory that was open to different interpretations. Even the President of the Board of Trade 'talks of looking towards certain principles, approaching nearer to a certain system'.

When ... the theory so highly vaunted, stripped of its disguises by the hand of time, presents itself in all its naked deformity, surrounded by sufferings and crimes, then, Sir, its advocates turn round upon us, and ask with much apparent simplicity, what it is we understand by free trade? We are to define its nature and its effects; in a word, explain their principles. This we think rather unreasonable. We presume to think the onus lies with them.

None the less, Sadler's pride had been too much wounded for him to leave the charge undefended. 'And if they mean', he continued,

that England is finally to be subjected to foreign competition of every kind, without those who so determine for her previously securing any corresponding advantages on her behalf, then we know what they mean. The proposition, notwithstanding the oracular responses of our inspired economists who are consulted on this occasion, is national degradation and ruin.... But, if after all, they are content to resolve their boasted theory into a set of fiscal regulations – if it is to end in an adjustment of the tariffs of the Custom-house ... – then, we say the very term as applied by themselves is a farce; and we do think that in determining these matters the testimony of the honest manufacturer ought to have been consulted.

Like Robinson, Sadler was not opposed to the principle of free trade when it was applied to industries that were in a position to withstand foreign competition.[55] Ideally, the management of social and economic policy allowed for a certain amount of active government direction and guidance, admitting free trade in some areas whilst retaining protection in others. This was not only a more sensible, it was a more humane approach, he believed, than one founded entirely on abstract principles.

A humane approach required governments to be cognisant of the social effects of economic policies. Critical of the government's narrow-mindedness in that regard, Sadler suggested that other factors beside economic ones ought to influence the decisions of ministers responsible for trade and commerce. Throughout the debate, there had been few references to artisans' wages and fewer still to the social implications of the change of policy. Mathias Attwood, regarded as one of the 'Sadlerian School', was one of the exceptions. As well as sharing Sadler's paternalistic beliefs, he enjoyed the same political affiliations. His seat of Boroughbridge was one of the many electorates under Newcastle's influence. Attwood was strongly paternalistic in his conception of parliament's social responsibilities and scathing in his criticism of the modern economists, whom he accused of being insensitive and inhumane. One of the fundamental errors of modern economic thought, he believed, was to assume that capital could be readily 'transferred from one branch of industry to another'. In reality, the money invested in equipment, machinery and buildings for one type of industry was not necessarily suitable or adaptable to another. The same could be said of the skills and experience people acquired in different trades and occupations. The trader 'will not abandon a station in which he has so many advantages, because you condemn it', declared Attwood:

> He will witness, year after year, the destruction of that capital which you expect him to remove; he will cling to the last remnants of his ruined fortune and blasted expectations; and, when, at length, he seeks in despair a new pursuit, little of his capital is left, and that will be wasted in the inexperience of a new undertaking.

Similarly, the labourer or the artisan is 'as strongly rooted' as his employer. Valued by his employer, his family and by himself for his efficiency and his skill, he 'will not abandon [such] advantages, to seek with his family and children, all difficult of removal, perhaps all skilful in their degree, a new occupation, where he will be helpless, inefficient, an incumbrance, and an obstruction'. The question, concluded Attwood, is 'whether we shall protect and support their industry ... or whether we shall abandon them to ruin: are we to deal with these men as a body of no importance to the general welfare, except as mere producers of bad silk goods at a dear rate, which we can buy on better terms from France?'[56]

Sadler expanded on the social theme. The deterioration in the quality of life for the labouring classes, particularly for those involved in textile manufacturing, was among the worst outcomes, he believed, of the new economy. Britain's 'commercial greatness ... is founded on the sufferings and miseries of our fellow creatures,' he declared. In defiance of Fitzgerald's explanation for the slump in the industry, Sadler maintained that foreign competition had 'condemned our operatives ... diminished their wages, and obliged them to encounter those increased exertions which have created, in connexion with immense imports, that glut which was its necessary and foreseen result'. Consequently, the infant has to be devoted at a still earlier age; and the wife taken from her natural and proper sphere, that of doing domestic duty, and sent to work; and still all this mass of exertion is often inadequate to obtain for the family a scanty and insufficient subsistence.

To illustrate the extent of this social regression, Sadler produced statistics from a range of social indices, including bankruptcy figures, poor rate returns and statistics on crime. In each case, the records indicated a worsening trend for the period after the free trade system came into effect. This was conclusive proof, he maintained, that free trade was 'accompanied by increasing labour, increasing poverty, increasing distress, increasing crime'.

The suggestion that wages should be linked to the cost of living was indicative of the underlying progressiveness of Sadler's paternalist philosophy. The price the labourer 'pays for the necessaries of life have or ought to have', he believed, 'something to do with the price of labour; to say nothing of that superior style of living which the English operative has hitherto enjoyed, as much to the advantage of the community as to his own'. Essentially, he was advocating a minimum wage, which, together with the principle of wage indexation, is one of the central tenets of the modern welfare state. The belief that it was possible for governments to implement measures that would bring about social improvement was equally progressive. Sadler was convinced 'that a better system would not only rescue [the working classes of England] from their distressed condition, but be still more beneficial to their employers'. The political economists did not share this optimism. Malthus's dire predictions and Ricardo's interpretation of Smithian economic doctrine had given rise to a good deal of pessimism and an almost fatalistic acceptance of the social repercussions of economic progress. The political economists did not believe it was possible for governments to effect socially beneficial changes. Moreover, the very notion was in itself offensive and conflicted with the belief in the need to foster individual responsibility and initiative. As a paternalist, Sadler emphasized the benefits of co-operation and mutual regard. 'By husbanding our resources, protecting our labour, and developing our mighty incalculable means', he declared, 'we have within ourselves the elements of prosperity'.

According to Sadler's holistic idealism, human existence was in harmony with the divine scheme of things. On the grounds that it implied God had made a fundamental error, he refused to accept that the population was expanding at a faster rate than the means for sustaining life. Similarly, the country's potential for social as well as economic improvement was in accordance with the divine plan. Prosperity might not be equally or evenly distributed but, Sadler reassured his parliamentary colleagues, 'there is, in every place which God and nature have formed, the constituents of internal happiness and prosperity':

> In the universal mechanism of the social system, of which necessity is the main spring, all the parts are so adequately and necessarily balanced, especially those of labour and demand, population and production, that nothing but the deviation from the dictates of sound policy and true benevolence can ever disturb or destroy its harmonious movements.

Sadler concluded his speech with a rousing appeal to the government to be mindful of its patriarchal and paternal duties:

> Let the legislature of the country, then, consult its proper character – let it assume that in which it would wish to appear before a confiding public – let it exhibit itself in the attitude of a kind parent, who, while exulting in the strength and vigour of his elder born, still extends his fostering care to the young and helpless branches of his family; and who, lending his patient ear and his soothing voice to their complaints, half removes the sorrow which he is perhaps unable wholly to cure, in the very act of commiserating it.[57]

This was Sadler's first major contribution to parliamentary debate of social and economic issues. There was no mistaking the direction of his thinking with regard to the social and paternal duties of government. Alexander Baring observed, in reference to Sadler and Attwood, that those 'who spoke so much against theories had themselves done nothing but favour the House with their own theories'.[58] John Maberly was critical of Sadler for the same reason.[59] Both Baring and Maberly recognized, albeit disparagingly, that Sadler's rejection or criticism of *laissez-faire* principles was derived from something more fundamental than simple disenchantment with the current system; it was derived from an alternative theory of society.

III

Sadler was first drawn into the debates on poverty in Ireland in April 1829, after the Chairman of the Emigration Committee, Sir R.J. Wilmot Horton, demanded an explanation for the 'scandalous manner in which he had misrepresented the opinions and the objects of the Emigration Committee' in *Ireland; its Evils and their Remedies*.[60] Sadler's primary reason for publishing this had been to discredit the committee's findings and dissuade parliament from accepting its recommendations for Ireland's 'redundant population'. The committee examined the feasibility of an emigration programme to help relieve Ireland of some of its paupers. In the preparation of its evidence, it had enlisted Malthus's help and its third, and most detailed, report for 1827 contained numerous references to his evidence.[61]

In his book, Sadler had declared that the 'wholesale deportations, now contemplated, are … unnatural, impolitic, and cruel'. He also wrote of 'terminating human misery, instead of relieving it'; of 'shipping [paupers off] to certain distress' and of the 'formidable ignorance of all the migration committees upon earth'.[62] The proposal for mass emigration conflicted with his belief in the value of community and kinship – of the physical and psychological attachment of individuals to their communities and the necessity for maintaining integrated social relations. He was dismayed that parliamentarians, '[i]magining the social edifice to be overloaded … actually propose to remedy the evil by removing a part of its foundations!' The term 'redundant population' was in itself objectionable for it implied that human beings were essentially worthless.[63] It assumed, moreover, that the country's resources were in danger of imminent depletion. 'I repeat, again and again', exclaimed Sadler,

> and, were it in my power, I would speak with a voice of thunder in the ears of those who, in conformity with the modern dogmas, are mainly instrumental in these deportations, that our fellow-subjects, at all events, cannot be superfluous till our lands are cultivated.

'And yet', he continued, 'we fancy ourselves as in a state of siege and are actually conveying our forces out of the citadel of the empire, in apprehension of a scarcity of provisions!'[64] For Sadler, the worst thing about policies, derived from Malthusian, abstract reasoning, was that they overshadowed 'those enlightened and liberal views which would dictate a better policy', and stood 'in the way of those patriotic exertions which might ameliorate the condition of that unhappy country'.[65]

Horton, 'who kept a careful record of the abuse and praise that he attracted as an emigration enthusiast', was deeply wounded by Sadler's assault on his committee, for he believed that a managed system of emigration was the best and most practical solution for ridding Ireland of its large pauper population.[66] He had maintained a professional interest in colonial settlement since 1821 when he was appointed Under-Secretary of State for the Colonies, a post he held for seven years. In 1823, he persuaded parliament to approve a trial programme of assisted emigration from Ireland to North America. Five hundred and sixty-eight men, women and children from southern Ireland took advantage of the scheme, which cost the state around £13,000. In 1825, an additional sum was voted and another 2,024 Irish migrants settled in Canada.[67] Encouraged by the success of these experiments, Horton's next step was to secure the appointment of a select committee to examine the feasibility of a programme of large-scale assisted emigration from the United Kingdom. This committee reported in May 1826, at a time when Britain was suffering the effects of widespread unemployment. The committee agreed that there were sound reasons for encouraging unemployed labourers and pauper families to emigrate to the colonies, where there were huge areas of unappropriated fertile lands and where a shortage of labour guaranteed that workers would be reasonably well paid. Because there had not been sufficient time in which to conduct a full inquiry, the committee was reluctant, however, to make any specific recommendations, other than stipulating that no state-sponsored scheme 'could be recommended to the attention of Parliament, which was not *essentially voluntary* on the part of the Emigrant, and which did not relate to that part of the community ... considered to be in a state of *permanent pauperism*'. In addition, it was felt desirable that any expenses incurred by the state 'should be ultimately repaid'.[68] In the light of the committee's caution, parliament was unwilling to commit any public money to establish a permanent programme.[69] Despite this setback, Horton remained committed to the idea, and in 1827 succeeded in getting approval for the committee's reappointment.[70] Throughout that year, it conducted a more extensive inquiry but this did not lead to any detailed proposal. In 1828 Horton tried, once again, to get the House to consider emigration as a possible solution to pauperism in

Ireland, but, faced with opposition from both pro- and anti-Malthusians, was forced to withdraw the motion.[71]

For political economists sceptical of the benefits of emigration, a major stumbling-block was the cost factor. Even Ricardo, whom Horton had consulted in the early days of formulating his scheme, was somewhat diffident, particularly in regard to the mortgaging of parochial Poor Law funds to provide the capital necessary for an extended programme of emigration.[72] He was 'not convinced', writes Barry Gordon, 'that the money used for financing the emigrants could not be better spent in giving them profitable employment at home'. There were also more fundamental reasons for the political economists' objections. The colonial system was associated with old-fashioned mercantilist policies, whereby colonies were established and maintained principally as trading outlets for the mother country. Now, that system was regarded as outmoded and financially burdensome and leading economists like James Mill and J.R. McCulloch argued, in line with Adam Smith, that the colonies should be given independence and the old colonial system dismantled.[73]

By contrast, Horton's 'interest in emigration', explains Peter Dunkley, 'arose from his belief in its value as a buttress to Britain's position as a world power'.[74] In his pamphlet, *The Causes and Remedies of Pauperism in the United Kingdom* (1829), written in reply to Sadler's critique of the Emigration Committee, Horton made a distinction between a regulated system of colonization and an unregulated 'casual, desultory and unprovided' process of emigration. The Emigration Committee's proposal was for a regulated system. This was spelt out in the committee's third report of 1827, which defined it as the difference

> between the planting of Colonists in a soil prepared to receive them, *aided by a small portion of capital*, to enable them immediately to take root and flourish, and the mere pouring of an indefinite quantity of labourers, as Emigrants *without capital*, into a country where there is a very small proportion of capital previously existing to employ them, and where, although, after much misery and privation, they may finally succeed, they are nevertheless subject to chances of failure and vicissitudes not experienced by the former class of persons.[75]

For this extensive and permanent programme of emigration to operate effectively and uniformly there had to be some form of centralized planning, which gave the Ricardian political economists another reason for being wary of the scheme. The committee had recommended the establishment of a board of emigration in London. It envisaged that this board would be 'placed under the direct control of an executive department of the State' and would be supported by agents acting under its authority in Britain and Ireland and in the colonies.[76] This would require a much higher level of government regulation and control than was generally acceptable to the economists. Indeed, it was reminiscent of Robert Owen's educational schemes for the labouring classes. In both cases there was a requirement for a high degree of paternal authority and control. Horton's response to arguments for introducing poor laws into Ireland was in that respect particularly revealing. 'I am of opinion', he wrote, that, whatever system of relief is finally decided upon, it 'should partake of the character of police, as well as of charity'.[77]

Given the difficulty Horton was having in convincing the political economists of the merits of his emigration scheme, it is little wonder that he was so exasperated by Sadler's charges. Alluding to his critic's use of emotive terms, like 'transportation' and 'deportation', and allegations of cruelty and heartlessness, there were no grounds, Horton declared, for suggesting that labourers would be coerced into emigrating.[78] The committee seemed to be genuine in its efforts to provide the labouring poor of Ireland with a means of escaping dire poverty. However, the mere mention of Malthus was sufficient to cloud Sadler's judgement and prevent him from discerning anything of value in its recommendations. Aware of this, Horton urged against any connotations being attached to the term 'redundancy' in the report. It merely was used to identify the problem of widespread unemployment in Ireland, which arose from the 'disproportion of the supply for labour to the demand', and its effect in forcing down wages. 'If Mr. Sadler had taken the trouble to read the Report and Evidence of the Committee,' he exclaimed,

> it is impossible but that he must have known that that Committee never argued, directly or indirectly, that Ireland did not produce sufficient 'edible products' (as he calls them), for her population; but that they limited their assertion of redundancy to the fact, that there were many thousands of able-bodied Irish labourers, who had nothing but their labour to offer in exchange for the means of existence; and who, as no demand existed for that labour, possessed no pecuniary means of purchasing those edible products.[79]

In Horton's opinion, Malthusian population theory was misunderstood largely because its advocates failed to make a 'sufficient distinction between the abstract existence or production of food, and the capacity of a certain part of the population to gain possession of food when produced'. Accordingly, the country's value as a potential source of food was only material when labourers had adequate work and thus an adequate income to purchase the food necessary to sustain them. Realizing the absurdity of grounding 'practical measures upon mere abstract theories', Horton explained that his policy was 'to endeavour to adjust abstract principles to the machinery of social life'. Malthus's claims about the pressure of population growth upon the production of food could only be understood, he concluded, in terms of the labourer's ability to purchase food.[80]

Sadler deflected Horton's attack with a standard response. His criticism was not aimed at the individual members of the committee but at the principles which underpinned their inquiries. He then produced, as evidence of the impolitic and 'anti-national' character of the committee's projects, statistics from the 1825 emigration experiment in Canada. According to Sadler's interpretation of these figures, sickness was more prevalent and the mortality rate much higher than it was for either England, Ireland or Wales during the same period. It was not necessary, he contended, when there were millions of acres in the mother country which had yet to be brought into cultivation, for the government to resort to such a drastic and costly undertaking. Sadler informed the House of his intention shortly to submit a proposal for the relief of Ireland's poor. This would not be a 'plan of wild theory', he explained, but one of 'real practical benevolence, calculated to prove an effectual and a speedy remedy for the evils of their present condition'. The prospect was somewhat daunting, however. Indeed, if it had not been for the taunts of Maberly, who had upbraided him for being too willing to badger the government and yet not so willing to come forward with anything constructive, he was not sure if he would have had the courage to take up the matter.[81] It was in fact another 12 months before he brought forward his proposal for Ireland. In the meantime, he was largely engaged in completing his book on population.

IV

Sadler made a considerable impact upon the House during the first two years of his parliamentary career. In terms of the development of paternalist social thought and the general reception of his ideas, two things are manifest. First, several members had begun to view his ideas as representative of a particular school of thought. Second, Sadler's critics were beginning to realize that such ideas, notwithstanding their lack of intellectual rigour, could be very appealing. Even before Sadler entered parliament and began establishing himself as leader of the Tory paternalists, his *Ireland; its Evils, and their Remedies* had made a favourable impression on several high-profile politicians and influential public figures. 'I feel … that to argue against views and notions so extravagant is a positive waste of time,' explained Wilmot Horton in his rejoinder to Sadler's critique,

> and, had I not known that Mr. Sadler's publication had captivated persons whose judgment and position ought to have protected them from its delusions, I would not have employed my time in the detailed refutation of such irrational principles.[82]

This might have been a reference to the Duke of Wellington, who is purported to have told Horton that Sadler was 'the only man that had written common sense about Ireland', or to the Earl of Darnley. In his motion of 1 May 1828 for the appointment of a committee on the distressed state of Ireland, Darnley recited Sadler's 'law of increase' as proof of the futility of emigration schemes.[83] By this 'law, which it was impossible to control', he informed their lordships, 'the increase of the population took place in an increasing ratio, as the numbers of the people diminished; and it followed, that the more they unpeopled Ireland, the more rapidly the population would increase'.[84] Not long after that, in July 1828, the *Quarterly* published Southey's highly favourable review of *Ireland; its Evils, and their Remedies*.

The fact that Sadler's thesis had drawn the teeth of Malthusian claims attributing Ireland's depressed state to the rapid growth of its labouring population was for Southey one of its most important achievements. He 'has proved by indisputable evidence', he declared, 'that the present condition of the peasantry of Ireland, however destitute and miserable, is still much superior to that of the population of the same island some centuries ago, when the number of the people did not exceed one million'.[85] Like Sadler, Southey believed that absentee landlords were 'responsible for much of the misery and degradation visible among their tenants'. An 'organized system for the maintenance and employment of the poor' would 'check the misconduct of middlemen', and restore an identity of interest between owners and occupiers. At present, he explained, the 'ownership of an Irish estate is vested in one person, and the management of it in another'.[86] Southey approved of Sadler's argument for a non-discriminatory system of relief in which able-bodied labourers would not be excluded. He also endorsed his claims about Ireland's vast untapped resources:

> She possesses, in no ordinary degree, all the natural requisites necessary to render her wealthy, prosperous, and happy ... All that is wanting is to give these inexhaustible resources a proper direction.[87]

Originally in favour of emigration schemes, Southey published a highly favourable review of the Emigration Committee's report in the March 1828 edition of the *Quarterly Review*. Referring to this article, H.J.M. Johnston, an historian of emigration policy, maintains that, 'oblivious of the idea that it would be an injustice to ask the poor to emigrate ... Southey accepted the evidence and recommendations of the Emigration Committees without reservation. In this he may have been exceptionally uncritical', adds Johnston, 'but his sentiments were of a kind that old-school Tories could respect.'[88] Johnston maintains that the *Quarterly Review* was consistent in its support of Horton's schemes. It was not. After reading Sadler's critique of the Emigration Committee's proposals, Southey began to reconsider the merits of assisted emigration and seems in fact to have acquired some quite powerful reservations. In a review of *Ireland; its Evils, and their Remedies*, published in the next issue of the *Quarterly*, he wrote,

> We are far from doubting that emigration is a subject which ought, at all times, to engage the serious attention of the rulers and legislators of this great colonizing empire; but we have many doubts indeed whether it be the one that has any claims to fix the studies and researches at this moment of the proprietors of the Irish soil, with the view of either bettering the condition of their peasantry or the amount of their rentals.... It is recommended, that the landowners of this country should raise loans – that is, should mortgage their manors *pro tanto* – in order to transport into the colonies the redundant population which incumbers an Irish estate, and, by that means, enable its owner to draw from it a larger rent, which he may expend in Paris, at Rome, or Naples. We are convinced that such a scheme never can be carried into effect: *at least, to such an extent as to render it worthy of any very serious consideration.*[89]

What makes these statements by Southey especially significant is that they come from one of the authors of the visionary pantisocracy scheme.

Perhaps the most forthright defence of Sadler's position came from *Blackwood's*, particularly from its editor, John Wilson, who wrote a glowing review of Sadler's *A Dissertation upon the Balance of Food and Numbers of Animated Nature* and strongly defended *The Law of Population* against the criticism of the *Edinburgh Review*.[90] Throughout Sadler's short parliamentary career, the *Blackwood's* circle remained strongly supportive. Robinson commended Newcastle for having 'used his parliamentary interest, not to aggrandize himself, but to serve his country – not to swell the ranks of apostasy, but to sustain the sinking cause of principle and independence – not to multiply the mercenaries of a ministry or a faction, but to confer their reward on genius and talent, and call them forth in support of the holy cause of religion and patriotism'. In Robinson's view, the 'leading men in cities and boroughs ... make no effort to find suitable representatives'. They are content to return 'such candidates as offer themselves'.[91] Similar sentiments were expressed by William Johnstone and Samuel O'Sullivan.[92] The *Blackwood's* correspondents' favourable impression of Sadler had as much to do with Sadler's paternal social outlook as with his ultra-Tory view of the constitution.

The first detailed account of Sadler's performance in the House appeared in O'Sullivan's review of the 1829 session for *Blackwood's*. Written in the wake of the Catholic emancipation crisis, this focused on Sadler's paternalist, protectionist response to social and economic issues rather than his efforts on behalf of the Protestant cause. He described Sadler's speeches as 'eloquent and argumentative, and replete with knowledge and principles'. He was particularly impressed by his handling of 'that pertinacious experimentalist', Wilmot Horton, and by his temerity in opposing those 'sages of the Satanic school in politics'. For the first time, declared O'Sullivan, the economists 'encountered an adversary by whom their favourite measures were opposed, and their most familiar axioms disputed'. O'Sullivan's praise for Sadler's paternal idealism reveals the extent to which Sadler's thinking chimed with *Blackwood's* protectionist, paternalist ethos. He emphasized the importance of social and economic interdependence to Sadler's assessment of economic issues, and recognized that harmonious relations and mutual obligation were fundamental to Sadler's understanding of social organization:

[Sadler] would not suffer the means to defeat the end, by making the stock-holders every thing, and the labouring community nothing; thus causing society to resemble an inverted cone, and to assume a position at once unnatural and precarious.

Sadler did not 'dispute the importance of the objects', added O'Sullivan, which the economists 'propose to themselves. He only disputes their paramount, or their exclusive importance'. Referring to the social implications of economic policies and the need to balance social with economic considerations, O'Sullivan observed that,

The economists seem to forget that there is a limit, beyond which capital cannot be advantageously employed, and that its best employment must ever consist with the multiplication of social comfort, and the diffusion of human happiness. Sadler would so regulate its use, as respects the employer, as to prevent its abuse, as respects those who are employed.[93]

These observations demonstrate that the Tory paternalists were not necessarily or not entirely opposed to modern economic theories.

On the other side, the *Edinburgh Review*, one of the leading promulgators of Ricardianism, was unmerciful in its condemnation of both Sadler's performance in parliament and his work on Ireland and population. This is hardly surprising, given Sadler's ultra-Tory perspective and the fact that he rarely missed an opportunity to hurl abuse at the political economists. The correspondents of the *Edinburgh Review* were prepared to go to considerable lengths, however, in exposing the errors of his arguments, which suggests that, like Horton, they were aware of the popular appeal of Sadler's powerful humanitarian, paternalist rhetoric. McCulloch's disparaging review of *Ireland; its Evils, and their Remedies* appeared in the July 1829 issue of the *Edinburgh Review*. This was after publication of the second edition of Sadler's book, which its enterprising publisher, John Murray, had arranged following the Newark by-election.[94] 'If Mr Sadler had not got a seat in the House of Commons, we scarcely think', wrote McCulloch,

we should have been tempted to notice his work on Ireland. Notwithstanding the *piquant* abuse of theorists and theories, the false reasonings and misrepresentations, the self-complacent gratulations and the appeals made in almost every page to vulgar feelings and prejudices, we doubt whether a hundred copies of this work would ever have been sold, had not the Duke of Newcastle taken the author under his protection.[95]

Sadler received a copy of the review while on holiday at Redcar. He assumed it was the work of Wilmot Horton and was not unduly perturbed by it. In fact 'he was vastly pleased', wrote Fenton, '& said I thought they might have ridiculed some grammatical errors as it was written in such haste … It is just what I could have wished, mere abuse.'[96]

The task of reviewing *The Law of Population* was given to Lord Macaulay. An uncompromising piece, from a formidable opponent, it opened with this damming statement: 'We did not expect a good book from Mr. Sadler; and it is well that we did not; for he has given us a very bad one. The matter of his treatise is extraordinary; the manner more extraordinary still.' Macaulay continued in that vein for the rest of the article. This time more eager to defend his position, Sadler wrote a detailed refutation. Macaulay replied with another trouncing, entitled *'Sadler's Refutation, Refuted'*.[97] Like Cobbett, Macaulay 'had no mercy for bad writers', but there were more vital reasons perhaps than straightforward intolerance for Macaulay's reprisal. Malthus was content simply to ignore Sadler's treatise, but Macaulay saw the necessity of defending his colleague's position. 'People here', observed Macaulay to the *Edinburgh Review's* Editor, Macvey Napier, 'think that I have answered Sadler completely. [William] Empson [a regular contributor to the *Review*] tells me that Malthus is well pleased, which is a good sign.'[98]

A scurrilous review of one of Sadler's minor publications, a pamphlet on the state and prospects of the country, appeared in the January 1830 edition of the *Edinburgh Review*.[99] It was work of Thomas Spring Rice, a Whig and member for Limerick. The main significance of this article lies in the fact that it was not simply critical of Sadler, it was critical of the 'Sadlerian School'. It underlined the extent to which Sadler's ideas were seen as belonging to a particular school of thought. The term 'Mr Sadler's School' was clearly derogatory, but, in outlining the traits of this school, Spring Rice touched on many of the leading ideas and principles governing Sadler's paternalist outlook. He caricatured a philosophy locked in some bygone chivalrous era and driven by anti-progressive and protectionist sentiments.[100] He was particularly disparaging in his criticism of the Sadlerians' view of the state and their preoccupation with the duties and responsibilities of parliament and government:

The vicissitudes of trade, each depression of the market, every bankruptcy at New York, or failure of the wheat crop at the Cape of Good Hope, is imputed to parliament, and to the ministers of the crown.

Spring Rice was anxious to disabuse the public of the idea that the current social and economic problems were the product of the government's programme of trade liberalization. Such suggestions, he urged, were not only erroneous they were irresponsible.[101] The Sadlerians were driven by overt anti-commercialism. They 'stigmatize competition as robbery and spoliation'; their leading principle 'is a denial of the benefits of cheapness'.[102] While he referred to Sadler and his colleagues as the 'new philosophers', he insisted that the bedrock of their philosophy was to be found in the obstructionist, reactionary ethos of the 'old Tory party'.[103]

The pamphlet reviewed by Spring Rice was the text of a speech which Sadler gave at a private function at the end of his first term in parliament. Needing time to recuperate from the rigours of parliamentary life and to complete his book on population, Sadler had taken his family to Redcar for a short recreational break. He was so anxious to finish his work that he had cancelled a meeting with Southey, which had been arranged by Lord Lonsdale several months earlier. Southey was very disappointed, for he had been looking forward to meeting Sadler, whose career he followed with great interest.[104] Sadler's recent notoriety ensured, however, that he would not be able to remain closeted at Redcar for very long. News of his whereabouts reached the nearby port of Whitby. A delegation from the town's commercial and shipping interests was sent to Redcar with a request, 'signed by nearly all the wealth and respectability' of the town, for him to speak at a public dinner to be convened in his honour. Impressed by his performance in parliament and attributing the difficulties in the shipping industry to 'idle and visionary theories', the people of Whitby felt that Sadler was someone who would faithfully represent the shipping merchants' interests. He willingly accepted the invitation. Indeed, he was flattered by the attention, particularly as he had had no prior connections with the town. With much pride, he said that it was 'one of the most unequivocal proofs ever tendered to any man that his public conduct had met with general approbation'.[105] The dinner, a 'splendid & sumptuous' affair, was attended by some 70 gentlemen from the town's business community.[106] Notwithstanding the social make-up of his audience, much of the speech was about the condition and suffering of the labouring poor, which was largely neglected, he believed, because the 'present legislative philosophy attempts to place the pyramid of national prosperity upon its apex instead of its base; its anxieties are about the summit, when it should be attending to the foundation'.[107] The gathering was reported to have listened with 'extraordinary attention' to his speech, which lasted an hour and three-quarters.[108] At its conclusion, it 'cheered him continually most enthusiastically', wrote Fenton, '& long as it was did not appear weary'.[109]

From the entries in Fenton's diary for this period, it is evident that Sadler was still very much in awe of his new status. This extract of a conversation between the two men on the Saturday after the Whitby dinner reveals much about Sadler's self-perception and his strong sense of public duty:

We had a very long walk on the sands. He was reviewing the events of the last 6 mon[ths]. Adverting to his personal success, he said he felt himself in so new & extraordinary [a] situation he could often hardly realize it. He feared he was over rated. Nothing brought home this conviction so much to his mind as the deep consciousness of his personal unworthiness. He could not believe that God almighty would make *him* the instrument of awakening the nation & directing the Governm[ent] to a better policy.[110]

Sadler seems to have imagined himself embarking upon a lone, albeit divinely ordained, crusade on behalf of the poor. Samuel Kydd maintained that his independence was such that he was 'of no party – he was of the nation'.[111] Yet it was evident that Sadler had connections with individuals who shared his Tory paternalist world-view. His critics, Spring Rice especially, recognized that his ideas were representative of a particular school of thought and the commentary in *Blackwood's* indicated that Sadler's paternal philosophy was in keeping with its social outlook. From Sadler's remarks to Fenton and his carelessly worded assurance to the House of his independence, it is evident that Newcastle did not feel the need to direct him in any way. As an aristocrat, Newcastle had little difficulty in upholding the paternal social outlook, which Sadler valued so highly. In 1819, striking frame-work-knitters in Nottingham appealed to the county's 'Nobility, Gentry and Clergy' and to Newcastle, the Lord Lieutenant of Nottingham, in particular, to support their claim for improved wages. Acknowledging that they had 'been so good as to look upon [him] as a friend', Newcastle went to Nottingham and personally 'advised the hosiers to grant the men the full price for their work that they were asking'.[112] This was an understanding of friendship in its traditional reciprocal and deferential sense. The fact that Sadler and Attwood not only enjoyed Newcastle's patronage but happened to share ideas about social responsibility was by no means coincidental.

Douglas Simes' study of the ultra Tories and their reaction to the Wellington Administration's betrayal demonstrates that the Ultras' response to social issues was underpinned by a profound sense of *noblesse oblige*.[113] This notion of honour and generosity not only fired the imagination of the Romantics but in men of high social and political status, accustomed to exercising authority and assuming great responsibility, it was taken to be a natural or instinctive attribute. The Ultra's disillusionment with the Wellington government traversed social as well as political issues. On 13 Feburary 1830, 'The state of the suffering amongst the lower orders is now dreadful', recorded Newcastle in his diary,

> the rigour of a long and hard winter is added to the most wretched distress – in all the great manufacturing towns a great proportion of the labourers are subsisting on charity alone … all suffer alike – all are becoming beggars – and yet the Duke of Wellington still maintains that no particular distress prevails in the country – He will before long be convinced of the contrary by a voice of thunder.[114]

The suggestion that the government was shirking its responsibilities in refusing to acknowledge the full extent of the distress among the labouring poor was a common paternalist theme, and one to which Sadler frequently alluded. So, too, was concern about the threat which continual neglect of the poor and their plight posed for social stability and order.

After the crucial 1831 general election, when the Tories suffered a resounding defeat over the reform issue, Sadler's interest in constitutional questions began to wane and he subsequently gave more attention to social issues. 'To his party in skirmishing debate' over the various clauses of the Reform Bill, observed Seeley,

> he proved of little advantage; not that his talents were unable to be turned to such a purpose; but because his whole soul was absorbed in other pursuits. Rapidly, therefore, his position in the house changed. A degree of disappointment naturally arose in some quar-

ters; the mere politicians, or political economists, or men of fashion, voted him more than ever 'a bore'; but the country at large soon began to comprehend his motives and to appreciate his character; and if he lost rank as a party leader; he gained it as a pure and simple-hearted philanthropist.[115]

After having been the subject of so much praise and optimism, it is not surprising that Sadler's abandonment of issues of great moment would have given rise to some displeasure among his political friends. It is evident from the letter to his son, Ferrebee, that he entertained no illusions about his political prospects in the unlikely event of his disavowing high-Tory principles. There is, in fact, a somewhat dispirited tone about this letter, particularly when it is set against the optimism and enthusiasm of his reverie after the Whitby speech. However, to reiterate the point made above, Sadler was embraced by the Ultras, and the *Blackwood's* circle in particular, for his protectionist, paternalist views on social and economic issues as well as for his high-Tory response to constitutional questions, and they were well aware from the outset of his career that the causes of distress among the labouring poor were of paramount concern to him. We now turn to Sadler's endeavours on behalf of the poor of Ireland and the agricultural labourers of England.

5
Ireland, Distress and Social Instability: Sadler Endeavours to Direct the Government 'to a Better Policy'

> Ill fares the land, to hast'ning ills a prey,
> Where wealth accumulates, and men decay;
> Princes and lords may flourish, or may fade;
> A breath can make them, as a breath has made;
> But a bold peasantry, their country's pride,
> When once destroy'd, can never be supplied.
>   Oliver Goldsmith, 'The Deserted Village' (1770)

Sadler announced at the end of the first parliamentary session for 1830 that he intended to bring in a 'bill to improve the condition of the Poor of the British Empire'. He did not, however, deliver the motion of which he had given notice. Instead, he moved for a resolution that would commit the House to accepting in principle the expediency and necessity of establishing a system of Poor Laws in Ireland. This was proposed 'as a preliminary to a general measure for bettering the condition of the labouring classes of the kingdom'. Lord Francis Leveson Gower, Wilmot Horton and Thomas Spring Rice all accused Sadler of misleading parliament.[1] In opting for a general resolution, Sadler had taken his lead from Villiers Stuart. When Stuart had raised the question of Poor Laws for Ireland in May of the previous year it had likewise been too late in the session for a protracted debate on the issue. He had, therefore, proposed a resolution that would have committed the House to a consideration of it in the next session. On that occasion Gower, together with Robert Peel and William Huskisson, objected to any resolution that 'pledged the House to a distinct line of conduct for a future session'.[2] Sadler's resolution, a slightly amended version of Stuart's, was obviously open to the same criticism.[3] 'Instead of a practical detailed measure', complained

Gower, he 'had come forward with a mere resolution, for which he could not expect to receive the support of the House.' As a committee on the state of the poor in Ireland was already in session it would be inappropriate, moreover, for the House to adopt any resolution that might pre-empt that committee's findings. The committee to which Gower referred had been initiated by Spring Rice. Sadler had declined Spring Rice's offer of seat on this committee; believing that there was little prospect of it recommending a system of Poor Laws for Ireland when the majority of its members were 'avowed opponents of the very principle'; he had also refused to act as a witness.[4]

Stuart had argued for a system of compulsory relief for Ireland in a fairly dispassionate manner, defending it largely on the grounds of 'sound policy'. It would, he believed, contribute to raising the expectations of the poor and to giving them a 'taste for the comforts and the luxuries of life', which, in turn, would help to stimulate the economy. Also, it would deter them from 'plunder and pillage' and thus make for a more stable and contented society. The social problems arising from widespread and long-term unemployment were not confined to Ireland.[5] The impact of Irish immigrants on the English labour market was one of the reasons why even the most ardent opponents of a compulsory provision for Ireland's poor were beginning to acknowledge that some measure of government intervention, whether in the form of make-work schemes or through assisted emigration, was becoming unavoidable.[6] Added to this concern was the matter of absenteeism. Stuart joined with those who believed that absentee landlords took a great deal from Ireland and gave nothing or very little back. Like most of these critics, he fashioned his argument in terms of the landowner's paternal duties and responsibilities:

> He thought that he was not going too far when he said, that in no country in the world, save in Ireland, would it be tolerated that the landlords should arrogate to themselves all the advantages of the labour of their fellow-countrymen, without giving any thing to them in return; and yet, without a system of Poor-laws, what was there to bind an Irish landholder to rescue his fellow-countryman from disease and poverty, or even from absolute starvation?[7]

The opponents of compulsory relief generally argued 'that there was no inherent right in the poor to demand maintenance at the hands of the rich'. It was not, however, necessary, urged Stuart, to defend the principle of poor relief in terms of rights. More importantly, by ensuring the security of property, a provision for Ireland would contribute to a stable and peaceful society. He accordingly 'called upon no one to vote with him on the mere ground of charity'. For he 'stood in need of no such auxiliary … as he knew he could prove that the interests of the land was as much identified with the prosperity of the higher classes as the interests of the labourer was with the land itself'.[8]

The 'rights of poverty' and absenteeism were the principal themes of Sadler's speech. Most of what he had to say on this issue would have been familiar to any member who had read his book on Ireland. Like Stuart, Sadler linked the relief of the poor with the protection of property, but he was more willing to defend this position in terms of moral obligation. His speech was characteristically emotive and alarmist, particularly in detailing the effects of Irish labourers flooding into England and in outlining the ruinous consequences of absenteeism. In defending a legal system of relief for Ireland, Sadler went much further than most. The argument that there were sound practical reasons for introducing a modified system of poor relief to assist the aged, the sick and the helpless was steadily gaining ground, but there was still considerable opposition to the idea of extending relief to able-bodied labourers. For Sadler, the rights of the poor could not be restricted, although the relief awarded to able-bodied labourers should be in the form of remuneration for labour. He also defended the poor against the charge that they were idle through choice. Disapproving of the racist and negative sentiments common among his countrymen towards Ireland and its people, particularly its peasantry, Sadler saw the necessity for defending the character of the Irish poor. The real culprits were absentee landlords:

> The poor creatures who take refuge here I do not blame. Absenteeism has deprived them of bread, and in its consequences driven them forth from their country; on the contrary, I would receive and relieve them, till a better system is established in their own country.[9]

Sadler's motion did not generate much debate, but William Duncombe, James Grattan, Sir Robert Thomas Wilson, William Henry Trant and John Berkeley Monck were all highly supportive. Monck and Grattan had long been advocates of a modified system of poor relief for Ireland. They were both highly critical of non-resident landlords. Grattan, a native Irishman and member for Dublin, had on many occasions found cause to bring the subject of distress in Ireland to the attention of parliament. Monck said it would be 'an act of justice and right, and not of charity'. Wilson agreed with his colleagues that sooner or later a system of Poor Laws must be introduced into Ireland. Sir Charles Wetherell, who numbered among Sadler's ultra-Tory colleagues, would not on this occasion give him his support. He was opposed to a system of Poor Laws in Ireland, 'when they gave so little satisfaction in their method of working in this country'. Wetherell's comments and the criticism of Gower and others about Sadler's handling of the issue were sufficient to persuade him to withdraw his motion.[10]

However, Sadler was not likely to abandon an issue in which he had invested so much time and thought. At the commencement of parliament in June 1831, Sadler indicated that he would be again pressing for a legal provision for Ireland. He felt that the King's Address had treated the issue in too vague a manner.[11] The new Whig government, like its predecessor, was reluctant to enter into any arrangement that would compel the propertied classes to contribute to the relief of paupers. It preferred, in keeping with the prevailing economic wisdom, to adopt policies that 'would encourage the flow of capital into Ireland'. After repeated demands for something be done about Ireland's distress, the Chancellor, Lord Althorp, had the previous March laid a proposal before parliament for a permanent loan fund to help finance public works in Ireland. Loans would be strictly reserved for projects of local improvement, and priority would be given to those that offered prospects for immediate and future employment. This measure was not calculated to impress the proponents of compulsory relief. Althorp was more concerned, however, to reassure the hard-line *laissez-faire* advocates. It has been 'said that it would be imprudent, and contrary to the principles of good government', he observed,

for England to advance money for this object; for that if the works contemplated were likely to be profitable, capital would be devoted to them without any extraordinary impulse. But experience of the condition of Ireland showed that such was not practically the fact there; capital was, indeed, increasing but not to the extent that must be desired by every well-wisher to the United Kingdom. It would, therefore, not be thought contrary to principle, or to those views that ought to guide an enlightened Government, to give an artificial direction to capital by the application of the powers of the Legislature.[12]

Several members, including Sadler, complained about the measure's inadequacy and insisted that the only hope for Ireland was to adopt 'a well-regulated system of Poor-laws'.[13]

In recent years and particularly after the passing of the Catholic relief bill, the Irish question had been the subject of countless debates in both Houses. After years of complaints about the negligence of the wealthy classes in Ireland, particularly of the large body of non-resident landowners, the argument that the government should take the matter in hand was gaining wider acceptance. Any examination of the various arguments for and against government intervention must be to some extent complicated by the political realignments following the transition from a Tory to a Whig ministry, but it is clear that even the most hard-line opponents of compulsory relief had begun to waiver. Sir John Newport, the long-serving member for the City of Waterford, had declared in March 1827:

> the majority of [Ireland's] poor had a propensity beyond the people of almost any other country, to live without labour. A system of provision like the English poor-laws, would have the effect of encouraging that propensity to a great extent; for, if it was once held out to them, that they could live, under any circumstances without labour, he was convinced that no labour would be done.[14]

In April the following year, he again insisted that he 'would protest against the introduction' of Poor Laws for Ireland.[15] Two months later, however, he admitted that it 'was the duty of government to show some attention to the state of Ireland' and acknowledged 'that Ireland had a claim on the country, at least to an advance of money for public works, as a large proportion of the wealth of Ireland was brought over to this country and expended here'.[16] Finally, in July 1831 Newport conceded that

> he had fully made up his mind, that a modified system of Poor-laws was absolutely necessary for Ireland. He had come reluctantly to that opinion, but, seeing that a crisis was at hand for Ireland – seeing that a large part of the revenue of the country was taken away by absentees, while the peasantry were left to starve, he had been compelled to conclude, that the time was come, when a portion of the produce of Ireland must be appropriated by the law to relieve the wants of the people. Something must be done, and speedily.[17]

George Dawson, a former Tory representative of Londonderry, who had served as a treasury secretary in Wellington's administration, had likewise been long opposed to compulsory relief for Ireland. If 'the poor-laws were introduced into Ireland', he observed in 1822, 'the result would be, that the poor would have to support the poor'.[18] Five years later, he was still 'raising his voice against' their introduction, for he believed that the various accounts which had been related to parliament about the prevalence of distress in Ireland were grossly exaggerated.[19] He also objected to the advancing of public money for public works, insisting that these should be left to 'private and individual enterprise; and he was sure that sufficient resources existed in Ireland to encourage and promote such objects, without any assistance from government'.[20] The following year, when Villiers Stuart introduced his motion for the relief of Ireland, Dawson was still adamant that a Poor Law for Ireland 'would be the greatest evil which could befall the country'. Curiously, however, he took the opportunity of apprising the House 'of the work on Ireland which had lately been produced from the pen of the hon. member for Newark':

> That work was, in his opinion, not only the best, but the most intelligent and interesting which had ever been published upon the subject, and, although he could not agree with the hon. member in every respect, he had felt much surprise to find an English gentleman so well acquainted with the affairs of Ireland, and one who, possessing that knowledge, had treated the subject with much fairness and liberality.[21]

By March 1831, '[h]aving considered the subject much', Dawson finally accepted that the condition of the Irish poor could not be ameliorated 'unless some system of Poor-laws were adopted'.[22] His change of heart, like Newport's, coincided with the accession of the Grey government, but it was a major concession none the less.

How much Sadler's book contributed to Dawson's about-face on this issue is a matter of speculation, but Sadler was certainly regarded by some members of parliament as an authority on Ireland.[23] Lord Darnley, an outspoken proponent of compulsory relief for Ireland, used extracts from *Ireland; its Evils, and their Remedies* to support his motion of May 1828 for a select committee on the state of Ireland.[24] Sadler's book had only just been published but was immediately regarded as an authoritative analysis of the Irish problem. In a debate on the state of County Clare and other parts of Ireland suffering from a shortage of basic provisions, James Grattan declared that 'the export of produce was the most miserable kind of export, and that most to be deprecated, and [he] agreed with the sentiments contained in the best book ever written on Ireland – that by the hon. member for Newark – in which he said, that when there was distress the export of corn and cattle ought to be stopped, and applied to feed the people.'[25]

There were pragmatic as well as humanitarian reasons for the emergence of a more conciliatory attitude towards Ireland. Parliamentarians were becoming increasingly concerned about the country's social instability. Several riots had recently taken place in the west of Ireland, where near-famine conditions prevailed. In his address to parliament on 21 June 1831, the King described these as 'local disturbances, unconnected with any political causes'.[26] A number of petitions seeking redress for Ireland's poor were subsequently tabled in parliament. Lord Althorp and Edward Stanley, the Secretary for Ireland, acknowledged that serious problems existed in that country, but they were wary of making any pledges and seemed to be at a loss to know how best to deal with the matter.[27]

On 29 August 1831, Sadler was finally afforded an opportunity to deliver his second motion on Ireland. Taking advantage of the increasing apprehension and feelings of insecurity that existed among the propertied classes following the recent civil unrest, Sadler dwelt on the 'political consequences of thus habitually neglecting the distresses of the people'.

> I need not give a catalogue of the barbarous appellations by which Ireland has been successively disturbed and afflicted. They have all sprung immediately ... from those local oppressions which have tormented and desolated Ireland, and to which Government itself has been accessory, by affording no relief to the distresses thus constantly occasioned.[28]

As before, Sadler wanted the House to agree to a resolution on the principle of compulsory relief for Ireland's poor, prior to his bringing forward a detailed proposal. Again he stressed the poor's right to relief and invoked a range of authorities, including Edmund Burke, John Locke, Sir Matthew Hale and William Blackstone, in support of his claim that this right was grounded in the laws of God and of nature. He maintained, in addition, that a compulsory provision for the poor was defensible in terms of common law and of common sense and was, moreover, the foundation of a civilized and humane society.[29]

Fundamental to Sadler's resolution on Ireland, was the belief that a poor relief provision for Ireland must include assistance for unemployed labourers. Most members, however, were reluctant to sanction a comprehensive and non-discriminatory Poor Law for Ireland, and for those who had only just come to accept the necessity of a compulsory provision it was generally out of the question. There were practical reasons for this. While it was now accepted that there was a strong humanitarian case for assisting the sick and the aged, some doubted whether the country had sufficient resources to provide relief for the unemployed as well. For landowners in particular, one of the most powerful arguments against a Poor Law for Ireland rested on the conviction that within a few years of its implementation a parochial rate would consume the whole of the country's rental income. The Emigration Committee's unequivocal acceptance of Malthus's views in that regard had done little to dispel such fears. The reports of 1826 and 1827 warned that the country's resources could not continue to keep pace with the apparently unrelenting expansion of its peasant population.[30] These authoritative claims were enough to convince the Earl of Limerick that if a system of poor relief was introduced into Ireland, 'every thing would tumble down, and leave all on the same hopeless level of poverty'.[31]

To Sadler, such deluded reasoning failed to take into account not only the productive potential of some 5 million acres of still uncultivated land in Ireland, but the reciprocal benefits of giving relief to the poor, particularly when it was given in exchange for labour. In the cultivation of waste lands, for instance, 'the production of a part of these only', he explained,

> would demand the exertion of every individual pronounced redundant in Ireland, and by increasing the demand, would raise the remuneration of labour, improving the food, the clothing, the habitations of the lower classes, and in one word, bestowing plenty, and conferring peace on the whole community.

A system of relief, far from acting as a drain on the country's resources, would thus be of considerable national benefit:

> The increased comforts of the Irish labourer and agriculturist would augment to an equal extent, that of the English operative and manufacturer, the products of whose industry would be increased in demand, and heightened in value, by so beneficial a policy. The

market thus created by the improved condition of seven or eight millions of our fellow subjects, would infinitely outweigh in value, those casual and uncertain openings to our commerce, whether in the Old World or the New, which distant countries may occasionally and reluctantly afford.... The public revenue would at the same time enlarge with the increasing prosperity – the heavy load of taxation would be no longer oppressively felt – the triumphs of the plough would succeed those of the sword, and bury the national grievances for ever.

The propertied class needed to understand, Sadler declared in conclusion, that 'it has duties to perform as strictly and righteously due, as those it exacts from poverty'.[32]

This time, with attention focused on the state of Ireland, Sadler's motion prompted several lengthy responses and more statements were made in support of the resolution than against it. Lord Althorp and Edward Stanley, together with Thomas Spring Rice (who had since been appointed a Treasury secretary) and Colonel Robert Torrens, were the principal opponents of the motion. Both Althorp and Stanley realized that the case against a compulsory provision for Ireland was becoming increasingly difficult to defend. Althorp admitted in fact that Sadler himself had succeeded in 'shaking the opinions of many who before were decidedly hostile to the introduction of any system of Poor-laws into Ireland'.[33] Stanley seemed poised to concede defeat on the issue. He realized that 'opinion in favour of Poor-laws was every day gaining ground in Ireland, and that to an extent which no Government could or ought to oppose'.[34] None the less, the spectre of Malthusianism left ministers extremely wary of, in Torrens words, 'entering upon a path whose termination no man could see, and from whose windings and labyrinths there could be no retreat'.[35] While Althorp conceded that the Irish were suffering and that Sadler had given a 'true account' of their circumstances, he felt it was necessary to

remind the House, that on this and other subjects, calculated to excite greatly the feelings of the people, there was a great liability to exaggeration; if not as to the extent or degree of the distress, at least as to its progress; and although it was quite true, that at the present moment Ireland was in a state of very great distress, yet that country was, on the whole, in the progress of improvement.[36]

Torrens, a committed political economist, upbraided Sadler for advocating 'this measure without reference to the principles' of political economy.[37] He was convinced that the introduction of a Poor Law in Ireland would lead to the destruction of the propertied classes in that country, and indeed of civilization itself:

> [T]his partition of rent and profit amongst the people would speedily destroy all leisure, would put a stop to every species of intellectual culture, and would confine each and all to the business of providing for merely animal wants. Not a single mind would be left to cultivate at the field of thought; the progress of knowledge would be arrested; nay, so far from the human mind being, under such circumstances, capable of further advances, the attainments already achieved would speedily be lost; arts, literature, and science would be no more; and the darkest barbarism return.[38]

Spring Rice objected on principle to a resolution of this nature. 'It was very easy to say that a system of Poor-laws ought to be established in Ireland, but it was ridiculous for the House to affirm that, unless it was acquainted with the nature of the measure to be introduced.'[39] Notwithstanding his barely disguised antipathy towards Sadler and his principles, Spring Rice had long opposed the establishment of a legislated system of relief for Ireland.[40] Like Torrens, he feared it would be impossible to back away from such a commitment once it had been made. He was also mystified that Sadler could speak of the advantages of a comprehensive provision for Ireland, regardless of the fact that there was continual argument over the administration of the Poor Laws in the southern counties of England, where the practice of giving relief in aid of wages to able-bodied labourers 'had long been rejected as most pernicious'.[41]

Most of the members who supported Sadler's motion were representatives of electorates in Ireland. Sir John Burke, the member for Galwayshire, one of the besieged counties in the west of the country, believed 'that the time was come for introducing Poor-laws into Ireland'. Colonel Standish O'Grady (Limerick) and Dominick Browne (Mayo) urged Sadler to withdraw his motion for a resolution and to bring forward a bill immediately. After all that had been said and written on the subject, O'Grady affected surprise that anyone should doubt the propriety of introducing Poor Laws into Ireland. He added that such a 'measure would make all property contribute to the support of the poor which the landlords had created'. Richard More

O'Ferrall (Kildare) could not see 'why there should be one law for England and another for Ireland'. As a landed proprietor, he would 'prefer a diminished income with a contented peasantry, to being surrounded, as at present, with a famishing population, and finding his whole property insecure'.[42] Richard Lalor Sheil, a Catholic and member for Louth, would have been reluctant, given his religious beliefs, to ally himself too closely with Sadler, but he clearly shared his disdain for the political economists and believed that absentees had drained the 'life-blood' of the country.[43] Nicholas Philpot Leader (Kilkenny) agreed with Althorp that Sadler's writings and speeches had 'given a powerful aid and impulse to the question of the relief of the people of Ireland'.[44] Leader reiterated Sadler's arguments about the responsibilities of the state and the need for a more interventionist, social role for government:

> It was the first duty of the Government to see that the people had support and employment and support and employment could only be ensured to them by a large assessment levied upon the lands of absentees, and upon those of other proprietors.[45]

The government had the power if not the will or disposition to effect a significant improvement in the condition of the poor:

> [It] ought to open every new avenue to agricultural improvement, assist the people by opening new roads, forming new canals and harbours; it ought to remove every possible local tax and burthen, to lighten the duties on timber, and on articles which, in a naked country like Ireland, would assist in sheltering the houseless poor, and wanting which, were insuperable impediments to civilization and comfort.[46]

Finally, in reference to Althorp's claim about Ireland's economic progress, he drew attention to its social relativity: 'There was a great difference between improving the condition of the landlords, by increasing the export of cattle and provisions, and improving the comfort and happiness of the people.'[47] The Irish members were joined by John Weyland and George Robinson. Weyland, author of a defence of the English Poor Laws, reiterated Sadler's concerns about the effects of absenteeism in draining the country of its resources and investment capital which otherwise would be sufficient, he believed, 'to furnish ample employment for the people'.[48] Robinson urged

Sadler to persevere, 'fully believing that he would reap, at no distant period, the fruits of his benevolent labours'.[49]

Unfortunately, there was not much chance of Sadler reaping the rewards of his efforts on this occasion as there were a number of members who, though not hostile to the principle of legislated relief for Ireland, none the less refused to give him their support. There were several reasons for this. Some were disappointed that Sadler had opted for a resolution, rather than a concrete proposal. Lord Morpeth agreed with Sadler that 'it was the duty of the resident Gentlemen of Ireland, to look to the comfort of those persons by whom they were surrounded'. But, as he was under the impression that Sadler would be seeking leave that evening for a bill he refused, somewhat peevishly, to vote for the resolution.[50] Before bringing forward his motion, Sadler had, in fact, stated that his intention was 'merely to take the opinion of the House on the propriety of adopting measures for the relief of the poor of Ireland'. This was to reassure Althorp, who was reluctant to set aside time for a detailed discussion of the state of Ireland's poor.[51] Other members objected to Sadler's advocacy of a non-discriminatory policy. George Strickland 'could not bring his mind to consider sturdy labourers as the objects to whom the property of the community was to be given'. Under the English Poor Law, he added, 'every man out of work might demand relief, and he was sure, nay, he defied contradiction, when he asserted, that to introduce laws founded on that principle into Ireland would be the ruin of that country'.[52] Sadler thus faced opposition from members on both sides of the debate. He refused, however, to withdraw his resolution and Althorp's motion, carried by a small margin of 12 votes, for postponing rather than defeating it prevented all further discussion of the issue that session.[53]

Sadler's third motion on Ireland was delivered some ten months later, on 19 June 1832. In the meantime, he had become the chief parliamentary spokesman for the factory reform movement. His speech was much shorter and somewhat half-hearted. Again, he argued for a compulsory system of relief on the grounds that the fundamental requirement of 'a just Legislature' was to protect the rights of property and to provide 'by law for the relief and support of the destitute and comfortless'.[54] Predictably, his unwillingness to venture a concrete proposal gave rise to further criticism from both opponents and supporters of the measure.[55] Sadler firmly believed, however, and probably rightly, that until the House reached an understanding on the principle of compulsory relief for the poor, there was little prospect of its approving any measure for that purpose irrespective of its details. It was in fact too late, even if the House agreed to a resolution, for any lengthy debate of a bill that session. Sadler's continuing reluctance to introduce a detailed proposal prompted questions about his motives. 'He seemed merely desirous', suggested Stanley 'to put on record his adhesion to the benevolent principles which he had, on former occasions, fully developed to that House.'[56] Daniel O'Connell bluntly stated that certain members had credited Sadler 'for too great a share of philanthropy in favour of Ireland – they gave him too much glorification for his extra purity and disinterestedness of purpose, without making a proper estimate of the benefits which they were to receive in return.' If 'the rich were compelled to support the poor', he added, 'their hatred for that class would be increased, and this, in itself … would be a great evil.'[57] Realizing that he was fighting a losing battle, Sadler's commitment to the cause was obviously flagging and a number of speakers objected to the cursoriness of his speech. However, from the perfunctoriness with which members tendered him their support it was evident that the issue had lost momentum generally.[58] The motion failed by 19 votes, with 58 voting in favour and 77 against.

II

1830 and 1831 were years of extreme hardship for people in England as well as in Ireland. This depression, wrote Edward Edwards in *Blackwood's*, 'seems to be universal; it extends throughout every district of the country; it affects every interest; it pervades the whole mass of our industrious population; involving in one common ruin the agricultural, the manufacturing, and the trading classes'.[59] Both Wellington's and Grey's administrations were for much of this period either embroiled in debate about discontent in Ireland or being pressed to deal with the insurrectionary behaviour of agricultural workers in England. The 'Captain Swing' disturbances began in Kent in August 1830 and over a period of three months ricocheted through the southern counties, leaving a trail of burnt-out ricks and wrecked machinery. The severity of the measures used to subdue the rioters was indicative of the propertied classes' apprehensiveness at these outbreaks of violence. Yet, it was recognized at the time that widespread unemployment and distress had triggered the unrest. The labour-saving threshing machine had been the rioters' prime target. Another correspondent of *Blackwood's*, William Johnstone, fearful of the political consequences of social unrest, urged the government not to ignore the despair which had sparked the riots:

> Let it be shewn by all those who have property, and have a mind to keep it, that they are not unmindful of the condition of those who have none; and let them rather endeavour to stop with food, than with unnourishing argument, the mouths of those who complain, that they are willing to work, but can get no bread.[60]

The number of petitions tabled in parliament in the period leading up to these outbreaks of violence was almost overwhelming. They came from cotton weavers complaining about the state of their industry; from agriculturists seeking remission of taxes on malt and beer; from communities appalled by the state of the poor in their districts; from the depressed commercial and shipping interests; from manufacturers and operatives in Scotland and the northern counties, and from citizens concerned about the increase in crime. Both administrations seemed reluctant, however, to take any decisive steps to deal with these wide-ranging concerns. They refused to believe that distress was as extensive as the petitioners claimed. In the debate on the King's Address in February 1830 Sadler joined his colleagues in rebuking the government for its insensitivity and narrow-mindedness. He objected to

> the constantly repeated metaphor that the sun of prosperity was diffusing its rays throughout the community. Hope was constantly held forth to the people. They could no longer, however, subsist on hope; they must have relief.[61]

Soon after this, Edward Davenport introduced a motion for an inquiry into the state of the nation. This developed into an arduous debate which lasted several nights, but achieved little.[62] Entrusted with a petition, signed by 1,500 inhabitants of the city, Sadler was prominent in representing the interests of Leeds. Given his business connections and intimate knowledge of the place and its people, he was acutely aware of the effects of the depression on a community, whose prosperity depended on the stability of the manufacturing and commercial sectors.[63] His advocacy of protectionism and trenchant remarks about the Tory government's economic policies, particularly its mismanagement of the currency issue, evoked some angry and disdainful replies.[64] The member for Newark 'would find employment for our agriculturists', suggested Thomas Whitmore, 'by making the people eat dear bread, and prohibiting the importation of foreign corn'.[65] Sadler readily upbraided ministers for their lack of initiative, remarked Thomas Courtney, yet offered no solutions of his own. If he continued with this unconstructive criticism he 'would denounce him as a wordy man, without meaning, who did not do his duty to his constituents'.[66] Several of Sadler's ultra-Tories colleagues came to his defence. Sir Richard Vyvyan believed Sadler 'was perfectly sincere in the principles he advocated and was much respected by a very large portion of the community'.[67] Sir Charles Wetherell, spoke of his abilities 'as a writer and as a reasoner – striking in his eloquence – well versed in ancient and modern learning, and accomplished in his mode of applying that learning'. This prompted an outburst of derisive laugher from members on the other side of the House, and Wetherell was hard-pressed to complete his well-intentioned panegyric.[68] Daniel O'Connell, who did not always agree with Sadler, particularly on the question of compulsory relief for his countrymen, promptly sprang to defend a man 'whose talents he respected, and whom he was sorry to hear ridiculed'.[69]

The government was becoming increasingly irritated over the Tory paternalists criticism of its commercial policy. Sir Richard Vyvyan, Robert Waithman and Sadler were fond of vitriolic comment, but they never, complained Huskisson, came forward with any constructive proposals nor 'tell us what they mean by Free Trade'.

> Do they know the changes which have been made in our commercial policy, since the restoration of peace? If they do, why not point out to this House specifically the alterations of which they disapprove, and move, as it is fully competent for them to do, for the repeal of the particular Acts by which they have been effected, and for the revival of Acts, now no longer upon the Statute Book, by which industry and trade would again be placed under their former regulations?[70]

To that 'school of which the honourable Alderman [Waithman] and the honourable Member for Newark are now the acknowledged chiefs', I have one short answer, continued Huskisson,

> If you resort at all to the foreign market, you must be content to sell your commodities for the prices which you can procure in competition with the like articles, the produce of any other countries. You cannot control their capital – you cannot regulate their industry –

and do you expect to improve the chance of meeting them at equal prices by subjecting your own people to restraints and burthens, from which those with whom they have to compete are free?[71]

Huskisson's exasperation was a reminder of the broad spectrum of issues – religious, social and economic – dividing the Tory Party. More importantly, it was a recognition of the political coherence of those who subscribed to protectionist, paternalist ideals and of Sadler's leadership of that group in the Commons.

It was not until October 1831, nine months after some 19 Swing rioters had been executed, 505 sentenced to transportation and around 644 imprisoned, that Sadler finally sought leave to introduce a bill for 'bettering the condition of the labouring poor'.[72] Having taken to heart perhaps the complaints about his unconstructive criticism of government policy and failure to initiate any detailed plan for the relief of Ireland's poor, Sadler gave a much clearer and more detailed outline of the measure he had in mind. He confined his statements to the rural sector, promising to address urban unemployment at a later stage. In an age of unprecedented economic growth and social change, the government had a much broader function to perform, urged Sadler, than simply keeping the peace and protecting property. It was incumbent on the legislature, now that order had been restored to the country, to investigate and endeavour to redress the grievances which had inflamed the people's passions. The problems facing agricultural communities were largely a product of the new commercialism which had revolutionized and by degrees undermined the socio-economic structure of rural communities; unless government intervened there was little hope of such problems ever being alleviated, he believed. To illustrate the devastating effect of the 'system of demolition and monopoly' on established rural communities, Sadler indulged in a romantic idealization of the pre-industrial 'golden' age:

> [T]he revolution which has taken place in the state and condition of our agricultural poor in many parts of the country ... has hardly 'left a wreck behind' of all their former prosperity and happiness. Long placed in an enviable situation compared with those of any other country, from them our moralists drew their proofs of the equal dispensations of human happiness – our poets, their loveliest pictures of simple and unalloyed pleasures – our patriots, their best hopes as to the future destinies of the country; while their humble

abodes, the cottages of England, surrounded by their triumphs of their industry, were as distinguished by their beauty as were their inmates for their cheerfulness and contentment. Hope still brightened this humble, but happy condition, and the prospect of advancement in life was then ever open to the peasant's persevering industry, and the means were within his reach.

The inspiration for this portrayal of old England's once happy and contented peasantry came from Oliver Goldsmith's 'The Deserted Village'. The changes wrought by 'trade's unfeeling train', the dispossession of the peasantry, social decay amidst conspicuous wealth and a vanishing era of rustic simplicity were the principal themes of Goldsmith's poignant poem. For Sadler, the 'ignorant and selfish system of spurious political economy' had come to dominate mercantile and agricultural interests, so that there was 'no place for the poor, none for the little cultivator; none for the peasant's cow; no, not enough, in one case in ten, for a garden'. To add insult to injury, those who had pauperized the labourer also blamed him 'for being idle, when his work has been taken from him; for improvidence, when he can hardly exist'.[73] Thus, the deterioration in the standard of living of rural labourers was owing to the agricultural revolution and to the disappearance of the cottage economy. The labourers themselves were powerless to resist the forces that had left them destitute. It was up to the government, which had the means at its disposal, to restore them to their former happy and contented state. It 'is necessary to speak the real truth', declared Sadler,

> in order to rouse us to a sense of our duty, and quicken us in the discharge of it – this state of things is remediable – remediable by Parliament, which cannot, I fear, be held altogether guiltless of having permitted, if not produced it.

The overriding cause of the agricultural labourers' distress, he attributed to the advent of large-scale farming and its appropriation of common land and smallholdings. The enclosure movement had left the peasantry dispossessed of much of their land or means of subsistence, and ultimately of their ancient rights and privileges:

> [T]he rich man, who possessed a whole county, seized when he pleased upon the cottage and garden of his poor neighbour, in contempt of ... rights which ought to have been as sacred as his own.

Sadler was not opposed to enclosures, provided some provision was made for the poor and their rights were preserved. One comprehensive Act would have been more equitable, he believed, than the profusion of Private Acts which served the interests of wealthy individuals while totally disregarding the 'humbler rights' of their poor neighbours.[74]

The principle of equity was fundamental to Sadler's argument for government assistance. Although the paternal social ethic was still upheld in some quarters and within their own domain the aristocratic and landed classes were still mindful of their social responsibilities and obligations, the humanitarian influence of those enlightened and benevolent individuals did not extend much beyond their immediate spheres of interest.

> Individually I acquit them, and freely confess that in their personal and local sphere, the Aristocracy and landed proprietors of England are among the most attentive and benevolent individuals of the community; and that none are more anxious to prevent or to relieve the sufferings of the poor under their immediate notice and protection.

'But it is to those parts of the country', continued Sadler,

> which are far removed from their notice to which I particularly advert, where a false and pernicious system of management is suffered to prevail, and where the poor are consequently under the domination of a set of English middle-men, who often act as fully up to that character, and are as deserving of the name, as those of Ireland; and where a system of cruelty, oppression and extortion prevails, which has at length placed the labourers in different parts of the utmost limits of endurance, and in many instances pushed them beyond it.[75]

In other words, the individuals employed to run estates or look after absent employers' interests were men of a lower social status, possibly outsiders, who did not exhibit the same concern for the dependent classes as their superiors. Similarly, professional overseers and salaried guardians, whose brief was to reduce the cost of relief, had no real social obligation to those whom they relieved. In certain parishes, observed Sadler, the pauper is 'sold by auction' and 'reduced to the condition of a slave, or driven to the workhouse, where he is often treated worse than a felon'. The only way, therefore, of safeguarding the interests of the labouring poor as a whole was through state intervention and regulation. In setting forth his plan for the relief of agricultural workers, Sadler emphasized that there was nothing new in any of his propositions, other than the requirement that the legislature 'afford those facilities which shall render them universal'.[76]

Sadler's solution to the problem was to give agricultural labourers the means which would enable them to regain some measure of independence and self-worth. Under the modern monopolist system, the small cultivator had been reduced to the precarious and servile existence of a wage labourer. This new generation of agricultural workers did not even have the security of yearly contracts, which existed under the old master and servant relationship. Instead, labourers were hired as required and on a weekly basis. The advocates of the modern system had raised hopes among the poor of a better standard of living and higher wages. These benefits had not materialized. In the summer months, when work was readily obtainable, an oversupply of labourers kept wages low, and in the winter months, when there was little or no employment, those same labourers in order to survive were forced to make applications to the parish Poor Law authorities for assistance. Enclosures and the clearance of land had also resulted in a shortage of accommodation. Cottages had been systematically demolished 'and the plough-share now drives over many a little plot where once stood the bower of contented labour'. In place of the labourer's 'humble abode' was a miserable hut in which several families lived huddled together 'to the utter destruction of all peace, comfort, and decency'.[77]

Sadler saw the answer to these problems in a revival of cottage agriculture. Under his scheme, government assistance would be made available to parishes in the form of low-interest loans. These would be used to provide labourers with good quality accommodation at half or even a third of the rent currently paid under the speculative subletting system of 'thoughtless' and irresponsible landlords. Priority would be given to those areas where the shortage of accommodation was most acute. Labourers would also be provided with 'a good and sufficient garden', which in times of scarcity would give them some means at least of supplying their families' basic needs and in good times would help to improve the quality of their lives. Sadler regarded individualistic notions of self-help with some antipathy, but he recognized the importance of raising the expectations of the poor and of giving them some means of advancement:

[T]he advantage I ask for this class ... is the garden, properly so called, which the husbandman can call his own, in which he can display his taste and cultivate as he pleases; and where, surrounded by his family he labours not only for present but prospective advantages, where the feelings of hope and the consciousness of prosperity are alive within him, rendering him as happy as his master – feelings which, alas! are seldom gratified.

Finally, he wanted to revive access to a form of common grazing to give each family the opportunity of keeping a cow. This would be 'as a reward and distinction to the deserving poor', who would be 'selected for their good conduct, industrious habits, and honest endeavours to bring up their families without parochial relief'. The parish would need to provide access to grazing land, which entailed in effect a restoration of the labourer's right to common land. He added, somewhat brazenly given the sanctity of property rights, that parish authorities may have to appropriate the land necessary for this purpose. It was not unusual, added Sadler, in anticipation of his colleagues' objections, for private property to be surrendered to public purposes, such as the building of roads, bridges, canals and other works of similar utility.[78]

The initial outlay needed to establish a community of cottage agriculturists was to be offset by a significant reduction in poor rates. The rents on the cottages and allotments would cover the loan and interest repayments. Once these costs had been met the cottages and land would become the property of the parish. Sadler anticipated that in their management of this property parish officials would be more attentive to the needs of the poor than individual landlords. However, to be absolutely sure of this, he recommended a strict demarcation of responsibilities. In addition to the existing parochial officers, the church wardens and overseers of the poor, each parish would appoint a 'Guardian' or 'Protector of the Poor', whose primary role would be to ensure that the provisions of the Act were faithfully and impartially upheld. The Guardians would select appropriate sites for the construction of cottages; ensure that reasonable quality land was set aside for allotments and make certain that rents were fixed at a reasonable rate. It would be up to them, also, to determine which labourers were to be given the privilege of keeping a cow. The guardians' authority would be restricted to the daily management of the scheme. They would not be responsible for either the collection or allocation of funds. Sadler concluded with his customary entreaty to the House to honour its social obligations:

> Let the House, then, assume its noblest character, that of the
> protector of the poor, and, seeking that the suggestions of human-
> ity, and the dictates of policy have long been disregarded, let the
> law once more interpose its sacred shield, and protect the defence-
> less and the wretched from the miseries which they have too long
> endured.[79]

No more than about 50 members listened to Sadler's speech, but
most of those who joined the discussion thought that his plan merited
closer attention and voted in favour of introducing a bill. Several
members, including Lord Althorp, Joseph Cripps and John Briscoe,
concurred that cottages and plots of land would be highly advanta-
geous to the poor, but they were wary of making the state responsible
for ventures which, in Briscoe's words, 'would be much better effected
by private arrangement amongst country gentleman'. A number of
members supported Sadler's claims that the government's duty was to
safeguard the interests of the poor. George Robinson felt that the
'poor deserved the attention of that House, and that House was bound
to afford it them'. John Weyland 'fully agreed with [Sadler], that it was
the absolute duty of the Government to endeavour … to restore the
poor man his former advantages'. Thomas Estcourt 'was anxious
something should emanate from Government, to show … that the
Government was desirous to alleviate and remedy, in part, at least, the
effects of a highly injudicious system of dispensing the Poor-laws in
the south of England'. Mathias Attwood, complaining about the inor-
dinate amount of time which had been spent in debating political
reform, was pleased that the House was 'resuming its proper duties
and its proper business – that of inquiring into the situation of the
people – that of looking into the state of the country'. Attwood and
several other contributors to the debate realized that what was needed
to appease the lower classes was a demonstration of the government's
willingness at least to tackle social and economic problems. 'If the
House desired to lead the people, and have their confidence', observed
Attwood, 'it must inquire patiently and deliberately into the causes of
their distress, and make that their first business.' Sadler also received
strong support from Henry Hunt, the radical member for Preston. In
response to Daniel Whittle Harvey's suggestion that the only measure
which would give relief to the poor was the reform of parliament,
Hunt maintained that this 'subject was of much more importance to
the people than the Reform Bill. It was a delusion to hold out that the
poor would derive any benefit from the Reform Bill.'[80] The digression

gave Wetherell an opportunity to fire a broadside at the critics of nomination boroughs. 'He defied them to show any county Member, any Member for a town, however large, who could surpass, or even equal, his hon. friend in the industry, the ability, the information, the resources of heart or understanding, which he displayed on this occasion.'

Concluding the debate, Sadler reiterated the point made by Attwood and others that it was important for the government to show sympathetic understanding of the people's suffering and its anxiousness to do something about it: 'Let them be taught again to entertain feelings of respect and affection towards their superiors – feelings which, he must do them the credit to say, he believed they were anxious to renew'. Although Sadler had no difficulty in obtaining leave to introduce his bill it was too late in the session for anything concrete to emerge from his endeavours. He had intended bringing forward his proposal sooner, but other business had prevented him from doing so.[81] When parliament reconvened in January 1832, Sadler was already engrossed in the issue that was to dominate the remainder of his time in parliament, namely factory reform and child labour.

From the above analysis, we see that the notion of equity – the idea that protection should be extended to every member of the labouring classes and that all should be treated in a just and equitable manner – was crucial to Sadler's enlarged view of the state's paternal, social role. Fundamentally centralist, it was critical to his defence of the poor's right to relief, his argument for a compulsory provision for Ireland and for state-funded schemes to assist agricultural labourers. It was also the basis of his argument for a single Enclosure Act. In defending the notion of a regulated factory system, Sadler extended the idea and argued that a uniform system would protect the interests of employers as much as employees. In an examination of this argument we see the culmination of his thinking as an advocate of state paternalism.

6
Sadler's Ten Hours Bill and Leadership of the Parliamentary Factory Reform Campaign

> ... few men have, in their day and generation, been more useful
> than Michael Thomas Sadler – 'though dead he speaketh'.
>
> Samuel Kydd, 1857[1]

Most of the literature detailing the 1830s phase of the factory reform issue concentrates upon the extra-parliamentary Ten Hours Movement, led by Richard Oastler. There is no detailed modern analysis of Sadler's contribution. In fact, his involvement has largely been overshadowed by the prominence given to Lord Ashley, who took over as leader of the Tory paternalists in 1833 after Sadler failed to secure a seat in the newly reformed House of Commons. One explanation for this neglect of Sadler is that the post-reform period is characterized as the beginning of an era in which parliamentarians became more responsive to demands for social reform and were increasingly less hostile to the notion of government regulation.[2] In this contrasting of the two periods, Sadler is very often associated with the less enlightened parliamentarians of the pre-reformed House of Commons. Thus, Maurice Walton Thomas argues that the ten hours bill 'was in some respects a retrograde measure':

> There was not a word about education; the existing provision for
> inspection, rudimentary as it was, was ignored; and children of
> nine were to be condemned to work the same hours as those twice
> their age.[3]

The same criticism, a reiteration of the complaints of the factory commission appointed by the Whig government in 1833, is made by Oliver MacDonagh in *Early Victorian Government* and more recently by

Clark Nardinelli in his analysis of child labour in the industrial revolution.[4] What these historians fail to recognize, however, is the extent to which Sadler's thinking on this issue carried the factory debate forward. Indeed, in many respect his paternalist ideas served as a bridge between the two periods.

A.V. Dicey linked the Tory humanitarianism of the pre-reform parliament to the growth of collectivism subsequent to the passing of the 1832 Reform Act. He described Sadler as the 'theorist of the factory movement', suggesting that he 'introduced into the factory movement ideas which pointed to socialism'. There are many references in Sadler's speeches and publications to the unequal division of property and to the inequitable distribution of capital in favour of the wealthy minority. This type of argument, coupled with descriptions of the oppressive conditions under which the labouring classes existed, was certainly reminiscent of socialist rhetoric. For Dicey, Sadler's defeat and Macaulay's triumph in the 1832 contest for the seat of Leeds were indicative of the fundamental changes taking place in the social and political ethos of the nation:

> This conclusion of the conflict was appropriate; it was fitting that the brilliant representative of liberalism should share the general triumph of individualism. It was also fitting that the representative of expiring toryism and as yet unrecognised collectivism, should suffer a repulse.

Notwithstanding the triumph of liberal individualism, Dicey's interpretation suggests that a kind of dialectical transition from Tory humanitarianism to collectivism had taken place. 'Humanitarianism ... was the parent', he explains, 'if socialism was the offspring, of the factory movement, and that movement from the first came under the guidance of Tories.'[5] The notion of a dialectical transition reinforces the claim that Sadlerian paternalism was a crucial link between the pre- and post-reform periods. It certainly underlines the need for a closer examination of Sadler's contribution to the factory reform issue. We begin with an account of Oastler's launching of the extra-parliamentary Ten Hours Movement and Sadler's elevation to the leadership of the factory campaign in the House of Commons.

I

Sadler was approached by Oastler and delegates from three of the leading 'short time' committees at the end of 1831 and formally invited to head the ten hours campaign in the House of Commons.[6] Sadler had informed the House in October that he would be following up his bill for improving the condition of agricultural labourers with a similar appeal on behalf of the manufacturing poor.[7] He had also told Oastler that if Hobhouse had not taken up the cause of the factory children that session he would have done so himself.[8] Both Sadler and his brother Benjamin had been concerned about the effects of factory employment on women and children since parliament first began investigating the issue in 1816.[9] It was through Sadler that the Rev. George Stringer Bull first became acquainted with horrors of the factory system, back in 1823. The 'poor of this country have not a more firm and unflinching friend', he observed, 'than Michael Thomas Sadler.'[10]

Strangely enough, it was not Sadler, with whom he had been acquainted since the 1810s, but John Wood who first brought the issue to Richard Oastler's notice. Oastler's famous missive on 'Yorkshire Slavery' (16 October 1830) is usually cited as the genesis of the extra-parliamentary Ten Hours Movement. Oastler claimed that it was written the day after he first learned of the plight of the factory children. He had lived in the vicinity of a manufacturing district for some ten years and yet had been unaware of the true nature of the factory system. Indeed, he had not given much thought to the question. Like many of his contemporaries, he had assumed that the growth of towns and the spread of factories were indicative of the country's progress and improvement. 'Now on a sudden', writes Cecil Driver, author of a biography of Oastler, 'he was learning something of the implications of this prosperity, and the shock was great.'[11] Oastler's admission of ignorance has reinforced the view among historians that the 1830s marked the beginning of a more socially conscious age.[12] But one wonders whether it was really so startling a discovery. Oastler's account of this momentous occasion and its effect on both himself and John Wood, written some 20 years after the event, reads like an evangelical conversion experience. 'My friend was in bed', recollected Oastler,

> but he was not asleep; he was leaning upon a table beside his bed. On that table was placed two candles, between them was the Holy Bible. On my advancing towards the side of his bed, he turned towards me, reached out his hand, and, in the most impressive and affectionate manner, pressing my hand in his, he said, 'I have had no sleep to-night. I have been reading this book, and in every page

I have read my own condemnation. I cannot allow you to leave me without a pledge, that you will use all your influence in endeavouring to remove, from our factory system, the cruelties which are regularly practised in our mills'.... I promised my friend that I would do what I could. I felt ... that we were, each of us, in the presence of the Highest, I knew that that vow was recorded in Heaven.[13]

This 'awakening', which prompted Oastler immediately to turn his attention from negro slavery to 'slavery' in Yorkshire, occurred some seven years after Sadler had brought the subject to Rev. Bull's notice. The question of whether or not Oastler had only just become aware of the problem is of course a matter of conjecture, but Wood's revelation seems to have been the trigger needed to galvanize Oastler into action. Moreover, he would have recognized that an indictment of the factory system from someone of Wood's standing, and with inside knowledge of the system, was bound to make a strong impression on the public, more so, perhaps, than the concerns of a social reformer.

Oastler was not the first person to draw a parallel between negro slavery and the factory system. Cobbett, Southey and other social commentators had preceded him. In 1825, when Hobhouse's first factory regulation bill was under consideration, several members, including one of the leading abolitionists in the House of Commons, William Smith, pointed out that negro slaves worked fewer hours and were treated more humanely than children employed in English factories.[14] Sadler had also referred to the enslavement of women and children in one of his first speeches in parliament on the silk trade.[15] In fact, the term 'slavery' was widely used, writes Seymour Drescher, 'to highlight a whole range of discontents from agricultural distress to cruelty to animals, and to characterize all of England under the unreformed parliament'.[16] Oastler was, none the less, an effective publicist of the idea. His provocative and intensely patriotic letter exploited the social conscience which the emancipationists had aroused in Yorkshire, the heartland of the anti-slavery campaign. He rounded on the county's representatives, Lord Morpeth, Henry Brougham, William Duncombe and Richard Bethell, for having neglected their own compatriots who were existing in a state of servitude *'more horrid'* than colonial slavery.[17] (Whilst not wishing to labour the point, one cannot avoid observing that if Oastler had only just become acquainted with the plight of the factory children, this upbraiding of his fellow emancipationists was somewhat hypocritical.)

II

Hobhouse was given leave in February 1831 to bring forward his factory apprentices bill. Under its provisions, the employment of children under the age of nine would be prohibited in mills and factories. The hours of labour for young persons up to the age of 18 would be restricted to 11½ on weekdays and to 8½ on Saturdays, with 1½ hours set aside each day for meal-breaks. Also, the under-18s would have been precluded from night work.[18] One of the major obstacles to the bill was its inclusiveness. It embraced all textile factories and mills, irrespective of the size or nature of the operation and regardless of location. The Scottish manufacturers, in particular, were apprehensive about the effects of these provisions, especially the no night-work clause, on their smaller and less technologically advanced mills. For proprietors of water-driven mills, especially, the need for flexibility regarding the commencement and duration of their employees' shifts was considered to be imperative. Horatio Ross, member for Aberdeen and principal advocate for the Scottish manufacturers, presented a petition against the bill from the city's woollen manufacturers. They wanted the Scottish woollen and flax trades to be exempted.[19] A few days later Hobhouse countered this with petitions from manufacturers in Manchester and Glasgow urging parliament not to exclude the Scottish manufactories. Similar appeals had come from Dundee and other parts of Scotland.[20]

Hobhouse was well aware of the difficulties involved in getting approval for a comprehensive measure of reform in this area. His bill of 1825, far more conservative in its objectives and scope than the 1831 proposal, had been likewise strongly resisted by the non-interventionists.[21] Indeed, at that time, Hobhouse had been somewhat indifferent to a suggestion that the proposal ought to be extended to woollen and flax manufactories. He 'had found so much difficulty', he responded 'in making regulations for cotton mills, that he thought that single object was enough for a single person'.[22] The only concession he was able to obtain from the House was a reduction of the hours on Saturdays from 12 to nine. Hobhouse was disappointed, 'it grieved him to find that any opposition should be given to a proposition, that children should not be forced to work in cotton mills for more than eleven hours'.[23]

However a modest gain, Hobhouse reasoned, was better than no gain.[24] Once it became apparent that many of the provisions of his latest bill would be likewise unacceptable to non-interventionists and representatives of the manufacturing interest, he again bowed to pressure and agreed to a series of amendments. The Act assented to in October 1831 was a shadow of his original proposal. The policy of confining regulation to the cotton industry was, if anything, reinforced. The hours of labour for minors up to the age of 18 were limited to 12 on week-days and to nine on Saturdays. The period defined as the night shift was reduced by two hours, which made the no night work clause less effective, particularly during the winter months. Bitterly disappointed, the ten hours campaigners had difficulty hiding their resentment. Oastler savagely criticized Hobhouse for his weakness in not persisting with the original proposal.[25] 'Certainly the present Act is far from being so extensive', wrote Hobhouse in its defence, 'either in its operation or in its restrictions, as I could wish, but it was the opinion of the deputies of the operatives, that it secured many advantages, and was a decided improvement of the former legislation on the subject.'[26]

Sadler had not been particularly prominent in defending Hobhouse's bill, but he had been in frequent contact with Oastler. This low-key support prompted one pamphleteer to suggest that Sadler's sudden prominence as leader of the campaign in the House was mere opportunism.[27] Publicly Sadler defended the proposal, but privately he felt that it did not go far enough. 'I not only concur with Mr. Hobhouse's factory bill', wrote Sadler to Oastler in September 1831, 'but as I have expressed to him over and over again, I go much beyond it.'[28] A veteran parliamentarian, Hobhouse was far more pragmatic and circumspect than Sadler. The intention to press on with a ten hours bill was not only futile but irresponsible, he believed.

> Those acquainted with the real state of the question, so far as parliament is concerned, know very well that nothing can be more idle than to talk of the possibility of limiting the hours of labour to *ten* for five days, and to eight on the Saturday – and I was, and am surprised to find ... that the worthy member for Aldborough should appear to concur in views so extravagant, and which can only end in disappointment.[29]

Sadler, in turn, criticized Hobhouse for his unconvincing and ineffective handling of the issue. The 'question of factory labour', he told Oastler, 'never has been taken up with sufficient energy in parliament'.

Of more concern to Sadler, however, was the Act itself. This was a case in which parliamentary intervention had proved counter-productive.

The law 'as at present carried is not only nothing, but actually worse than nothing'. It endorsed the very thing which the advocates of the ten hours bill were endeavouring to remedy, namely the overworking of children. *'I had rather have no bill'*, he declared, *'than one that would legalize and warrant their excessive labour.'* It not only gave employers more scope for oppression, but exonerated them of any moral responsibility for the health and welfare of their young employees, for

> if parliament deliberately takes twelve hours, or even eleven hours per day, labour for children, the private individual responsibility of the employers seems done away with in great measure: they will argue, and feel, and act under the impression that, if those who seek only to serve the children prescribe those hours, it would be worse than folly not to abide by them; deliberately considered, as they must have been.

To Sadler, this was an issue over which there could be no compromise, for 'ten hours can never be receded from by those who love children, or who wish to obtain the approbation of Him who was indeed their friend and lover'.[30]

III

Sadler wasted no time in bringing forward his ten hours bill. Leave was granted on 15 December, less than two months after the enactment of Hobhouse's bill. In part, this haste was because of the imminent proroguing of parliament. In Leeds, the parties were already lining up their candidates and Sadler had willingly accepted the Tories' nomination. There were personal as well as pragmatic reasons, however, for his eagerness to take charge of the issue. Since entering parliament and particularly after the failure of his efforts on behalf of Ireland's poor, Sadler had been in need of an issue of substance, preferably of national proportions, which would enable him to focus his energy and passion and, more importantly, to promote his paternalist ideas and principles. The factory reform question was ideal for that purpose. Moreover, it suited his temperament. From an early age he had shown a proclivity for highly controversial and challenging issues.

The bill was certainly contentious. Embracing all branches of textile manufacture, it was the most ambitious factory reform proposal that had yet been laid before parliament.[31] It proposed, in line with the existing cotton factory regulations, that the minimum age at which children should be allowed to commence work in factories and mills would be nine years. The working hours of children between the ages of nine and 18 would be restricted to ten hours on week-days and to eight hours on Saturdays. All persons under the age of 21 would be precluded from working nights. It also included regulations to protect the health and safety of all employees and proposed stiff penalties for any transgressions of the proposed Act by employers, including gaol terms of up two months for repeat offenders.[32]

The bill's second reading was scheduled for 16 March 1832. Throughout February, numerous petitions were tabled in parliament, most of them in favour of the bill. Notably, a significant number of the members who supported Sadler's proposal did so on the grounds that protection of minors was one of the primary duties of the legislature. However, because several members had serious misgivings about the social and economic implications of the proposal, Sadler was cautioned against acting too hastily. These members did not necessarily oppose the bill, but thought it advisable to have the issue thoroughly investigated by a select committee. Sadler was, therefore, given leave to proceed with the second reading of his bill on the understanding that it would then be submitted to a select committee.[33]

For opponents of factory regulation, the principle of non-interference between masters and men was fundamental. Typically, this was the position of the doctrinaire political economists but it was also upheld by some paternalists. Cobbett, for instance, objected to governmental interference in what he considered was the masters' sphere of authority and responsibility.[34] Set against the principle of non-interference was the equally authoritative and well-established principle of state-protection of minors as a moral and constitutional obligation of the state. The concept of the free agent had been central to the factory regulation issue since Sir Robert Peel introduced his bill in 1816. The purpose of that measure was to extend the scope of the 1803 Factory Act, which offered protection only to pauper apprentices. Peel's second Factory Act (1819) embraced 'free' as well as pauper children. Those children, in other words, who were not wards of the state and who had the benefit, in theory if not in practice, of parental guidance and care. Oastler's broadside on 'Yorkshire slavery' took the question of the free agent a stage further and maintained that both the parents and their children were the victims of an oppressive and avaricious system. He also claimed that the factory master, unlike the slave-driver, had no vested interest in ensuring the health and welfare of his workers.[35]

Those who argued in terms of free will seemed, in Sadler's opinion, to be unaware of the difference between an abstract idea and the actual circumstances of the mass of the people. This is where Sadlerian paternalism foreshadowed some of the ideas that would ultimately become the bedrock of socialist philosophy. In the real as opposed to ideal world, explained Sadler, labourers were almost wholly dependent on the will of the propertied classes. The 'unequal division of property, or rather its total monopoly by the few', he explained, left

> the many nothing whatever but what they can obtain from their daily labour; which very labour cannot become available for the purpose of daily subsistence, without the consent of those who own the property of the community, all the materials, elements, call them what you please, on which labour is to be bestowed, being in their possession.

If optimum conditions prevailed and the demand for labour equalled its supply, then labourers would be in a position to bargain with their employers. But it was absurd to suggest that such ideal conditions currently existed in Britain. On the contrary, the unequal distribution of labour coupled with inadequate wages meant that one part of the labouring population was over-worked whilst the other was either unemployed or under-employed. On the one hand, therefore, labourers were reduced to slavery and, on the other, to pauperism. The labourer, 'call him as free as you please, is often almost entirely at the mercy' of his employer. 'He would be wholly so', added Sadler, 'were it not for the operation of the Poor-laws, which are a palpable interference with the market of labour.' The purpose of legislation, as he understood it, was to guard the weak against the strong; '[h]ence have all laws, human and divine, attempted to protect the labourer from the injustice and cruelty which are too often practised upon him'. By focusing attention on the wider implications of the free agent idea, his purpose was not to provide grounds for interference with the labour market, but to demonstrate that if adult labourers were dependent upon the 'will of others', then children could hardly be regarded as free agents.[36]

Linked to this issue of free will was the question of whether a child's welfare and conditions of employment were strictly the responsibility of its parents. Oastler's suggestion that parents were no more free than their children and that both were victims of predatory masters was not one endorsed by every advocate of protection. In the debate of

Hobhouse's first factory regulation bill in 1825 several members had suggested that it was not just factory masters from whom these children needed protection. Their parents were also at fault. Sir Francis Burdett spoke of 'helpless children ... sacrificed to the avarice and cupidity of their unfeeling parents'.[37]

Sadler regarded both categories of parents as 'victims' – in the Rousseauian determinist sense – of the system. The first group, identified by Oastler, consisted of parents who were so destitute that they had no choice but to send their children to work in factories. They either had no work themselves or their wages were insufficient to cover the family's living expenses. Moreover, it was not unusual, claimed Sadler, for overseers of the poor to withhold aid to families who refused to allow their children to work in factories. 'It is mockery', he exclaimed,

> to contend that these parents have a choice; that they can dictate to, or even parley with the employer, as to the number of hours their child shall be tasked, or the treatment it shall be subject to in his mill; and it is an insult to the parental breast to say, that they resign it voluntarily – no, Sir, 'Their poverty, and not their will consents'.

The second group had no idea of parental responsibility nor sense of moral feeling. 'Dead to the instincts of nature and reversing the order of society, instead of providing for their own offspring, they make their offspring provide for them.' But nor should these parents be blamed for their behaviour. It was the system that was at fault, for 'to so disgusting a state of degradation does the system lead, that they make the certainty of having an offspring, the indispensable condition of marriage, that they may breed a generation of slaves'. This was further grounds, Sadler maintained, for state intervention, for under constitutional law any child who suffered from mistreatment at the hands of its parents was entitled to look to the state for protection. It was 'high time', he concluded, 'that the Legislature should interfere and rescue from the conspiracy of such fathers, and such factory-masters ... these innocent victims of cruelty and oppression'.[38]

While the treatment and well-being of children in factories was of primary concern, Sadler also recognized that their poor physical and mental state was not solely nor necessarily due to factory masters wilfully mistreating them. The nature of the work itself – the 'wearisome uniformity of the employment, the constrained positions in which it is pursued, and, above all, the constant and close confinement' – also needed to be taken into consideration.[39] These aspects were linked to the wider socio-economic changes of the eighteenth and nineteenth centuries and the introduction of new technology and processes. Sadler compared the pre-industrial organization of labour – when 'the incipient manufactures of the country were carried on in the villages and around the domestic hearth' – with the modern factory system, where children

> no longer performed their tasks, as before, under the parental eye, and had them affectionately and considerately apportioned, according to their health and capacities, but one universal rule of labour was prescribed to all ages, to both sexes, and to every state and constitution.[40]

New inventions served a worthwhile purpose if they helped to improve the quality of people's lives. Indeed, the advent of new technology was heralded as the beginning of a new era in which the duration and intensity of labour would be considerably lessened. In reality, however, hours were longer and conditions of employment less satisfactory than they were prior to its introduction. The increase in the average working day had coincided with a diminution in the number of holidays and thus in the time available for physical, mental and spiritual rejuvenation. He looked 'forward to the period when machinery' will restore 'to the mass of our fellow beings those physical enjoyments, that degree of leisure, those means of moral and mental improvement, which alone can advance them to that state of happiness and dignity to which, [it was] their destiny to attain'.[41] In addition to the detrimental effects of long hours on the health of children, many accidents resulted from overwork and fatigue. Added to this was the inherent drudgery of the work, for it was 'not so much the degree', Sadler explained, 'as the duration of their labour that is so cruel and destructive to these poor work-children'.[42] These comments were for the benefit of those who believed that factory work was no more physically demanding than other forms of manual labour and that the factory workplace was better than many others. Indeed, there were many occupations where the work required of labourers was thought to be far more strenuous and liable to cause injury or debilitating illnesses than the operation of machines in textile factories.[43] Dismissing these claims, Sadler described the noisy, crowded and suffocating environment typical of factories.[44]

Sadler also addressed the wider social implications of the factory system. Crime statistics had risen in conjunction with the spread of factories and in manufacturing towns, generally, there was a high proportion of orphaned and illegitimate children, many of whom had been left fatherless because of the high mortality rate among adult spinners, who rarely lived beyond the age of 40. In the new factories, children were given work in preference to adults and the practice of apprenticing pauper children to cotton factories was, according to Sadler, still common.[45] The lack of moral standards among the operative class was of particular concern. Unsupervised night work encouraged sexual intimacy between young persons, and prostitution was rife in some of these mills.[46] These problems were compounded by the fact that inflexible and protracted work schedules made it almost impossible for youngsters to profit from any religious instruction or moral guidance. Sunday was the only day in which they were free to recuperate from the week's toil. They were too exhausted, explained Sadler, to attend either church or Sunday school. Unlike the Benthamite social reformers, he placed less stress on the type of education which he thought these children ought to receive and more upon the fact that there was little opportunity for them to attend school even if they were willing to do so. Finally, he touched upon the populationists' concerns about 'improvident' marriages and examined the social consequences of the system in evolutionary terms:

> Infantile labour leads to immature marriage, which crowds the generations upon each other, and, together with the great discoveries in medicine, may have increased the numbers of people; but, as far as the system has prevailed, it has diminished the athletic and active proportion of them, and given us in their stead a weak, stunted, and degenerate race, and so lessened the relative proportion of those who have to bear the general burthen, and fight the battles of the country.[47]

Sadler's description of the tyrannical behaviour of some manufacturers and overseers was an important but not a central part of his speech. He spoke of the imposition of fines for lateness or unsatisfactory work and produced a leather thong of the type which he claimed was commonly used to punish young offenders. With much feeling, he suggested that any overseer who dared to lay the factory thong 'on the almost naked body of a child', should be compelled to 'tread the wheel for a month; and it would be only right', he added, 'if the master who, knowingly tolerates the infliction of this cruelty on abused infancy ... should bear him company'.[48]

Sadler had argued for legislative intervention on behalf of agricultural workers on the grounds that without it there could be no just and equitable treatment of the poor. This was because not all masters were endowed with the same understanding of their social duties and could be relied on to respect their workers' rights and interests. Similarly, because of the variety of circumstances existing in different types of mills, the manner in which labourers of whatever age were treated and the length of hours expected of them, were factors which depended on the humanity and interests of the individual employer or his overseers. On this occasion, however, Sadler emphasized that employers were themselves subject to forces which were beyond their control for he had come to realize that the oppressors of the poor were not, in the strictest sense of the term, free agents either. They were beholden to the competitive system. If the 'humane masters' tried to regulate the trade, they would simply be forced out of it, he explained:

> for these, it is quite clear, cannot control others less humanely disposed. They are, indeed, in the present state of things, as little free agents as the children whom they employ.[49]

In other words, in order to remain competitive, manufacturers had to operate in accordance with the rules of commerce, even if it meant overworking children. This determinist argument underlined one of the fundamental weaknesses of the individualists' *laissez-faire* response to social problems and represented a major development in Sadler's understanding of the paternal responsibilities of the state.

Government regulation was required, Sadler believed, to prevent the effects of fluctuations in trade and manufacture falling to 'an undue and distressing degree upon those who were least able to sustain' them; it was required, in other words, to ensure a balance and harmony of interests. Anthony Forder points out that the policy of balancing social with economic objectives, which characterized the postwar welfare, capitalist state, is essentially an accommodation of nineteenth-century *laissez-faire* philosophy. Referring to measures aimed at sustaining full employment and to the planned economy of the 1960s, he suggests that such policies were intended 'to make capitalism more effective within its own terms by reducing uncertainty and maintaining stability'.[50] In 1832, Sadler recognized that regulation of the economy was in the national interest. He questioned the justice of a system which, on the one hand, 'allowed owners to throw out of employment all these children at a day's notice' and, on the other, thought 'it proper that they should be permitted to work them for an unlimited number of hours the moment it suits their purpose so to do'.[51] Again, as in the case of agriculturists, he doubted whether the majority of manufacturers could be relied on to consider let alone protect the interests of their employees. They subscribed to a creed which encouraged self-interest and were suspicious of any policy that might lead to a diminishment of their profits. Certain manufacturers had already attempted to agitate workers against his bill by intimidating them with threats to cut wages immediately it was enacted. Those same individuals affected to be concerned about the impact of the proposed legislation on the well-being of the labouring class. Their claim that the Corn Laws and protectionist policies were the real source of labourers' problems was likewise, he declared, full of cant:

> Why, these individuals ... have during the operation of these laws, rapidly amassed enormous fortunes; yet, during the whole period they have never found an opportunity, either of increasing the wages or diminishing the toil of these little labourers, to whom they owe every farthing they possess; they have constantly done the reverse – and they talk of Corn-laws as their apology.[52]

Sadler concluded his speech by outlining some of the provisions which he had omitted from the bill. The first concerned inadequate safety standards in mills and factories. Stressing the need for socially responsible management, he suggested that proprietors or managers of mills ought to pay a heavy penalty if serious accidents occurred as a result of unguarded machinery. To address the deficient levels of education among the manufacturing poor, he proposed that factory children be relieved of an hour's labour each day, or six hours on one day to enable them to receive 'the rudiments of instruction and education, the expense of which upon the modern system would have been nothing, especially if shared between the mill-owner and parish'. Lastly, he was keen to see the abolition of all night work for adults as well as children.[53] Realizing, however, that it would be impolitic to include these provisions, and 'feeling assured that the present attempt is *only the commencement of a series of beneficent measures on behalf of the industrious classes*', all he proposed on this occasion was 'the remission of infant and youthful labour'.[54] In other words, Sadler looked on this as a first step in a programme of far-reaching social reforms in which manufacturers were to be made accountable for their employees' welfare and watched over by the state. Obviously, he did not at that stage know that he would shortly lose his seat in parliament and thus the opportunity to realize his visionary scheme, but the fact that he had such a vision needs to be borne in mind when considering the government's subsequent handling of the factory question.

Lord Althorp admitted that Sadler had established strong grounds for an inquiry. If the claims which had been made proved correct, then some measure of regulation was evidently necessary. However, some of the statements contained in Sadler's speech struck him as too fantastic to be taken on trust and not enough consideration had been given to the implications of the proposals. Notwithstanding Sadler's good intentions, the proposed reforms would create more problems, he believed, for the labouring poor than they solved. If the House imposed restrictions on the hours of employment of children, it was almost inevitable that wages would be reduced and there was a strong possibility that the children would simply be discharged.[55]

The strongest statement against the proposal came from John Thomas Hope. He acknowledged that, in many respects, children were not free agents, but insisted that the responsibility for safeguarding their interests lay with their parents not parliament. Indeed, he 'could not comprehend how it was possible, by legislative enactments, to supply the place of parental affection'.[56] Sadler's claims about the harsh effects of the factory system on the well-being of children were largely based on evidence from the 1816 Select Committee on Child Labour. Hope countered this by citing contrary evidence from the inquiries conducted in 1818 and 1819 by the House of Lords. Comparing the statements of the medical authorities called before the respective committees, Hope showed the extent to which medical opinion was divided on the issue. The arguments raised by proprietors of water-powered mills, who feared that compliance with the proposed measures would force them to shut down or relocate, were an example, he believed, of the possible, though unintended, consequences of legislative regulation.[57] Finally, he pointed out how easy it would be to flout the regulations by employing two teams of children to work in relays and at half the current rate of pay. The workmen who were responsible for hiring their own assistants would simply 'exchange the children from one mill to another so that they might by such means be constantly employed, and, of course they could derive no benefit' from the proposed regulations. A number of members from textile manufacturing areas joined Hope in voicing opposition to the motion. James Mackenzie (Ross) maintained that Sadler had not established sufficient grounds for either the bill or an inquiry. William James (Carlisle) declared that taxation and protectionist policies, particularly the Corn Laws, were the real source of the labourers' problems. John Kearlsey (Wigan) thought that the bill would cause more harm than good and that much of what Sadler had said about the conditions in factories was exaggerated. Lord Morpeth advised the 'friends of the measure' to resist making any lengthy statements at this juncture since the government had already given an undertaking not to oppose the bill's second reading. He suggested that they 'reserve their strength until it should be necessary to exert themselves in support of' the bill. Of the ten members who indicated that they would support the motion, five warmly approved of Sadler's endeavours; the remaining four accepted that there were grounds for an inquiry but, like Althorp, had some misgivings about certain of the bill's provisions. The debate was terminated by Lord Nugent, who pointed out that members had been needlessly discussing the principle of the bill, which had already been endorsed by the House.[58]

IV

Sadler worked very hard on the committee appointed to examine his ten hours bill.[59] He was later censured for what was said to be a dictatorial and extremely biased handling of the investigation. The evidence favourable to the bill was certainly given a high priority, and because of the large number of operatives called as witnesses there was no time left before the proroguing of parliament for the committee to hear evidence from manufacturers.[60] Most of the operatives came from Leeds where the Ten Hours Movement had a strong foothold. Sadler was also heavily criticized for allowing it to become involved in the preparation of witnesses.[61] A list of the committee's questions was prepared by the West Riding Central Committee and circulated to all the 'short time' committees. It also sent out details of the committee's preferences with regard to the operatives to be selected as witnesses. Those summoned by the committee were later compensated from funds which had been raised by the movement specifically for that purpose.[62] Receiving nine shillings a day plus travelling expenses, some critics felt that the operatives had been given a substantial reward for their trouble.[63]

Historiographical analyses of Sadler's committee largely concentrate on its depiction of the cruel and harsh treatment of factory children.

J.L. and Barbara Hammond's heart-rending account of the lot of a factory child was drawn largely from the committee's report and focused on the system's most brutal aspects. 'In some mills', they wrote, 'scarcely an hour passed in the long day without the sound of beating and cries of pain.'[64] The Hammonds' 'victim' thesis was reviewed by W.H. Hutt in 1926. He pointed out that their highly subjective and sympathetic description, which had become the standard interpretation of the early nineteenth-century factory system, was based on a document of questionable merit. The committee had been stage-managed, in Hutt's opinion, by Sadler and his supporters in a desperate bid to get the ten hours bill through parliament.[65] Even the champion of the working classes, Frederick Engels, realized that Sadler's methods were suspect, observed Hutt. Sadler had, in Engels' opinion, 'permitted himself to be betrayed by his noble enthusiasm into the most distorted and erroneous statements, drew from his witnesses by the very form of his questions, answers which contained the truth, but truth in a perverted form'.[66] This view is supported by Maurice Walton Thomas, while Clark Nardinelli states that the report was 'designed to present the factory system in the worst possible light'. He also joins the Hutt school in criticizing the Hammonds for giving too much credit to the 'obviously biased testimony of Sadler's witnesses'.[67] E.P. Thompson defends the 'victim' thesis, though he concedes that Sadler's committee was biased and that the Hammonds and other historians who dwell on the evils of the factory system 'may be criticized for drawing upon it too uncritically'. There is no doubt that the Ten Hours Movement was involved in the preparation of witnesses and evidence and clearly the manufacturers were not given an opportunity to state their case. 'But it does not follow that the evidence before Sadler's Committee can therefore be assumed to be untrue. In fact', adds Thompson, 'anyone who reads the bulk of the evidence will find that it has an authenticity which compels belief.'[68] This division among historians mirrors contemporary perceptions. As far as Southey was concerned, 'the whole cruelty of the factory-system has been at last fully brought to light by Sadler's committee'.[69] Andrew Ure argued, equally emphatically, that the report was a complete fabrication. 'Nothing', he declared, 'shows in a clearer point of view the credulity of mankind in general, and of the people of these islands in particular, than the ready faith which was given to the tales of cruelty exercised by proprietors of cotton-mills towards young children.'[70]

This debate over the committee's depiction of the mistreatment of factory children has effectively stifled much of the historical analysis of the 1832 committee. Certainly, the primary purpose of the committee was to inquire into the nature of children's employment in factories and the report is replete with claims which indicate that the abuse of youngsters was probably not uncommon. There is also ample evidence to support the claim that the hours of labour were extremely long, even by nineteenth-century standards, and that this had a detrimental effect upon the children's health. Clearly, the mistreatment of factory children was a fundamental consideration, but it was not the only consideration. A whole range of issues and paternalist themes were explored by the committee. Unfortunately, because the committee did not have time to complete its work and produce a written report, it lost the opportunity of providing a summary of the proceedings or of drawing conclusions which would have influenced subsequent appraisals of its findings. It is somewhat ironic, therefore, that historians have none the less confined their examinations of the evidence to one or two of its most contentious aspects.

The committee's inquiry was, as Hutt and others have noted, unashamedly partisan. The nature of that bias, however, particularly the extent to which it reflected the Sadlerian paternalist philosophy, has been left unexplored. Sadler's authoritative handling of the committee ensured that most of the arguments supporting his ten hours bill were reaffirmed by the 1832 'report'. Accordingly, the social implications of the factory system, its impact upon the quality of life of the labouring poor, the protection of the helpless, the rights of the poor and the importance of ensuring a balance and harmony of interests were prominent themes. Sadler adopted three distinct lines of interrogation. The first illuminated the 'evils' of the existing factory system in relation to the moral, psychological and physical well-being of the manufacturing poor. This also addressed the long-term regressive effects of the unregulated system upon the well-being of society. The second showed that under the competitive system both workers and masters were powerless to institute the changes necessary to reverse or arrest the socially divisive trends. The third demonstrated that a regulated system would be of considerable benefit not just to the children but to the manufacturers and indeed to society as a whole.

The effect of the factory system on the character and behaviour of the manufacturing poor was examined in the light of its disruption of social relations and of domestic organization. It was commonly accepted that night work and the confinement of large numbers of young people in a closed environment encouraged moral impropriety and prostitution. Factories were also associated with alcohol abuse and petty crime. These social problems, urged countless witnesses, were compounded by the fact that there was no incentive for the children to acquire even a rudimentary education. They were too exhausted to attend evening school and needed Sundays to recuperate. The Rev. Bull acknowledged that, notwithstanding the benefits of religious and moral instruction, it was unreasonable to expect children who worked incessantly for six days of the week to have to spend the seventh day in a school-room. The witnesses reiterated Sadler's argument that children needed time for rest and recreation as well as for mental and moral improvement.[71]

The overall impression of the report was that unregulated factories were 'nurseries of vice', breeding a generation of social misfits.[72] The following is a sample of many exchanges alluding to the implications for society at large of this social and moral decay:

> Do you think that [the factory system's] effects are beginning to be very serious to the general interests of society, and to the prospects of future generations? – Yes; and I think that the factory system, after it has a little more pervaded society, will be attended with very alarming effects.

The witness, Daniel Fraser, agreed with the inquirer's suggestion that the system encroached upon the domestic life of the manufacturing poor and interfered with parental guidance and care.[73] The operatives were encouraged to speak of the emotional pressures of factory life on both the children and their parents. Joseph Firth, who had started work in a cotton factory at the age of six, spoke of the huge emotional and psychological gulf which existed between parents and their children as a result of long periods of separation. Parents became devoid of feeling and the children grew more resentful.[74] Peter Smart admitted that as an overseer he was inclined to inflict the same punishment on the children under his charge as he had himself experienced. 'I went as an overseer; not as a slave, but as a slave-driver.'[75] Bull was particularly concerned about the effect of the system on the minds of impressionable young people:

> I conceive that when a young person, a young woman for instance, is reared up in such a system of excessive labour, she becomes in consequences of it reckless in character, loses self-respect, and ... is an easier prey to the seductions with which she may be surrounded.[76]

The system was, in Bull's view, responsible for a significant deterioration in the quality of the manufacturing poor's domestic environment and social relations. The majority of the females employed in factories were 'as unfit as they possibly can be', he observed, 'to fill the important station of a cottager's wife'. Their incompetence, for instance, in the basic art of needlework compelled them to waste money on ready-made clothes. Indeed, much of the parochial relief paid to the poor in these communities could be traced, he believed, to the 'failure of the cottager's wife in managing, as she should do, the general arrangements of her household'.[77]

Practically every witnesses who had had personal experience of factory life was asked to make some comment about the discipline and punishment of children. These revelations of victimization and brutal behaviour are central to the historiographical debate on the issue. Yet, historians on both sides take little account of the reasons why Sadler and his committee drew attention to mistreatment. Sadler's principal objective was to demonstrate that young children were physically incapable of performing the extensive hours of labour demanded of them. The witnesses were guided into explanation which revealed that chastisement generally took place towards the end of the day when the children were most fatigued and finding it difficult to maintain the pace required to keep the mill operating efficiently. The following is typical of the responses which the committee succeeded in extracting from many of the operatives:

> Had you generally to be stimulated to your work in the evening, when you became fatigued? – Yes, in a general way in the evening; we had window-bottoms, they were very convenient places to sit down upon; and we used to get upon them and fall asleep, and then the overlooker used to come and shake us by the ear, or give us a rap with the strap, and for a time we resorted to our work to repair what was wrong, but if we could see an opportunity we got to the window-bottom again.[78]

The Rev. Bull verified the factory workers' claims. In answer to the suggestion that much of the cruelty in factories was to be attributed to the children's inability to 'perform the duties that are exacted of them, for such an undue length of time', 'I have no doubt', he replied, 'because I have asked children myself sometimes whether they have got strapped, and they have said "Yes" … and I have inquired at what part of the day they get that punishment, and have found it to be towards the close of the day, when they get tired and fatigued, and cannot perform their work so well.'[79] These particular inquiries thus focused on the fact that children were ill-equipped to work for such long periods of time. Less attention was given to the nature or extent of the beatings and disciplinary measures. Their purpose was spelt out by John Wilson in *Blackwood's*. 'With more sleep and more rest, there would be far less punishment – there would then be no call for cruelty.'[80] Similarly, the impact of the work on the physical well-being of the children was closely linked to their inability to work continuously for 12 hours or more. The medical witnesses confirmed that respiratory diseases, weak constitutions and physical deformities, common among factory operatives, were primarily a consequence of the extensive hours of labour that they had been subjected to since early childhood.[81] Several of these witnesses corroborated Sadler's argument that it was not the arduousness of the work but the drudgery and prolonged confinement which produced those ill-effects.[82]

The second line of interrogation addressed the extent to which self-interest and commercialism had pervaded the system. It centred on the concept of the free agent and Sadler's view that the manufacturers were themselves subject to constraints. Many of the factory workers informed the committee that the labourers generally, and the parents of the factory children in particular, were strongly in favour of the bill. Their statements repudiated the anti-interventionists' claims that operatives were opposed to intervention because they feared, and had been told, that it would lead to a reduction of their wages. These inquiries were designed to reveal the extent to which labourers were beholden to their employers. Sadler's argument that employees and employers did not meet on equal terms, fundamental to his rejection of the free agent idea, was the substance of the following exchange with James Paterson:

> Supposing the hands were to make any remonstrance as to their utter incapacity to endure this length of labour, and were to make known their case as to the effect it has upon their health and upon their welfare, what would be the result? – The result would be, that they must go about their business, that the master would get other people to work the mill if they would not do so, and that has been the case.

Paterson was an overseer of a mill in Dundee. The inquirer drew attention to the fact that in Scotland there was no system of compulsory relief. Paterson agreed that the labourer either worked or starved. He also confirmed that parents were anxious to see a remission of labour for their children and were willing to accept a reduction of wages.[83] So too did John Hanson, a spinner from Huddersfield. Hanson was also invited to consider whether operatives, particularly those who would come within the provisions of the bill, could be regarded as free agents:

> No, I cannot consider them so at all; for I think when circumstances are such that a man has no employment, and cannot get any, he is forced to submit to almost any thing; for when there are too many labourers in the market, the master has only to say to those who are employed, 'Do so and so', and they are obliged to do it, or be in the situation of those out of employment; and least of all are the children free agents; they are obliged to submit to every regulation or imposition of the master.[84]

Benjamin Bradshaw, a cloth-dresser from the Leeds district, reaffirmed Sadler's claim that some parishes refused poor relief to unemployed parents who refused to send their children to work in the mills. If the age restriction was enacted the parish would be obliged, explained Bradshaw, to provide those families with parish assistance.[85] Bull maintained that in most cases it was necessity which compelled parents to subsist on the earnings of their children. He admitted that some parents were unscrupulous but, like Sadler, he did not believe that they were entirely to blame for their actions:

> I ... conceive that in many cases the parents themselves are exceedingly degraded, and do not show that kindness and affection towards their children which they ought to show; and I have traced it in many instances to the fact of their having been brought up in the same system, which I apprehend tends to harden the best feelings of our nature.[86]

This line of questioning also took into account the pressures under which spinners and overlookers operated, particularly if their earnings were linked to productivity. Some were paid by the piece, others were contracted to produce a certain quantity of material within a given period of time. The children employed to assist the spinners and adult workers were, as a consequence, coerced and bullied into working longer hours. George Dawson, who had started his working life as a piecer and had spent 34 of his 41 years in mills, gave an example of a mill where

> the quantity of work required by the master to be performed by the spinners was such that it could not be done without the children being extremely injured with fatigue; and they were also very ill beaten by the spinners for whom they pieced, and abused in order to make them work the length of hours, and to perform the work.[87]

Whilst considerable evidence was marshalled against the factory system, Sadler's purpose was not so much to condemn factory work as to establish grounds for government intervention and regulation of factories. Accordingly, the committee's third line of interrogation concentrated on demonstrating that regulation was in the national interest. In seeking leave for his ten hours bill, Sadler had pointed out that the fluctuations in the textile industry were primarily due to the constant rivalry between manufacturers. He also noted that these fluctuations bore particularly heavily on 'those least able to sustain their effects'.[88] The manufacturers' preoccupation with maintaining profitability and competitiveness precluded all other considerations. This and other arguments connected with the paternalist idea of the harmony and balance of interests were clearly evident in the report. John Hanson, a spinner of many years' experience, maintained that

> competition has now so far affected the profits of the present machinery, that the owners of it, in their wish to restrain the benefits and profits to which they have been accustomed, resort to long hours, and the excessive labour of children.[89]

Hanson thought that the bill would have the effect of

> keeping machinery to its proper influence and its proper direction; that it would cause its productiveness to be, as it ought to be, given to the public. I do not think that all our great inventions, and all the power of steam, and all the arts and sciences, ought to be monopolized by a few individuals, when we see that the effect is to injure society.[90]

Several witnesses were encouraged to talk about the commercial benefits of regulation and the counter-productive effects of excessive hours of labour. It was suggested, for instance, that at the end of a shift there was a noticeable deterioration in the quality of the work and an increase in the amount of wastage.[91] Joseph Sadler agreed with the inquirer's suggestion that the bill 'would equalize the labour, and at the same time insure more work was done in the same length of time, and that work done better, and with less waste'.[92] This principle of equalization or equilibrium cropped up frequently, particularly in terms of the distribution of labour. Sadler had anticipated that this would be one of the major benefits of his bill.[93] The report was replete with statements to that effect. If a 'man works fifteen hours a day', explained one witness, 'he is doing the half day work of a man who ought to have had ten hours a day, besides his own, and that man is loitering in the streets because he is pushed out of labour by the man who does his work, and he himself is kept by the poor rates'.[94] Hanson spoke of the monopolization of wealth by the major textile producers and its implications for the agricultural interest. 'I think that the great mischief arises from these two interests not being properly balanced; that the tendency of our manufacturing interest has been to increase too rapidly and to too great an extent; and that it does not properly circulate the products and the proceeds of agriculture.'[95] The Rev. Bull likewise thought that 'if capital, instead of being amassed into large heaps, were distributed into smaller ones, it would be far better for the operatives, and for all classes.'[96]

It was not machinery or factories as such which bore the brunt of much of the criticism in the report; rather, it was the fact that individuals were being driven like machines. Richard Oastler was asked if it was 'necessary, in order to secure the object of this bill, to restrain the moving power'. The point at issue, he responded, was 'whether that principle which says you shall not inflict an injury on a poor child, shall be made to bend before the mercenary feelings of the rich men of the present day; that is to say, whether life or property deserve legislation best'.[97] The Rev. Bull explained that he had not 'declared war ... against a factory system as such, but against *the existing* factory system'. He thought that a properly regulated system would in fact be of great advantage to the poor.[98] Hanson was also asked to consider whether the problems identified by critics of the system were a consequence of the introduction of new machinery and technology:

No, I never pretend to argue or to say that machinery abstractedly is an evil; I think it a great benefit; but I do think ... that when it is introduced too rapidly, and runs into monopoly, so as to render the operatives ... of little value to his employer, frequently producing stagnations in trade, and thereby throwing numbers out of employ, then machinery becomes an evil; and that has been the case with us.[99]

There is little doubt that Sadler was in complete control of the 1832 inquiry. His ideas are in evidence on every page of the report. Each witness was carefully guided into giving answers that reinforced his paternalist philosophy. The leading members of the Ten Hours Movement gave set speeches and made observations that endorsed his thinking. When Richard Oastler was asked to consider whether the operatives would settle for a restriction of 11 hours, both the question and Oastler's response echoed Sadler's view of the regressive effect of Hobhouse's Act.[100] In answer to the suggestion that the ten hours bill was a compromise measure, the Rev. Bull maintained,

> Certainly I should say that if we had to choose, I conceive humanity and proper regard for the interests of our fellow-creatures would have induced us, if possible, to have made a greater limitations than ten hours a day; I conceive that ten hours a day is the least possible limitation which will prevent the factory system from greatly counteracting my labours as a clergyman.[101]

Asked several times to elaborate on this point, it is clear that Sadler wanted contemporaries to understand that this bill was a cautionary first step. Acceptance of this measure would open the way for other and more ambitious proposals for improving the condition of the labouring poor. The government's efforts to regain the initiative on this issue suggests that they were aware that this bill would not settle the issue. They were also mindful of the fact that even the most ardent advocates of *laissez-faire* had begun to see the sense of some measure of regulation. Sadler and the paternalists had forced parliamentarians to reassess their understanding of the duties of the legislature and parliament. The idea of selective interventionism had, as a consequence, gained acceptance as a viable alternative to the steadfastly minimalist view of government authority and responsibility.

V

Sadler's chairmanship of the 1832 committee marked both the apogee and the demise of his political career. The committee sat for four months, from 12 April to 7 August, parliament was prorogued in

October and the general election took place in December. When the Tories began canvassing in Leeds Sadler was already physically and emotionally exhausted. The intense rivalry between the Whigs and Sadler's supporters continued unabated throughout the campaign, which proved to be more acrimonious and nerve-wracking than either of the Newark contests.[102] The poll was headed by John Marshall, the son of a highly respected and prosperous flax spinner in Leeds. There was little doubt, given his business and family connections, that Marshall would be returned. The main contest was between Sadler and his old rival, Macaulay.[103] Macaulay had been drafted in by 'The Association for Promoting within the County of York the Free Return of fit Representatives to Parliament'. Edward Baines, the proprietor of the *Leeds Mercury*, figured prominently in the formation of this association. The *Mercury* supported Marshall and Macaulay's campaign while its Tory rival, the *Leeds Intelligencer*, promoted Sadler's. Given their opposition to the Reform Bill, The Tories had had difficulty finding suitable candidates, particularly in the West Riding where the pro-reform movement was well organized. However, the movement for social reform had also gained a firm foothold in this region and Sadler, 'a man who stood ... for privilege and tradition on the one hand, and for the improvement of the lot of the unprivileged and necessitous on the other', was a strong candidate.[104] It none the less rankled Sadler's opponents that the 'supporter of the Boroughmongers' should have the temerity to offer himself to an electorate, which, if the Tories had had their way, would not have been granted the privilege.[105]

The issues at the centre of the Leeds campaign were complex but fairly neatly aligned. The Whigs spoke for middle-class radicalism and the manufacturing interest, focusing on political reform and the abolition of negro slavery; the Tories spoke for factory labourers and the labouring poor, concentrating on social reform and the abolition of 'infant slavery'. The contest also laid open the division among Evangelicals. The Wesleyan movement had invested considerable time and energy in the campaign for the abolition of negro slavery and Macaulay was regarded as one of its most able champions. The Rev. Richard Watson, a leading member of the Wesleyan Connexion, was thus anxious to secure his return to parliament. Watson wrote to the Superintendent of the Leeds Circuit praising Macaulay and disparaging Sadler. The letter was passed around several chapels in the neighbourhood of Leeds. It eventually reached the local press and was duly published.[106] As a young man, Sadler had allied himself with the abolitionists. He assisted Wilberforce in 1807 in the Yorkshire campaign. But he now had other priorities and Oastler's letter on 'Yorkshire Slavery', with its trenchant criticism of the pro-abolitionists, had effectively divided the two issues. Macaulay refused to accept that the circumstances of factory labourers bore any resemblance to those of negro slaves:

> [T]he freeman cannot be forced to work to the ruin of his health. If he works over hours, it is because it is his choice to do so. The law ought not to protect him; for he can protect himself.

Macaulay acknowledged, however, that children did not necessarily have such a choice. They were subject to the authority of parents who might not have their best interests at heart. Macaulay was at this time less dogmatic in his opposition to government intervention than when he reviewed Southey's *Colloquies* some two years before.[107] He conceded the principle of Sadler's bill, but had considerable reservations about its details. He failed to comprehend, for instance, why anyone should think it was necessary to legislate to protect the interests of a 20 year old.[108]

Sadler was presented as a candidate of the people whose primary objective was to defend the interests of the labouring poor. The Tory 'statement of principles' was published in the form of an Address to Sadler from the Huddersfield Short Time Committee:

> we feel confident you will not consider us too presumptuous in calling you *our* friend notwithstanding the great disparity of condition and circumstances there is betwixt you and us; and especially when we reflect on your devotedness to the cause of suffering humanity and consider those noble and energetic disinterested appeals you have so frequently made to the government in behalf of the poor of this country, we are encouraged not only to recognize you as a *friend* but also to look on you as a *father* who is ever wishful to promote the welfare and happiness of his children.[109]

For Driver, this letter was the genesis of the 'Radical-Tory fusion'.[110] Yet, it is plain from the text of the letter that this alliance was in the spirit of deference and hierarchical responsibility, not of democracy. The celebrated radical and member for Preston, 'Orator Hunt', visited Leeds during the campaign and urged his fellow radicals to support Sadler, who was 'ten thousand times more disposed to assist the working classes' than 'the briefless barrister'.[111] Until the principle of universal suffrage was admitted, social reform was of more value, Hunt believed, to the labouring classes than political reform.[112] The Ten Hours Movement organized huge rallies in support of Sadler, but many of the people attending these were unable to give him more than symbolic support.[113] If 'a still lower class of voters were admitted under the bill', observed the *Intelligencer*,

> Mr. Sadler's supporters would be more than proportionally increased, so completely are the operative classes satisfied that the Honourable Gentleman, of all our public men, is the Most thoroughly imbued with the spirit which 'careth for the poor and lowly'.[114]

When Sadler observed in his post-election speech that 'the people are entirely without representation', his supporters would have understood that he was referring to the unenfranchised labouring poor.[115] Sadler did not believe that a parliament dominated by political economists and representatives of the manufacturing class could be relied on to protect the interests of the working classes.[116]

VI

Notwithstanding his failure to secure a seat in the newly reformed House of Commons, Sadler's presence was felt in spirit if not in fact. The committee's report was published in January 1833, and immediately parliament resumed in February Ashley reintroduced Sadler's ten hours bill and the factory issue again became the subject of exhaustive discussion. Ashley assumed responsibility for completing Sadler's work with considerable trepidation. 'It is very cruel on Mr. Sadler', he wrote to Oastler, 'that he is debarred from the joy of putting the crown on his beloved measure; however, his must be the honour, though another may complete it.'[117] Ashley had not been involved in the 1832 campaign. Indeed, until delegates from two of the West Riding's 'short time' committees deputized the Rev. Bull to seek his help, he had not even known of the existence of Sadler's committee.[118] Ashley continued to pay tribute to the efforts of Sadler and his colleagues.[119]

The report had an immediate impact. A few years later, Charles Wing claimed that it 'was the evidence brought before ... Sadler's committee that first awakened the public to the enormities of the system'.[120] The slave trade was shocking enough, declared Southey, 'but this white slavery has arisen in our own days, and is carried on in the midst of this civilized and Christian nation'.[121] Even the renowned political economist, John Ramsay McCulloch, was deeply disturbed by the report's revelations. 'I look on the facts disclosed in the late Report as most disgraceful to the nation', he told Ashley, 'and I confess that, until I read it, I could not have conceived it possible that such enormities were committed.'[122]

However, the emotion aroused by the report did not help the factory reformers' campaign. Defenders of the manufacturing interests argued that it was grossly misleading and insisted on further inquiry to clear manufacturers of the imputation that they were cruel and heartless.[123] The Sadlerites pointed out that this was unnecessary. The inquiry had shown that it was not the manufacturers who were the source of the problem.[124] 'It is against the system [that Sadler] fights', explained *Blackwood's*, 'not against the men who have got involved in it by the operation of causes hard to resist, and which he thoroughly understands.'[125] Notwithstanding these reassurances, the critics of the bill continued to press for further inquiry. Contrary to the report, they argued that the social and economic problems outlined in the report were the product of regulation and protection not of the competitive system. Again, the Corn Laws and high taxation were cited as the real source of the labourers' distress.[126]

It was evident, however, that there was no longer any possibility that the government could avoid intervention. Even the most ardent critics of regulation acknowledged that parliament had little choice in the matter given the public outcry.[127] The debate now centred on the nature and extent of that interference, and whether government should act on the information already gathered or complete the investigation begun by Sadler. The inquiries undertaken by the Commons in 1816 and by the Lords in 1818 and 1819 were considered by the opponents of regulation to be out-of-date. It was said that the conditions in factories had long since improved. The new generation of mills were much larger and more technologically advanced than their predecessors; also, factory environments were much less oppressive and more attention was given to cleanliness. While it might be possible to find a few small mills run in this antiquated fashion, these were isolated cases. The committee was thus criticized for using evidence of harsh treatment and appalling conditions which belonged to another era.[128]

From the government and anti-interventionists' point of view, one the most compelling reason for completing the inquiry was to restore public confidence in the system. At the same time, it was evident that Lord Althorp was keen to regain the political initiative and to discredit Sadler and the Tory paternalists. In the context of a political analysis that is not a particularly startling observation but it is one which has not received a great deal of attention. Two factors stand out. First, the government made sure that it had complete control of the 1833 factory commission inquiry. Second, the report prepared by the government's commissioners suggested that Sadler's proposal was neither as progressive nor as humane as its proponents seemed to think. Naturally, the commissioners' political perspective and view of the factory issue accorded with the ministers from whom they received their brief. Indeed, the Treasury Secretary, Thomas Spring Rice, considered it to be the 'duty of government' not only 'to select proper persons as Commissioners, [but] to appoint the places to which they should go, and to point out the subjects on which they should collect evidence'.[129] The Sadlerites and pro-interventionists were highly critical of the government's methods. The investigation was held *in camera* and there was no verbatim report of its proceedings. Wilson Patten's motion for the appointment of a commission was agreed to in April. It scraped through with a majority of one vote. Two months later, the government had still not disclosed the names of the commissioners nor their terms of reference. Althorp claimed he had forgotten that he had given an undertaken to lay the commissioners' instructions before the House.[130] The second reading of Ashley's bill was scheduled for 17 June, but debate was postponed until its committee stage when the commissioners' report was to be made available.[131] Sir Robert Inglis was incensed that when the bill finally came up for discussion, at the beginning of July, the majority of members had had no prior opportunity to peruse the report.[132]

Historians generally present the commission report, with its vindication of manufacturers, as a counterbalance to the bias of Sadler's report.[133] Some suggest that the commissioners handled their inquiries in a more dispassionate and even-handed manner.[134] Less attention is given to the similarities between the two reports and to the fact that their evaluation of the issue was not that far apart.[135] The commissioners went to great lengths to prove that claims about the manufacturers' cruelty and hard-heartedness were either untrue or misdirected. The report is replete with examples of the masters' kind and benevolent regard for the children.[136] The incidents of brutal behaviour were presented as the exception rather than the rule. The workmen, particularly spinners, were accused of being the main culprits.[137] The commissioners responded to what the Sadlerites had already insisted was a misconception of the committee's findings. It was not the masters' ruthlessness but the baneful effects of the system under which they operated which Sadler and his colleagues sought to expose.

The argument central to Sadler's inquiry, that excessive hours of labour were not conducive to the health and welfare of young children, was strongly supported by the commissioners. They found that the 'effects of labouring during such hours are, in a great number of cases',

> permanent deterioration of the physical constitution; the production of diseases often wholly irremediable; and the partial or entire exclusion (by reason of excessive fatigue) from the means of obtaining adequate education and acquiring useful habits, or of profiting by those means when afforded.

They also endorsed the view that the children in question 'are not free agents, but are let out to hire, the wages they earn being received and appropriated by their parents and guardians'. The commissioners concluded that these were strong grounds for legislative interference.[138] They did not believe, however, that the paternalists' measure would succeed in mitigating any of these problems. It was an ill-devised proposal which would not give the children the protection they obviously needed. Based on the evidence of medical witnesses who had appeared before the 1832 committee, Sadler and his colleagues had settled on a minimum of ten hours labour for children and young persons. Yet, many of those witnesses, the commissioners observed, had in fact admitted that ten hours labour was too long. One witness was quoted as recommending eight hours. In other words, the commissioners' report implied that the evidence in favour of shorter hours had been disregarded. It also dwelt on the paternalists' failure to make any provision in their proposal 'for the occupation of any part of the time of children for their own benefit, either before or after their hours of labour, and taking no charge of their education, elementary or moral'. The effect of the factory system on the moral character of the manufacturing poor was the most serious evil which the commissioners had encountered in their investigation. They concluded that the ten hours bill was not intended to protect the interests of the children. Its real objective was to limit the hours of adult labourers.[139]

During the second reading of Ashley's bill, Althorp informed the House of the commission's overall impression that 'some of its clauses went further than was necessary, and some of them did not go far enough'.[140] At the committee stage he attempted to take charge of the whole issue. He outlined a series of amendments, based on the commissioners' recommendations and likewise intended to demonstrate the shortcomings and impracticality of the paternalists' measure. He also moved for the appointment of a select committee to consider the various revisions. Having conceded that the government must take the matter in hand, Althorp was anxious to ensure that the proposal did not go too far. His first and most important proposition was to limit children under the age of 13 to an eight hour day. By this measure, he explained,

> the protection to children, properly so called, would be increased, while adults, who were in a state to decide for themselves should be left unshackled and unrestricted.

Keen to show that the government was genuine in its endeavours, Althorp suggested that an extension of Hobhouse's Act to all areas of textile manufacturing would suffice to protect the interests of those children who were above that age. He also questioned whether it was fair to exclude the silk industry. This work, he admitted, was not as severe or as unhealthy as other branches of textile manufacturing but, since it required the employment of large numbers of children, it ought to be given some consideration. His second proposition focused attention on the paternalists' failure to tackle the education issue. It was self-evident, he thought, that the moral and mental improvement of factory children ought to be the 'one great and paramount' objective of any legislation in this area. His third was designed to ensure that manufacturers complied with the law. Again, it revealed a fundamental weakness in the existing proposal. He suggested that consideration be given to the feasibility of establishing a 'system of inspection throughout the mills where child labour was used'. Finally, Althorp challenged the idea that manufacturers should be made responsible for the safety of their employees. If an accident resulting in the death of an employee could be attributed to the master's negligence, then the incident should be treated, the paternalists believed, as a case of manslaughter. Althorp defended the rights of the manufacturers and argued that such a penalty would be an unfair and intolerable imposition.[141]

Sadler's explanation that the bill was a compromise measure was reiterated by Ashley. He likewise felt that any attempt to introduce a more stringent measure would be futile.[142] Ashley welcomed the enforcement mechanism. Once again, the only reason he had not pressed for a similar arrangement was that he was 'afraid of giving additional offence to the opponents of the measure'. As to the provision of education, 'he only wished that the noble Lord ... would push forward and provide suitable education for all classes of children among the lower orders, whether employed in factories or otherwise'. He was not likely to disapprove of the eight hour restriction for the under-13s but he had some reservation about its impact on their earnings. He also made it very clear that he would continue to 'hold to his own proposition with regard to the children beyond that age'. Referring to Althorp's questioning of the safety standards clause, Ashley rightly observed that his objections were contrary to the advice of his own commissioners, who had recommended strict penalties for such offences.[143] Notwithstanding these concessions, Ashley was clearly suspicious of Althorp's motives. If these propositions had been brought forward at an earlier stage of the bill, the matter would have been resolved sooner. He also strongly objected to Althorp's proposal for another select committee. After so much prevarication, the public was entitled to an open and frank discussion of the issue. The most practical way of achieving that was to proceed as planned with a full committee of the House. In fact, given the depth of public feeling on this issue, even the most ardent political economists were inclined to agree with Ashley. Joseph Hume felt that the bill 'ought to be discussed, clause by clause ... in order that the public might know all [its] bearings and principles'.[144] The motion for a select committee was accordingly rejected.

Despite this setback, Althorp was still determined to thwart the paternalists' bill. Two weeks later, when the House went into committee on the bill, he immediately moved an amendment to the clause limiting the labour of persons under-18 to a ten-hour day, substituting the number 13 for 18. He then effectively gave the House an ultimatum. If it rejected this amendment in favour of Ashley's proposal, he 'should probably have no other Amendments to propose'. Ashley had clearly been outmanoeuvred by Althorp. Even Colonel Torrens, who had formerly shown little regard for Sadler's paternalist endeavours, recognized the perversity of the Minister's stand:

[The operatives] prayed the Legislature to limit the labour of their children to ten hours, and they were willing to submit to the diminution of the wages of their children to that extent. No, says the noble Lord, we will not grant you what you ask, but we will grant more: we will limit the labour of children under thirteen to eight hours, and reduce their wages in this greater proportion.

Althorp's amended version of the bill was regarded by those who continued to object to all measures of interference as the lesser of two evils. One member's comment that 'no child ought to work ten hours a day' suggests that Althorp had succeeded in convincing some parliamentarians that his measure was the more humane of the two.[145] The committee voted resoundingly in favour of Althorp's amendment, giving him a majority of 145. Ashley had no choice but to surrender his bill to Althorp.

From the above analysis, it is evident that Sadler's advocacy of factory reform gave considerable impetus to the whole question of governmental responsibility. His speech proposing the ten hours bill established the terms of reference for ongoing discussion of the issue in which the role of the state became central. The revelations of the 1832 select committee made an enormous impact on a public, whose humanitarian sentiment had been aroused by the efforts of the anti-slavery campaigners. The committee's report was made available in January 1833 and thereafter the arguments against legislative intervention became almost impossible to defend. The Sadlerian factor influenced Lord Althorp's subsequent handling of the factory issue and it was manifest in the findings and recommendations of the 1833 Factory Commission. Its counter-measure, particularly the eight-hour provision for children under the age of 13, enabled the new Whig government to take charge of the issue and their keenness to do this was in itself indicative of the influence of the 'Sadlerian School'. In fact, in the absence of a comprehensive analysis of Sadler's ten hours proposal and of the government's opposition to it, the actions of Althorp and the commissioners in subsequently proposing a more radical measure appear, as Torrens suggested, somewhat perverse.

Conclusion: Towards a Realization of the Paternalist, Collectivist Idea of the State

Historical interpretations of the 1833 Factory Act and its implications for the subsequent expansion of government are broadly divided into two schools of thought. One side emphasizes that this was a landmark piece of legislation which initiated a new era of government policy based on Benthamite principles. Whilst acknowledging that Sadler and the Ten Hours Movement were responsible for launching the protest which prompted the government to take the issue in hand, this group stresses that the bill finally agreed on was an entirely new measure based on entirely new principles. In line with contemporary criticism, the ten hours bill is regarded as a dishonest measure which aimed to restrict the hours of all textile workers, not just infants, whereas the 1833 Act is considered to have attempted, at least, to address the fundamental problem, namely the overworking of children. This school promotes the idea that there was a radical shift in policy following the 1832 Reform Act and suggests that Jeremy Bentham's *Constitutional Code*, published between 1830 and 1832, is the key to understanding that phenomenon.[1]

The alternative, and generally more conservative, interpretation likewise acknowledges the innovativeness of the 1833 Factory Act and the extent to which Benthamite principles ultimately determined its principal features. The historians in this category also regard the Benthamite idea of a centralized state as being incompatible with Tory thinking. The main distinction between this and the former, essentially liberal, interpretation is that more emphasis is placed on the fact that the bill had its origins in the ten-hours campaign for reform. Also, this group attaches more significance to the continuity of ideas and stresses that, in addition to Benthamism, a whole range of influences fed into the development of the Victorian collectivist state.[2]

In both cases, however, the political context of the 1833 Act is not adequately addressed. Charles Poulett Thompson remarked, in support of Althorp's amendments, 'that sooner or later the people would learn who were their true friends'.[3] This illustrates the point central to the analysis in chapter 6 of the post-reform parliament's handling of the issue, namely that Althorp's measure was in large part designed to undermine the influence of the Sadlerites. Conscious of the momentum which Sadler's campaign had given to paternalist ideals, Althorp was keen to produce a measure that would reaffirm the government's reform credentials. He succeeded in convincing his parliamentary colleagues (and indeed many historians) that his measure, even from a strictly humanitarian standpoint, was a vast improvement on Sadler's and Ashley's bill.[4]

This failure to consider the political or parliamentary context of the issue is particularly problematic for the first group of historians, who largely view the 1833 Factory Act in terms of the transition of ideas. They argue, in the tradition of Halévy and Dicey, that this Act marked the ascendancy of Benthamite or Chadwickian influence in the formulation of social policy and correspondingly the final demise of the old aristocratic and protectionist ethos. The reasons for their emphasis on Benthamism are fairly straightforward. The commissioners in charge of the factory inquiry, Edwin Chadwick, Thomas Southwood Smith and Thomas Tooke, were committed political economists and disciples of Jeremy Bentham. Chadwick, a close associate of Bentham and contributor to the utilitarian *Westminster Review*, is generally regarded by these historians as the main architect of the 1833 Factory Act.[5] In the words of one steadfast adherent of this view,

> Those provisions which make it a landmark in administrative history – the appointment of inspectors, and the delegation to them of extensive powers – were the work, not of Shaftesbury or any of the leaders of the agitation, but of the Benthamite, Chadwick.[6]

The Act is thus generally regarded by historians of the pro-Benthamite school as essentially a realization of the administrative and tutelary principles outlined in the *Constitutional Code*. The *Code*'s guidelines for the administrative function of government included a number of new ministries which would regulate such things as education and health.[7] In fact, this idea of governmental departments to manage social affairs had been around for some time. In 1813, Robert Owen's

proposal for a state-funded system of education required the establishment of a new department of government, which would be
responsible for maintaining national educational standards.[8] The
suggestion that the introduction of inspection 'was an innovative and
dramatic step' likewise warrants some qualification. It was a device
that had been used before. Norman McCord explains that

> The voluntary educational societies already had teams of salaried
> inspectors of schools; in earlier years paid inspectors had been used
> to ensure product standards in a variety of trades and survivals of
> that regulation still existed within the textile industries affected by
> the 1833 Act.[9]

The idea certainly did not, as one historian has suggested, come
'wholly' from Chadwick.[10] Indeed, one need only cite the Report of
which Chadwick was co-author to show that the suggestion in fact
came from the manufacturers themselves:

> Some manufacturers have proposed that the inspectors, *who they
> think ought to be appointed to ensure compliance with any legislative
> regulation*, should have power to inspect factories, and direct what
> parts of the machinery should be fenced off, and that after such
> directions have been complied with, the manufacturer should be
> relieved from further responsibility.

Sadler would have applauded the commissioners' recognition of the
manufacturers' social responsibilities. They concurred 'in the proposition for giving such power to inspectors, but [they] did not concur in
the proposal to relieve the manufacturers from responsibility'.[11] The
manufacturers in question, who had apparently accepted the necessity
or perhaps the inevitability of regulation, clearly regarded the device of
an inspectorate as something which would operate in their interest.
They wanted to minimize the undue advantage which might be gained
by competitors who were unscrupulous enough to ignore any govern-
ment-imposed restrictions. Their views coincided with Sadler's point
about the inequality of circumstances and the need for uniformity in
the treatment of factory children, which was crucial to his argument for
a regulated system. He had stressed that it would be fairer to humane
masters if all manufacturers had to abide by the same restrictions.
    It is thus questionable, given that the idea was not completely
foreign to contemporary thinking, whether the notion of inspection

was the most important feature of the 1833 Factory Act. The significance which historians attach to the influence of Benthamism diverts attention from the fundamental concession made by the government, namely its acceptance of broad-scale interference between masters and servants.[12] As David Roberts observes, there was nothing in the *Code* about the regulation of hours. Bentham 'wished to regulate many things, but the economy was not one of them; he wished inspectors to guarantee that factories were sanitary, but not that working hours be limited'.[13] It would be reasonable, of course, for those who regard the introduction of an inspectorate as the most important feature of the measure to point out that the regulation of hours was likewise hardly unprecedented. The breach had already been made by the 1819 Factory Act. None the less, barring a few exceptions, the new restrictions included all mills and factories and applied to all adolescent workers between the ages of nine and 18. This was no minor concession.

Historians also make the mistake of referring to the bill as Chadwick's or the commissioners'.[14] Althorp certainly made use of some of the commission's recommendations but the final proposal put before parliament was his, not Chadwick's. Indeed, Chadwick was extremely disappointed with the measure, particularly as it contravened the hallowed principle of non-interference with adult labourers. The commissioners had recommended an eight-hour day for children under the age of 13. Althorp's additional 12–hour clause went far beyond their idea of what was an acceptable level of interference. Chadwick was also highly critical of Althorp's revision of their proposals for raising the children's level of education.[15] The commission had recommended that three or even four hours should be set aside each day for the purpose of teaching the factory children to read and write. Althorp thought that two hours would be sufficient, and probably that was more realistic than the figure his commissioners had proposed.

Why Althorp ignored the advice of his commissioners and introduced the 12–hour clause is a question which historians have not addressed. Halévy does not seem to regard it as particularly significant. He notes that Althorp's amendments incorporated the commissioners' suggestion of an eight-hour day for the under-13s, but his reference to Althorp's introduction of the 12–hour clause appears in a footnote, almost as an afterthought:

One concession was made to [the paternalists] and their friends. The principle of a maximum day of twelve hours up to the age of eighteen was introduced into the bill. That is to say, the provisions of the Act of 1831 were extended to the entire textile industry[16]

As well as the theoretical context, consideration must also be given to political praxis. Ministers recognized the potential power of the Sadlerian position in so far as it had raised Sadler's standing both within and outside parliament. Althorp's method of dealing with the problem was the well-tried one of apparently offering more than his opponents.[17] By doing this he achieved three things. He removed Sadler's link with the bill; he associated his name with a radical social measure and, by going beyond the recommendations of his own commissioners, who were seen as an instrument of the manufacturers, he could safely claim that he had acted impartially.

While parliamentarians were certainly influenced by predominant schools of political thought, they were also – particularly the more experienced – mindful of pragmatic considerations. It was noted in chapter 4 that Sadler's criticism of free trade policies had forced Poulett Thompson into acknowledging that what counted was 'not the principle of free trade, but the approximation of that principle'. Sir Henry Parnell had likewise urged that these policies were the work of practical men not of theorists, they were 'merely the first step towards a freer system'. In other words, these policies were not necessarily an endorsement of the extreme *laissez-faire* position.[18] Similarly, Althorp selected from the commissioners' report those proposals that suited his purpose and revised the measure in a way which undermined the Sadlerites but did not entirely alienate the anti-interventionists.

Three years later, however, when the proposal was about to come into full operation, Poulett Thompson, who 'considered the measure to be an evil forced on the Government and the House', moved for an amendment, which, if accepted, would have seriously weakened the Act. He proposed restricting the eight-hour day to children under the age of 12, rather than 13.[19] The support he received from ministers suggests that they were never entirely happy with the measure or sincere in their commitment to the eight-hour provision. Charles Wing certainly believed that that was the case. In protest, he published his well-known account of the progress of factory reform, the *Evils of the Factory System*. Wing selected extracts from the various parliamentary inquiries which supported the argument for regulation. The bulk of the evidence cited came from Sadler's Committee:

The inconsistency [observed Wing] of ministers, in bringing

forward this bill is obvious. They threw out Lord Ashley's ten-hours bill at the recommendation of their own commissioners, who gave it as the result of the evidence they had collected, that the labour of children ought to be restricted to eight hours, and that, therefore, a ten-hour bill would not afford them sufficient protection. And now these same ministers would drive back a large portion of these children to twelve hours.... Ministers have found themselves in a dilemma; either they must overwork the children, or underwork adults – and they have got out of the dilemma by determining to overwork the children. In their alarm, they have thrown consistency overboard; and the very same men who declared even ten hours' labour too long for a child in his thirteenth year, would now expose him to be worked twelve hours.[20]

Notwithstanding ministerial support, Poulett Thompson was only able to secure a two-vote majority on the bill's second reading. He decided that it would be prudent to withdrew the amendment.[21]

Although conservative interpretations of the 1833 Act take more account of the contemporary political scene, particularly the 'contest for popular opinion', these generally have more to say about the success of the extra-parliamentary ten hours campaign than about Althorp's attempts to regain the political initiative on the issue.[22] In fact, the problem one encounters with these assessments of Sadler's and the paternalists' role is almost the reverse of that which has been outlined as characteristic of liberal interpretations. Historians in the latter category, seeking a theoretical explanation for the emergence of collectivism, tend to neglect political praxis. Those in the former usually take into consideration practical aspects of the issue but, because they have difficulty reconciling the growth of 'centrally directed collectivism' with Tory thinking, their examinations of the theoretical context of the issue tend to dismiss or neglect its Tory paternalist dimensions. David Roberts maintains that

> the significance of the act lay not in the shift of administrative powers from local authorities to a central department but in the insistence that the central government can regulate private enterprise for the public's welfare.[23]

This principle was at the heart of Sadler's understanding of the paternal state. Yet, Roberts considers that, notwithstanding their rhetoric, the paternalists of Sadler's era, and indeed Sadler himself, did not have any conception of a centralized collectivist state:

> The paternalist writers were not always modest in the terminology. Just as Southey called for a 'parental government', so Michael Sadler called for a 'Protective State' and William Wordsworth for one that stood 'in *loco parentis* to the poor' ... Paternalist thought did have a strand to it that promoted government intervention. But it was a strand that was intertwined with a decided preference for local and private authorities. Sadler and Wordsworth, like Arnold, Helps, and Southey called for legislation, not government departments, and they looked for the execution of laws to the persons of station and rank in local spheres ... It is the intertwining in their thought of these various strands that makes the paternalists writers too ambivalent about demanding the intervention of an effective administrative state.[24]

Similarly, Oliver MacDonagh declares that Ashley 'failed entirely to recognize the revolutionary and collectivist implications of his own measure'.[25] Whilst this might be an appropriate assessment in Ashley's case, it is not in Sadler's.

One of the problems encountered by historians is that of explaining the growth of collectivist policies and the emergence of a centralized state in an era when enthusiasm for individualism and *laissez-faire* principles dominated political and intellectual discourse. J. Bartlet Brebner's solution to this paradox was to turn the 'triumph of *laissez-faire*' thesis on its head. He argued that Dicey in particular had misleadingly equated Benthamism with individualism, when in fact 'Bentham was the archetype of British collectivism'.[26] MacDonagh, adopting the conservative idea of evolutionary change, suggests that there was no rational basis for the growth of a centralized collectivist state. Social pressures forced governments to adopt policies which are now recognized as being essentially collectivist, but at the time, he argues, 'a large number of [such] measures ... slipped through unnoticed'. Hence his point about Ashley not being aware of the intrinsically centralist nature of the ten hours proposal. MacDonagh admits that the development of collectivism was assisted by ideas from the various political perspectives, including 'old Toryism'. However, like Roberts, he insists that

> there was no group or body in early Victorian England consciously and single-mindedly promoting collectivism; indeed, no group or

body had a clear understanding of its implications or extent, or perhaps even of its existence.[27]

Because Sadler did not refer specifically to an administrative state or speak in terms of government departments, it does not necessarily follow that his conception of a paternal government was merely rhetorical and essentially meaningless. In Sadler's speeches, there are so many references to the paternal responsibilities of government and parliament that it is hard to believe that the concept did not have some deeper meaning for him. Indeed, Sadler seems to have been the first parliamentarian to use the terms 'paternal' or 'protective' to describe government's social role. Roberts points out that in the 1840s the phrase 'paternal government' was widely used by parliamentarians.[28] The same could not be said of the 1820s. It was noted in chapter 3 that, notwithstanding the strong presence of paternalist ideas and attitudes in the discussion of social policy, there were no explicit references to a 'paternal government' or to the paternal responsibilities of parliament. Yet, soon after he entered parliament Sadler began referring to the paternal responsibilities of government and parliament and in a way that suggested he anticipated the need for a more interventionist and definite social role for government. The principle of centralization or collectivism is also implicit in Sadler's claim that legislation was necessary to ensure that the poor as a whole were treated in an equitable manner. Whether he was defending the regulation of factories, the provision of cottages and gardens for distressed agricultural workers or the principle of compulsory relief for Ireland, the fundamentally centralist concept of uniformity and fairness in the treatment of the labouring classes was crucial to his arguments for state intervention and regulation. Furthermore, in terms of perceptions of the notion of a paternal or protective government, it is unnecessary, indeed confusing, to make a distinction between the Benthamites' advocacy of more efficient government administration and the paternalists defence of legislation grounded in paternalist principles. Even if an Act designed to regulate the hours or conditions of child workers is administered at a local level, this does not alter the fact that, in allowing it to pass, parliament has in effect endorsed the paternalist argument for state intervention and regulation.

The major distinction between the Sadlerite and the Benthamite view of government lay not so much in their perception of whether its main functions should be directed from the centre or dispersed among local authorities, as in their underlying reasons for advocating a more active social role for the state. While Sadler emphasized the need to improve the quality of life for the labouring poor, the Benthamites showed more interest in improving the minds of the lower orders by social conditioning. From the Benthamites' individualistic perspective, once the poor were made aware of their responsibilities as individuals, they would acquire a sense of self-respect and this in turn would stimulate a desire for self-improvement. Hence, the education clause of Althorp's bill was regarded by many of his liberal and pro-Benthamite supporters as the most important aspect of the whole factory regulation issue. The paternalists were certainly conscious of the value to society as a whole of educating the lower orders, particularly in relation to their civic duties and responsibilities. Coleridge, in particular, had seen it as a means of securing an identity of interests between the different orders in society and of maintaining social stability. However, for them, education was largely a process of social interaction in which children learned from their parents, or servants from their masters. They were, therefore, wary of the highly regimented Owenite-type training schemes advocated by liberal reformers. Southey, in particular, was extremely critical of the factory school system introduced by Althorp's Act, believing that it contributed to dissolving the bonds between the mother and her child. He regarded it as lamentable that the mother was no longer required to provide guidance and instruction for her children, instead 'the duty is undertaken *for her* now – nay, it is *taken from her*'.[29]

For Sadler, education was an important but not a pre-eminent consideration. He included it in the list of reforms which he intended to take up once the ten hours bill had passed. But he frequently stressed that what the children needed more than anything else was free time and that time was as necessary to their recreational as to their educational needs. Similarly, the Rev. Bull and several other pro-Sadlerite witnesses for the 1832 Committee on Child Labour had stressed that it was unfair to expect children to attend classes or Sunday school when they were obliged to spend so much of their time confined in factories. In the debate on Althorp's bill, this point was taken up by Thomas Attwood, a brother of Mathias Attwood, whose paternalist outlook and associations with Newcastle are examined in chapter 4. The children, Attwood suggested, 'would derive more benefit from ... having those two hours for repose or healthful amusement'.[30] Boyd Hilton observes that the 'paternalists, far from seeking to *improve* their inferiors, sought merely to protect them from the stormy blasts'.[31] For Sadler, government's primary role was to improve the circumstances of the labouring poor. Once that had been achieved, the mental and moral improvement of the lower orders would automatically follow. Through his persistent advocacy of the state's social responsibilities and demands for social reform and improvement, Sadler's was an instrumental contribution to the institutionalization of paternalist, protectionist principles. His reach may thus be argued to extend to both the Victorian collectivist and the modern welfare state.

Notes

Introduction: Michael Thomas Sadler and 'the Revival of the Aristocratic Paternalist Ideal'

1 Harold Perkin, *The Origins of Modern English Society 1780–1880* (London: Routledge and Kegan Paul, 1969) pp. 218–70 ff.
2 *Ibid.*, p. 237.
3 *Ibid.*, pp. 243–4.
4 *Ibid.*, p. 241.
5 *Ibid.*, p. 243.
6 Barry Gordon, *Economic Doctrine and Tory Liberalism, 1824–1830* (London: Macmillan, 1979) p. 87; Raymond G. Cowherd, *The Humanitarians and the Ten Hour Movement in England* (Massachusetts: Baker Library, Harvard, 1956) p. 9; R.K. Webb, *Modern England From the Eighteenth Century to the Present* (London: George Allen & Unwin, 1969) p. 241; J.R. Poynter, *Society and Pauperism. English Ideas on Poor Relief, 1795–1834* (London, Routledge and Kegan Paul, 1969) pp. 148, 308–9.
7 Norman Gash, *Aristocracy and the People, Britain 1815–1865* (London: Edward Arnold, 1979) pp. 193–4; Elie Halévy, *The Liberal Awakening 1815–1830* (London: Ernest Benn Ltd, 1926, 1961) p. 283.
8 Geoffrey Carnall, *Robert Southey and his Age* (Oxford: Clarendon Press, 1960) pp. 190, 193; Poynter, *op. cit.*, pp. 308–9; E.P. Thompson, *The Making of the English Working Class* (Harmondsworth: Penguin Books, 1980 edn) pp. 377–8.
9 *Ibid.*, pp. 378–80.
10 Perkin, *op. cit.*, pp. 243–4.
11 J.C.D. Clark, *English Society 1688–1832: Ideology, Social Structure and Political Practice during the Ancien Régime* (Cambridge, 1985). Joanna Innes, 'Jonathan Clark, Social History and England's "Ancien Regime"', *Past and Present*, 115 (May 1987) 165–200; John Money, 'Provincialism and the English "Ancien Regime": Samuel Pipe-Wolferstan and the "Confessional State", 1776–1820', *Albion*, 21, 3 (1989) 389–425.
12 Clark, *op. cit.*, pp. 4, 7, 64–5, 71, 90.
13 *Ibid.*, p. 65.
14 *Ibid.*, p. 73.
15 *Ibid.*, pp. 4, 7, 90, 92, 350, 409, 411.
16 David Roberts, *Paternalism in Early Victorian England* (London: Croom Helm, 1979) p. 1.
17 *Ibid.*, pp. 26–7.
18 *Ibid.*, pp. 1–2, 189.
19 John Stuart Mill, *Principles of Political Economy* (1848), *Collected Works of John Stuart Mill*, III (Toronto: University of Toronto Press, 1977) bk. iv, ch. vii, pp. 758–60.
20 Roberts, *op. cit.*, pp. 38–47.

1: Continuity and Change in the Revival of Paternalist Social Thought

1 Harold Perkin, *The Origins of Modern English Society 1780–1880* (London: Routledge and Kegan Paul, 1969), p. 243.
2 Jean-Jacques Rousseau voiced similar sentiments in the *Discourse on Inequality*, Alan Ritter and Julia Conaway Bondanella, eds, *Rousseau's Political Writings* (New York and London: W.W. Norton and Co., 1988) p. 42.
3 Samuel Taylor Coleridge, *The Statesman's Manual* (1816) and *A Lay Sermon Addressed to the Higher and Middle Classes on the Existing Distresses and Discontents* (1817), *The Collected Works of Samuel Taylor Coleridge*, VI (London: Routledge and Kegan Paul, 1972).
4 Coleridge, *The Statesman's Manual*, pp. 7, 39, 40.
5 William Hazlitt, 'Coleridge's Lay Sermons', *ER*, XXVII, LIV (December 1816) 449.
6 Coleridge, *The Statesman's Manual*, pp. 39, 40.
7 Coleridge, *A Lay Sermon*, pp. 144–55 ff.
8 *Ibid.*, p. 163.
9 *Ibid.*, pp. 169–70 ff.
10 *Ibid.*, p. 189.
11 *Ibid.*, p. 207.
12 *Ibid.*, pp. 170–4, 193–4.
13 *Ibid.*, p. 223.
14 *Ibid.*, p. 161.
15 *Ibid.*, pp. 219–20.
16 *Ibid.*, pp. 215–16.
17 *Ibid.*, pp. 226–7.
18 *Ibid.*, pp. 228–9.
19 *Ibid.*, p. 216.
20 Samuel Taylor Coleridge, 'Essay IX', *The Friend, II* (1818), *Works*, IV, 1 (London: Routledge and Kegan Paul, 1969) p. 252.
21 Edmund Burke, 'Thoughts and Details on Scarcity' (1795), *The Works of the … Edmund Burke*, IV (London: Oxford University Press, 1907) p. 3.
22 Samuel Taylor Coleridge, *On the Constitution of the Church and State* (1829, 1830), *Works*, X (Princeton, NJ: Princeton University Press, 1976) pp. 25, 27, 29, 31, 44, 88ff.
23 *Ibid.*, p. 69.
24 *Ibid.*, p. 29.
25 *Ibid.*, p. 54.
26 'If … [citizens] are trained early enough never to consider their own persons except in terms of their relations with the body of the state, and not to perceive of their own existence, so to speak, except as part of that of the state, they may finally succeed in identifying themselves in some way with this greater whole, in feeling themselves members of the home-land, in loving it with that exquisite sentiment which every isolated man feels only for himself, in perpetually lifting up their souls towards this great objective, and thus in transforming into a sublime virtue that dangerous disposition from which all our vices arise.' Jean-Jacques

Rousseau, *Discourse on Political Economy*, Ritter and Bondanella, *op. cit.*, p. 73.

27 Samuel Taylor Coleridge, *Two Addresses on Sir Robert Peel's Bill* (April 1818), Edmund Gosse, ed. (London, 1819) pp. 8–9.
28 [Samuel Taylor Coleridge], 'To the Editor of the Courier', *Works*, III, 3 (London: Routledge and Kegan Paul, 1978) p. 155; see also *Lay Sermons*, p. 229.
29 John Colmer, *Coleridge, Critic of Society* (Oxford, 1959) p. 44.
30 Robert Southey, 'On the State of the Poor' (1816), *Essays, Moral and Political*, I (Shannon, Ireland: Irish University Press 1971) p. 214.
31 Robert Southey, 'On Emigration' (1828), *Essays*, p. 224; 'On the State of the Poor, the Principle of Mr. Malthus's Essay on Population, and the Manufacturing System' (1812), *Essays*, pp. 98, 11; *Colloquies*, II, p. 234.
32 Robert Southey, *Sir Thomas More: or Colloquies on the Prospects of Society*, II (London: John Murray, 1829) pp. 246–7, 250.
33 Robert Southey, *Letters from England* (1807), Jack Simmons, ed. (London: Cresset Press, 1951) p. 209.
34 Southey, *Colloquies*, II, p. 253.
35 Southey, 'On the State of the Poor' (1816) pp. 175–8.
36 *Ibid.*, pp. 179–81; see also 'On the Means of Improving the People' (1818), *Essays*, pp. 113–14.
37 Southey, 'On the State of the Poor' (1812) pp. 112–13.
38 Southey, *Colloquies*, I, pp. 100–1.
39 Southey, 'On the State of the Poor' (1812) pp. 95, 142.
40 Southey, *Colloquies*, I, p. 111.
41 Southey, *Colloquies*, II, p. 420.
42 Thomas Babington Macaulay, 'Southey's Colloquies on Society', *ER*, L, C (January 1830) 565.
43 *Ibid.*, 546.
44 John Dennis, ed., *Robert Southey: The Story of his Life written in his Letters* (London: George Bell and Sons, 1894, pp. 27–8.
45 Macaulay, *op. cit.*, p. 565.
46 Southey, *Colloquies*, II, p. 73.
47 Southey, 'On the State of the Poor' (1816) p. 212.
48 Southey, *Colloquies*, I, 142.
49 Southey, 'On the Means of Improving the People' (1818) p. 160.
50 Southey, 'On the State of the Poor' (1816) pp. 223–6.
51 *Ibid.*, pp. 219–23, 237, 244–5; 'On the Means of Improving the People' (1818) p. 173; *Colloquies*, I, p. 170.
52 *Ibid.*, p. 193; 'On the State of the Poor' (1812) p. 144.
53 Southey, 'On the State of the Poor' (1816) p. 183.
54 Southey, *Colloquies*, II, p. 78; 'On the State of the Poor' (1812) p. 146; 'On the State of the Poor' (1816) p. 230; 'On the Means of Improving the People' (1818) p. 137.
55 Southey, 'On the State of the Poor' (1812) p. 149.
56 Robert Southey, *Journal of a Tour in Scotland*, in Anne Taylor, *Visions of Harmony: A Study in Nineteenth-Century Millenarianism* (Oxford: Clarendon Press, 1987) p. 82.
57 Southey to Ashley (12 May 1832), Edwin Hodder, *The Life and Work of the*

Seventh Earl of Shaftesbury, I (London: Cassell and Company, 1886) pp. 195–6.

58 Robert Owen, *A Statement Regarding the New Lanark Establishment* (1812) p. 17, *A New View of Society* (1813) p. 58 and *Address Delivered to the Inhabitants of New Lanark* (1816) p. 124, Gregory Claeys, ed., *Selected Works of Robert Owen*, I (London: William Pickering, 1993).
59 Owen, *A Statement*, p. 16.
60 *Ibid.*, pp. 17–19; *A New View of Society*, pp. 56–8, 64, 66; *Address* (1816) pp. 124–5.
61 *Ibid.*, p. 134.
62 Owen, *A Statement*, p. 14.
63 Owen, *A New View of Society*, p. 28.
64 In 1813, Jeremy Bentham together with a number of prominent Quakers and educationists, including William Allen and Joseph Fox, helped Owen finance a takeover of the New Lanark mill. This was after Owen's existing partners began to object to his visionary methods. Their refusal to allow construction of the Institution prompted Owen to resign as manager of the mill and surreptitiously set about organizing a new partnership. *A New View of Society* was privately circulated in 1813 as a prospectus for New Lanark. Robert Owen, *The Life of Robert Owen* (1857), *Works*, IV, pp. 140–9; *A Statement*, pp. 13–15.
65 Robert Owen, *Mr Owen's Speech at a Public Dinner at which He Presided, Given to Joseph Lancaster* (1812), *Works*, I, p. 9.
66 Owen, *A New View of Society*, pp. 75, 92–4.
67 Jeremy Bentham, *An Introduction to the Principles of Morals and Legislation* (1798), *The Utilitarians* (New York: Anchor Press) p. 18.
68 Robert Owen, *Permanent Relief for the British Agricultural and Manufacturing Labourers, and the Irish Peasantry* (1822), *Works*, I, p. 352.
69 Owen, *A New View of Society*, pp. 48, 64.
70 Owen, *Address* (1816) p. 126.
71 Owen, *A New View of Society*, p. 53, fn. b.
72 Owen, *Report to the County of Lanark; An Address to the Working Classes* (1819), *Works*, I, pp. 281, 332–4.
73 Reprinted in William Reitzel, ed., *The Progress of a Plough-boy to a Seat in Parliament as Exemplified in the History of the Life of William Cobbett* (London: Faber and Faber) 1933, pp. 264–5.
74 Karl W. Schweizer and John W. Osborne, *Cobbett in His Times* (Leicester: Leicester University Press, 1990) pp. 154–5; Martin J. Wiener, 'The Changing Image of William Cobbett', *The Journal of British Studies*, XIII, 2 (May 1974) 135–54.
75 Cobbett, 'A Letter to the Luddites', *PR* (30 November 1816) 677, 681; see also *Rural Rides* (1830), George Woodcock, ed. (Harmondsworth: Penguin Books, 1967) pp. 317–18; *The Progress of a Plough-boy*, pp. 234–6, 251–2.
76 Cobbett, *PR* (13 April 1816) 452; *Rural Rides*, pp. 261, 273, 289, 460.
77 William Cobbett, 'To the Working Classes of Preston', *The Poor Man's Friend or Essays on the Rights and Duties of the Poor*, II (London, 1829).
78 Cobbett, *PR* (7 April 1821) 15.
79 Cobbett, *PR* (2 November 1816) 559; see also *The Poor Man's Friend*, I.
80 Cobbett, *Cottage Economy*, p. 3. His argument was reminiscent of Burke's

'Thoughts and Details on Scarcity' (1795).

81 Cobbett, 'To the Stocking-weavers of Leicestershire, Nottinghamshire and Derbyshire', PR (14 April 1821) 114–15.
82 Cobbett, *PR* (2 November 1816) 545–6, 560; *PR* (14 April 1821) 97–8.
83 According to Cobbett's understanding of this doctrine, in a state of nature, self-preservation was the paramount consideration. This 'law of nature teaches every creature to prefer the preservation of its own life to all other things … At length this state of things became changed: men entered into society; they made laws to restrain individuals and following, in certain cases, the dictates of their own will; they protected the weak against the strong; the laws secured men in possession of lands, houses, and goods, that were called THEIRS; the words MINE and THINE, which mean my own and thy own, were invented to designate what we now call a property in things … Now civil society was formed for the benefit of the whole. The whole gave up their natural rights, in order that every one might, for the future, enjoy his life in greater security. This civil society was intended to change the state of man for the better. Before this state of civil society, the starving, the hungry, the naked man, had a right to go and provide himself with necessaries wherever he could find them. There would be sure to be some such necessitous persons in a state of civil society. Therefore, when civil society was established, it is impossible to believe that it had not in view some provision for these destitute persons.' *The Poor Man's Friend*, II.
84 Cobbett, *PR* (14 April 1821) 118.
85 Cobbett, *The Poor Man's Friend*, IV.
86 Cobbett, *Rural Rides*, pp. 254, 261, 273, 289, 458–60 ff; *PR* (13 April 1816) 451–2; *The Poor Man's Friend*, IV and V.
87 Cobbett, *Rural Rides*, pp. 100, 140–1, 471, 473.
88 Cobbett, *PR* (7 April 1821) 10–12.
89 *Ibid.*, 14; *Rural Rides*, pp. 226–7; *The Progress of a Plough-boy*, pp. 238–40.
90 Cobbett, *PR* (14 April 1821) 102.
91 Ian Dyck, *William Cobbett and Rural Popular Culture* (Cambridge: Cambridge University Press) 1992, pp. 56, 73.
92 *Ibid.*, pp. 125, 71, 125–51.
93 Indeed, there were occasions when Cobbett seemed to view class-based relations with some abhorrence. In answer to stocking weavers seeking protection from competition, he declared, 'You are for an aristocracy in trade; you are for Lords of the Loom; you are for shutting out your own brother workmen, you own kindred and children; and, as for yourselves, you, if you adopt these sentiments are guilty of an abandonment of the chance of adornments in life. You are for cutting off the chain of connection between the rich and the poor. You are for demolishing all small tradesmen. You are for reducing the community to two classes: Masters and Slaves'. *PR* (14 April 1821) 85.
94 Schweizer and Osborne, *op. cit.*, pp. 150–1.
95 Cobbett, *Cottage Economy*, pp. 2–3.
96 Cobbett, *PR* (20 November 1824) p. 477.
97 Cobbett, *PR* (14 April 1821) 102, 122 [emphasis added]; see also *PR* (2 November 1816) 570–1, 671; *Rural Rides*, pp. 262, 409, ff.; *The Progress of*

a Plough-boy, pp. 220, 252.

98   Cobbett, *PR* (2 November 1816) 571–2; see also *PR* (14 April 1821) 102, 127–8; *The Poor Man's Friend*, V.

99   Cobbett, *PR* (7 April 1821) 6; see also *PR* (20 November 1824) 454.

100 Cobbett, *The Progress of a Plough-boy*, p. 105.

101 *Ibid.*, p. 233.

102 Cobbett, *PR* (20 November 1824) 479–80.

103 James Mill, Preface, *Elements of Political Economy* (1826), Donald Winch, ed., *James Mill: Selected Economic Writings* (London: Oliver and Boyd 1966). It ran to three editions, published in 1821, 1824 and 1826 respectively.

104 *Ibid.*, p. 182.

105 *Ibid.*, pp. 179, 181–7.

106 Barry Gordon, *Political Economy in Parliament 1819–1823* (London: Macmillan, 1976) p. 17.

107 *Ibid.*, p. 4.

108 Winch, *op. cit.*, pp. 192–3.

109 Nasseau William Senior, 'An Introductory Lecture on Political Economy' (1827), Selected Writings on Economics (New York: Augustus M. Kelley, 1966) pp. 10–11.

110 *Ibid.*, p. 23.

111 'Review – Ricardo on Political Economy', *Blackwood's*, I, II (May 1817) 176.

112 Perkin, *op. cit.*, p. 245.

113 'Ricardo and the Edinburgh Review', *Blackwood's*, IV, XIX (October 1818) 58.

114 *Ibid.*, 59.

115 'On the Influence of Wages on the Rate of Profits', *Blackwood's*, V, XXVI (May 1819) 171.

116 David Robinson, 'Public Distress', *Blackwood's* XIX, CXI (April 1826) 429–46; William Johnstone, 'The State and Prospects of the Country', *Blackwood's*, XXVI, CLVII (September 1829) 464–73.

117 David Robinson, 'The Repeal of the Combination Laws', *Blackwood's*, XVIII, CII (July 1825) 23.

118 *Ibid.*, pp. 21–2, 24–5ff; 'The Combinations', *Blackwood's*, XVIII, CV (October 1825) 463–78.

119 Henry Brougham, 'Scientific Education of the People', *ER*, 41 (October 1824) 96–122; 'Mechanics' Institutes', *ER*, 42 (August 1825) 499–504; 'Supposed Dangers of Knowledge', *ER*, 43 (November 1825) 242–8.

120 Robinson, 'The Repeal of the Combination Laws', 26.

121 Robinson, 'Brougham on the Education of the People', 531, 549ff.

122 William Johnstone, 'Our Domestic Policy', *Blackwood's*, XXVI, CLIX (November 1829) 768.

123 William Johnstone, 'The State of the Country', 464–6; 'Condition of the Lower Orders', *Blackwood's*, XXVII, CLXI (January 1830) 90–2.

124 *Ibid.*, 93.

125 Johnstone, 'The State of the Country', 92; 'Our Domestic Policy', 768–9.

126 Johnstone, 'Condition of the Lower Orders', p. 94.

127 *Ibid.*, 92–6.

128   David Robinson, 'The Poor Laws', *Blackwood's*, XXIII, CXL (June 1825) 924.

129   Edward Edwards, 'The Influence of Free-Trade upon the Condition of the Labouring Classes', *Blackwood's*, XXVII, CLXV (April 1830) 556, 558ff.

130   *Ibid.*, 564; Robinson, 'The Poor Laws', 926, 935–6.

131   Edwards, 'The Influence of Free-Trade', 559–60.

132   *Ibid.*, 565.

133   Robinson, 'The Poor Laws', p. 925; 'Political Economy. No. IV', *Blackwood's*, XXVII, CLXI (January 1830) 31–2.

134   *Ibid.*, 29; 'Political Economy. No. I', *Blackwood's*, XXVI, ClVII (September 1829) 510–23.

135   *Ibid.*, 516.

136   *Ibid.*, p. 110; see also David Robinson, 'Political Economy. No. II', *Blackwood's*, XXVI, CLVIII (October 1829) 671–87; 'Political Economy. No. III', *Blackwood's*, XXVI, CLIX (November 1829) 780–808.

137   Robinson, 'Political Economy' (January 1830) 47; (September 1829) 511.

2:   Sadler's Protectionist, Paternalist Social System and the Foundation of His Social Agenda

1   Robert Benton Seeley, *Memoirs of the life and Writings of Michael Thomas Sadler* (London: R. B. Seeley & W. Burnside, 1842) p. 34.

2   *Ibid.*, pp. 1–6.

3   *Ibid.*, pp. 403–5, 650–62.

4   T.B. Macaulay, 'Sadler's *Law of Population, and Disproof of Human Superfecundity*', *ER*, LI, CII (July 1830) 298.

5   Seeley, *op. cit.*, p. 14.

6   M. T. Sadler, *An Apology for the Methodists, being a copy of a letter to the Reverend Henry Stokes, Vicar of Doveridge, Derbyshire* (Stockport, 1797). An original of this pamphlet could not be located, but extracts of it are reproduced in a late nineteenth-century account of Sadler's life written by a descendant of the family and former vice-chancellor of Leeds University, Sir Michael Ernest Sadler, 'Michael Thomas Sadler, M.P. F.R.S., A Sketch of his Life and Opinions' (MS, Brotherton Library, University of Leeds, 1896) pp. 6–13.

7   Mary Howitt, *An Autobiography edited by her daughter Margaret Howitt*, 1 (London, 1889) pp. 101–2.

8   Sadler, *op. cit.*, pp. 8–9.

9   Quoted in M.E. Sadler, *op. cit.*, p. 11.

10   R.J. Morris, *Class, Sect and Party: The Making of the British Middle Class, Leeds 1820–1850* (Manchester: Manchester University Press, 1990) p. 209; Seeley, *op. cit.*, pp. 11–12, 29.

11   Mrs. Gaskell, *The Life of Charlotte Brontë* (London: John Murray, 1862) pp. 84–5.

12   Seeley, *op. cit.*, pp. 13–16.

13   John Mayhall, *The Annals of Yorkshire*, 1 (Leeds: Joseph Johnson, 1862) p. 397.

14   Arthur Stanley Turberville, 'Leeds and Parliamentary Reform, 1820–1832',

Thorseby, XLI (Leeds, 1954) p. 19.

15 Admissions Book, 1766–1828, Leeds Corporation (West Yorkshire Archives, Sheepscar, Leeds).

16 Tuberville, *op. cit.*, p. 19.

17 Seeley, *op. cit.*, p. 15.

18 J. Myers Gardner, *History of the Leeds Benevolent or Strangers' Friend Society 1789 to 1889* (Leeds, 1890) p. 8.

19 Emily Hargrave, 'The Leeds Volunteers (1820)', *The Publications of the Thoresby Society*, XXIV (Leeds, 1919), pp. 451–68.

20 *Ibid.*, p. 455.

21 *Ibid.*, p. 451.

22 *Ibid.*, pp. 457, 464–8.

23 E. Kitson Clark, *The History of 100 Years of Life of the Leeds Philosophical and Literary Society* (Leeds: Jowett & Sowry, 1924) pp. 5, 12.

24 *Ibid.*, pp. 7–11, 20–2; Mayhall, *op. cit.*, pp. 274–6.

25 Kitson Clark, *op. cit.*, pp. 11–16.

26 Edward Baines, *On the Moral Influence of Free Trade, and its effects on the Prosperity of Nations* (London, 1830).

27 Seeley, *op. cit.*, p. 33.

28 M. T. Sadler, A Dissertation upon the Balance of Food and Numbers of Animated Nature (London: John Murray, 1830)

29 For a list of the society's discussion papers and public lectures, see Kitson Clark, *op. cit.*, pp. 151–219.

30 Seeley, *op. cit.*, p. 17.

31 Michael Thomas Sadler, 'The Speech of M.T. Sadler at the Meeting held at the Parish Church Leeds ... 1813, on the Catholic Question' (MS, Leeds, Central Library); Roman Catholic Relief Bill, *PD*, 2nd ser., XX (17 March 1829) 1149–71.

32 Sadler, 'Speech', pp. 1–2, 8.

33 *Ibid.*, pp. 4–5.

34 *Ibid.*, p. 12.

35 *PD*, 2nd ser., XX (17 March 1829) 1150.

36 Sadler, 'Speech', p. 8.

37 Linda Colley, *Britons Forging the Nation 1707–1837* (London: Pimlico, 1992) pp. 11–54.

38 *Ibid.*, pp. 1–9.

39 John Stuart Mill, *Principles of Political Economy* (1848), *Collected Works of John Stuart Mill*, III (Toronto: University of Toronto Press, 1977) bk IV, ch. VII, p. 758.

40 William Paley, *The Principles of Moral and Political Philosophy* (London: R. Faulder, 1785) bk III, ch. IV, p. 199; Michael Thomas Sadler, *Ireland; its Evils, and their Remedies; being a Refutation of the Errors of the Emigration Committee and Others, Touching that Country* (London: John Murray, 2nd edn, 1829) pp. 211–12; The Law of Population: *A Treatise in Six Books; in Disproof of the Superfecundity of Human Beings, and Developing the Real Principle of Their Increase* (London: John Murray, 1830) p. 345; see also *PD*, 2nd ser., XXI (12 June 1829) 1791; 3rd ser., VIII (11 October 1831) 499.

41 *Ibid.*, 3rd ser., I (14 December 1830) 1156–7.

42 Sadler, *Ireland*, p. 20.

43 *Ibid.*, p. 2.
44 *Ibid.*, p. xlviii.
45 *Ibid.*, p. xlix.
46 Sadler, *Law of Population*, p. 6.
47 *Ibid.*, p. 10.
48 *PD*, 2nd ser., XXII (5 February 1830) 155–7, 232.
49 Sadler, *Ireland*, pp. 97–8.
50 *Ibid.*, p. liii–vi; see also *Law of Population*, p. 11.
51 Sadler, *Ireland*, pp. 205–6. Cf. William Cobbett, *PR* (30 November 1816) 698.
52 Sadler, *Ireland*, p. 324.
53 *Ibid.*, pp. l-li.
54 *Ibid.*, p. 90.
55 *Ibid.*, pp. 54–5ff.
56 *Ibid.*, pp. lv, 54–6, 95, 458–60; see also *PD*, 2nd ser., XXIV (3 June 1830) 1296ff; *PD*, 3rd ser., III (30 March 1831) 1221–2; IV (21 June 1831) 208, 251; VIII (11 October 1831) 512–13.
57 *PD*, 3rd ser., VIII (11 October 1831) 512–13.
58 Sadler, *Ireland*, pp. 198, 202–3.
59 *Ibid.*, pp. 202–5.
60 Thomas Robert Malthus, *An Essay on the Principle of Population*, Donald Winch, ed. (Cambridge: Cambridge University Press) 1992, p. 101.
61 Sadler, *Ireland*, p. 203.
62 *Ibid.*, p. 207.
63 Sadler, *Law of Population*, p. 343.
64 Sadler, *Ireland*, pp. 208–12; *PD*, 2nd ser., XXIV (3 June 1830) 1299–1303.
65 Bertrand Russell, *History of Western Philosophy* (London: George Allen & Unwin, 1979 edn) pp. 606–10; George Sabine, *A History of Political Theory* (London: George G. Harrap & Co. Ltd., 1963 edn) pp. 429–30.
66 John Locke, 'An Essay Concerning the True Original, Extent, and End of Civil Government', *Two Treatises of Government* (1690), Peter Laslett, ed. (Cambridge: Cambridge University Press, 1960) bk III, ch. VI, sect. 131, p. 398.
67 Sabine, *op. cit.*, p. 431.
68 *Ibid.*, p. 433.
69 Sadler, *Ireland*, p. 211.
70 William Cobbett, *The Poor Man's Friend or Essays on the Rights and Duties of the Poor*, 1826–7, II (London, 1829).
71 Locke, *op. cit.*, bk I, ch. III, sect. 42, p. 206.
72 Sabine, *op. cit.*, p. 532.
73 Sadler's theory of indigence profited from these writers' enlarged view of the social compact. *Ireland*, pp. 210, 211–12.
74 See, for example, Frederick Page, *The Principle of the English Poor Laws Illustrated and Defended, by an Historical View of Indigence in Civil Society* (London: Hatchard & Son, 1822) p. 38; William Carmalt, *A Letter to the Honourable George Canning, On the Principle and the Administration of the English Poor Laws* (London: T. Cadell, 1823) p. 12; W. Copland, *A Letter to the Rev. C. D. Brereton, in Reply to His 'Observations on the Administration of the Poor Laws in Agricultural Districts'* (Norwich: S. Wilkin, 1824) pp.

70–2; George Ensor, *The Poor and Their Relief* (London: Effingham Wilson, 1823) pp. 205–50; John H. Moggridge, *Remarks on the Report of the Select Committee of the House of Commons, on the Poor Laws* (Bristol: Browne & Manchee, 1818) pp. 6–7.

75 Thomas William, *Means of Improving the Condition of the Poor in Morals and Happiness Considered, in a Lecture Delivered at the Minor Institute* (London, [1816]), p. 17.

76 Sadler, *Law of Population*, p. 344.

77 Malthus, *op. cit.*, p. 123.

78 Thomas Robert Malthus, *A Summary View of the Principle of Population* (1830), Anthony Flew, ed. (Harmondsworth: Penguin Books, 1970) pp. 268–9.

79 *PD*, 2nd ser., XXIV (3 June 1830) 1299–1300.

80 Sadler, *Ireland.*, pp. 212–19.

81 Thomas Chalmers, 'Causes and Cure of Pauperism', *ER*, 28, LV (March 1817) 1–31; 'Causes and Cure of Pauperism', *ER*, 29, LVIII (February 1818) 261–392.

82 Chalmers, 'Causes and Cure of Pauperism' (1817) 2, 6.

83 Chalmers, 'Causes and Cure of Pauperism' (1818) 270.

84 *Ibid.*, 269 and 'Causes and Cure of Pauperism' (1817) 16.

85 Sadler, *Ireland,* pp. 214, 216, 217.

86 *Ibid.*, p. 218.

87 *Ibid.*, pp. 230–2; Chalmers, 'Causes and Cure of Pauperism' (1817) 15–16.

88 Sadler, *Ireland*, pp. 286–7.

89 *Ibid.*, pp. xiii, 196–8, 221.

90 Malthus, *An Essay on the Principle of Population*, p. 101.

91 Sadler, *Ireland*, pp. 218–19.

92 *Ibid.*, p. 194.

93 *Ibid.*, p. 292.

94 *PD*, 3rd ser., VIII (11 October 1831) 501–2.

95 Sadler, *Ireland*, p. xlviii.

96 *Ibid.*, p. xiv.

97 Sadler, *Law of Population*, p. vii.

98 Sadler, *Ireland*, p. xviii; *Law of Population*, p. 359.

99 Sadler, *Ireland*, p. xxxiv; *Law of Population*, p. 22; see also *A Dissertation upon the Balance of Food and Numbers of Animated Nature* (London: John Murray, 1830) pp. 13, 19, 23ff.

100 Sadler, *Law of Population*, pp. 359, 397–630ff.; *Ireland*, pp. xxi–xxv, xxvi-iiff; see also *A Refutation of an Article in the Edinburgh Review ... Containing also, Additional Proofs of the Principle Enunciated in that Treatise, Founded on the Censuses of Different Countries Recently Published* (London: John Murray, 1830).

101 Sadler, *Ireland*, p. xix; see also *Law of Population*, pp. 20, 357.

102 *Ibid.*, p. xl.

103 *Ibid.*, p. xxxiii [emphasis added].

104 *Ibid.*, pp. xvi, xliii; *A Dissertation*, pp. 5, 13; *Law of Population*, pp. 3, 5–6.

105 *Ibid.*, p. 29.

106 Sadler, *Ireland*, p. xvi.

107 Thomas Babington Macaulay, 'Sadler's Law of Population, and Disproof

of Human Superfecundity', *ER*, 51, CLL (July 1830) 299–300ff.
108   Sadler, *Ireland*, p. xliv.
109   Sadler, *A Dissertation*, p. 7.
110   Sadler, *Ireland*, p. 193 [emphasis added].
111   *PD*, 3rd ser., VIII (11 October 1831) 503–4.
112   Sadler, *Ireland*, pp. 309–312.

3:   Parliamentary Debate of Social Issues, *c.* 1815–30: a Conflict between Liberal Utilitarianism and Aristocratic Paternalism

1   Samuel Taylor Coleridge, *On the Objections Which Have Been Urged Against the Principle of Sir Robert Peel's Bill* (18 April 1818) and *The Grounds of Sir Robert Peel's Bill Vindicated* (24 April 1818), Edmund Gosse, ed., *Two Addresses on Sir Robert Peel's Bill* (London, 1819).
2   Coleridge, *Objections* (18 April 1818), p. 1; John Colmer, *Coleridge, Critic of Society* (Oxford, 1959) pp. 44–5, 149.
3   John Russell, 'Distresses of the Country', *Edinburgh Review*, 26, LII (June 1816) 275.
4   *PD*, 1st ser., XXXIV (28 May 1816) 881.
5   *Ibid.*, 894; Curwen, J. C., *Sketch of A Plan for Bettering the Condition of the Labouring Classes of the Community and for Equalizing, and Reducing the Amount of the Present Parochial Assessments* (London: J. Bell [1817]) p. 14.
6   *PD*, 1st ser., XXXI (8 May 1815) 221–2; (2 June 1815) 581–4; XXXV (25 February 1817) 759–61.
7   *Ibid.*, XXXIV (28 May 1816) 902.
8   Thomas Robert Malthus, *An Essay on the Principle of Population*, Donald Winch, ed. (Cambridge: Cambridge University Press) 1992, pp. 324–5.
9   Report from the Select Committee on the Poor Laws, *PP*, VI, 462, (1817), p. 8.
10   *Ibid.*, pp. 4, 5.
11   *Ibid.*, pp. 10–13.
12   *Ibid.*, pp. 7–8, 14–16, 20.
13   *Ibid.*, p. 9
14   *Ibid.*, pp. 18–19.
15   Thomas Peregrine Courtenay, *A Treatise upon the Poor Laws* (London: John Murray, 1818) pp. 7–9ff.
16   *Ibid.*, p. 13; Malthus, *op. cit.*, pp. 110–23, 357–8. 'The obvious tendency', wrote Malthus, 'of the poor laws is certainly to encourage marriage; but a closer attention to all their indirect as well as direct effects, may make it a matter of doubt how far they really do this. They clearly tend, in their general operation, to discourage sobriety and economy, to encourage idleness and the desertion of children, and to put virtue and vice more on a level than they otherwise would be; but I will not presume to say positively that they tend to encourage population.' This admission appeared in an appendix to the 1806 edition of his Essay on Population. In the body of his work he continued to treat the Poor Laws as wrong in principle.

17 Courtenay, *op. cit.*, pp. 18–19, 33ff.
18 *Ibid.*, pp. 52–4.
19 *Ibid.*, pp. 56–8.
20 *Ibid.*, pp. 72, 86–7.
21 *Ibid.*, pp. 84–5.
22 *Ibid.*, pp. 88, 90, 94.
23 *Ibid.*, pp. 96–8.
24 PD, 1st ser., XXXVI (9 May 1817) 298.
25 Report of the Lords Committee on the Poor Laws, *PP*, V, 400 (1818), p. 8.
26 *Ibid.*, p. 10.
27 *Ibid.*, p. 11.
28 *PD.*, 1st ser., XXXVII (12 March 1818) 1057.
29 Report from the Select Committee on Labourers Wages, *PP*, VI, 392 (1824) p. 6.
30 George Long, *Observations on a Bill to Amend the Laws Relating to the Relief of the Poor*, (London: J. & W. T. Clarke, 1821).
31 *PD*, 1st ser., XXXVIII (7 May 1818) 573.
32 *Ibid.*, 574.
33 For details of the Parish Vestry Act (58 Geo. III, c. 69) and Select Vestry Act (59 Geo. III, c. 12) see Sir George Nicholls, *A History of the English Poor Law in Connection with the State of the Country and the Condition of the People* (1854, 1898), II (London: Frank Cass and Co. Ltd., 1967) pp. 180–3.
34 *PD*, 1st ser., XXXVII (12 March 1818) 1057.
35 Formerly, any justice of the peace was empowered to overrule the authority of overseers and order relief for up to a month to any 'industrious' poor person. For periods beyond that, the authority of two magistrates was required. In 1814 the legislation was amended to allow a single magistrate to order relief for up to three months. Under the Select Vestries Act, two magistrates were required and the period was again restricted to one month. Nicholls, *op. cit.*, pp. 116, 153, 182–3.
36 Peter Dunkley's research demonstrates that parishes' economizing efforts were frequently thwarted by magistrates ruling in favour of paupers. Peter Dunkley, 'Paternalism, The Magistracy and Poor Relief in England, 1795–1834', *International Review of Social History*, 24, 3 (1979) 371–97.
37 *PD*, 1st ser., XXXVIII (8 May 1818) 575–6.
38 *Ibid.* (25 May 1818) 916.
39 *Ibid.*, XXXIX (25 March 1819) 1157–8.
40 *Ibid.* (9 February 1819) 414.
41 *Ibid.* (25 March 1819) 1158.
42 *Ibid.*, XL (17 May 1819) 469.
43 *Ibid.*, 471–3; (25 March 1819) 1158. 47 members voted for the second reading and 22 for the amendment.
44 *Ibid.* (11 June 1819) 1125–30: 69 voted for the bill and 46 for the motion against it.
45 *Ibid.* (5 July 1819) 1514–15.
46 *Ibid.*, 2nd ser., V (8 May 1821) 573–82.
47 Daniel Defoe, *Giving Alms no Charity And Employing the Poor A Grievance to the Nation Being an Essay Upon this Great Question* (London, 1704) p. 9.
48 *PD*, 2nd ser., V (8 May 1821) 581.

49 *Ibid.* (24 May 1821) 987ff.
50 *Ibid.* (8 May 1821) 582.
51 *Ibid.* (24 May 1821) 988, 996–7; (2 July 1821) 1482–3.
52 *Ibid.*, 1479.
53 *Ibid.* (24 May 1821) 994.
54 *Ibid.* (2 July 1821) 1480.
55 *Ibid.* (8 May, 20 June 1821) 584, 1228.
56 *Ibid.* (24 May 1821) 996, 997.
57 Robert A., Slaney, *An Essay on the Employment of the Poor* (London: Hatchard & Son, 1819) and *Essay on the Beneficial Direction of Rural Expenditure* (London: Longman, 1824).
58 *PD*, 3rd ser., XXIV (26 April 1830) 38–54.
59 *PD*, 2nd ser., XIII (12 May 1825) 571.
60 Report from the Select Committee on that part of the Poor Laws Relating to the Employment or Relief of able-bodied Persons from the Poor Rates, *PP*, IV, 494 (1828).
61 Report on Labourers Wages (1824) pp. 3–8.
62 Report on the Employment or Relief of able-bodied Persons (1828) pp. 8–9.
63 *Ibid.*, 9–10.
64 W. R. Brock, *Lord Liverpool and Liberal Toryism 1820 to 1827* (London: Frank Cass & Co., 1941, 1967) p. 196; Allen Fox, *History and Heritage. The Social Origins of the British Industrial Relations System* (London: Allen and Unwin, 1985) pp. 7–11, 68–73.
65 *PD*, 2nd ser., IX (9, 21 May 1823); 149–50, 378; (9 June 1823) 811, 816; (11 June 1823) 832.
66 Second Report (relative to the silk and wine trade) from the Select Committee of the House of Lords, appointed to inquire into the means of extending and securing the Foreign Trade of the Country, *PP*, VII, 703 (June 1821) pp. 6–7, 17–23.
67 William Hale, *An Appeal to the Public in Defence of the Spitalfields Act* (London, 1822, New York: Arno Press Inc., 1972).
68 *Ibid.*, pp. 16, 20.
69 *Ibid.*, pp. 6–7.
70 *Ibid.*, pp. 15–16.
71 *PD.*, 2nd ser., IX (16 June 1823) 986–8.
72 *Ibid.* (16 July 1823) 1530–1.
73 *Ibid.* (17 July 1823) 1533–4.
74 *Ibid.*, XI (14 May 1824), 570–2; XII (21 May 1824) 792–3.
75 *Ibid.*, XVII (30 May 1827) 1060–2; XIX (1 May 1828) 260–2.
76 See, for example, *ibid.*, IX (30 May 1823) 706; XI (4 May 1824) 491; XII (22 March 1825) 1138; XIII (12 May 1825) 571.
77 *Ibid.* (1 May 1828) 261; (17 April 1828) 1543.
78 *Ibid.*, V (8 May 1821) 586; (1 May 1828) 261.
79 *Ibid.*, 1st ser., XLI (30 November 1819) 416–507; 517–70; (9 December 1819) 890–955; Edward Royle and James Walvin, *English Radicals and Reformers 1760–1848* (Sussex: Harvester Press, 1982) pp. 108–23; John W. Derry, *Reaction and Reform, 1793–1868, England in the Early Nineteenth Century* (London: Blandford Press, 1963, 1970) pp. 68–73.

80 Robert Owen, *Report to the Committee of the Association for the Relief of the Manufacturing and Labouring Poor* (March 1817), Gregory Claeys, ed., *Selected Works*, I (London: William Pickering, 1993) p. 153.

81 Robert Owen, *A New View of Society; or, Essay on the Principle of the Formation of the Human Character* (1813) in *ibid.*, p. 97.

82 *Report to the County of Lanark* (1820) in *ibid.*, p. 287.

83 *Ibid.*, pp. 304, 305.

84 *Ibid.*, p. 295; *PD*, 2nd ser., I (16 May 1820) 408.

85 *PD*, 1st ser., ILI (16 December 1819) 1189–1217. Sixteen members supported the motion, 141 opposed it.

86 *PD*, 2nd ser., V (26 June 1821) 1321–4.

87 *Ibid.*, I (16 May 1820) 395–422.

88 Slaney, *Employment of the Poor* (1819); *Beneficial Direction of Rural Expenditure* (1824), pp. 9–10.

89 *Ibid.*, pp. 104–9ff.

90 *Ibid.*, pp. 110–13.

91 *Ibid.*, pp. 120–4ff.

92 *Ibid.*, pp. 124, 127–8.

93 *Ibid.*, pp. 144–5, 158–63, 170–1, 20, 206ff.

94 *PD*, 1st ser., XXXVI (5 June 1817) 889–90.

95 Elie Halévy, *History of the English People in 1815* (London: Routledge & Kegan Paul, 1924, 1987) p. 297.

96 *Address from the Committee on the Society for Superseding the Necessity of Climbing Boys* (London, 1818).

97 Report from the Select Committee On Employment of Boys in Sweeping of Chimnies, *PP*, VI, 400 (1817).

98 *The Times* (21 August 1817) 2; (12 November 1817) 3; (1 May 1818) 4; (5 August 1818) 3; (3 March 1819) 3.

99 *PD*, 1st ser., XXXVII (9 February 1818) 216–17.

100 *Ibid.*, (18 February 1818) 506–7.

101 *Ibid.*, (2 March 1818) 690.

102 Report of the Lords Committee [on] 'An Act for the better Regulation of Chimney Sweepers and their Apprentices; and for preventing the Employment of Boys in climbing Chimneys', *House of Lords Sessional Papers*, XCV, 25 (1818) pp. 1–5.

103 *PD*, 1st ser., XXXVIII (14 May 1818) 649–50.

104 *The Times* (3 February 1819) p. 4.

105 *PD*, 1st ser., XXXIX (11 February 1819) 426–7.

106 *Ibid.* (12, 17, 22 February 1819) 430, 448, 450, 548–9.

107 *Ibid.* (17 February 1819) 451.

108 *Ibid.*, 449–50, 453.

109 The division for the second reading was 17 in favour and 14 against.

110 *PD*, 1st ser., XXXIX (8, 25 March 1819), 899–903, 981–4.

111 Report of the Lords Committee on Chimney Sweepers (1818), p. 2.

112 'Resolution unanimously adopted at a General meeting of Master Chimney Sweepers' (25 July 1816) reprinted in Report of the Select Committee on Chimney Sweepers (1817) pp. 50–1.

113 The bill was defeated by 20 votes, 12 in favour and 32 against. *PD*, 1st ser., XXXIX (31 March 1819) 1269; IL (24 May 1819) 668–70.

114 See Sydney Smith's analysis of the Lords' report, 'Climbing Boys', *Edinburgh Review*, 32, LXIV (October 1819) 309–20.
115 *PD*, 1st ser., XXXIII (3 April 1816) 884.
116 Robert Owen, *The Life of Robert Owen written by Himself, with Selections from his Writings and Correspondence* (London: Frank Cass & Co. Ltd, 1967) pp. 115–17.
117 *PD*, 1st ser., XXXI (6 June 1815) 624.
118 Report of the Minutes of Evidence taken before the Select Committee on the State of the Children employed in the Manufactories of the United Kingdom, *PP*, III, 397 (1816).
119 See, for example, the evidence of Matthew Baille, p. 29; Astley Cooper, p. 33; Christopher Pemberton, pp. 34–5; George Leman Tuthill, pp. 43–4; Sir Gilbert Blane, p. 45.
120 *PD*, 1st ser., XXXVII (19, 23 February 1818) 559–60, 581–2.
121 See Lord Henry Lascelles (Northallerton) and Sir James Graham (Hull), *ibid.*, 560, 582.
122 *Ibid.*, 581.
123 See George Philips and Kirkman Finlay (Malmesbury), *ibid.* (19, 23 February 1818) 561, 562, 583, 587–8; (10 April 1818) 1261ff.
124 *Ibid.*, XXXVIII (27 April 1818) 347.
125 *Ibid.*, XXXVII (19 February 1818) 565; XXXVIII (17, 27 April 1818) 172, 346.
126 *Ibid.*, XXXVII (10 April 1818) 1260–1; XXXVIII (27 April 1818), 349.
127 *Ibid.*, XXXVII (23 February 1818) 586.
128 *Ibid.*, XXXVIII (27 April 1818) 353–9.
129 *Ibid.*, XXXVII (17 April 1818) 172; XXXVIII (27 April 1818) 370–1.
130 Minutes of Evidence taken before the Lords Committee [on] 'An Act to amend and extend an Act made in the Forty-second Year of His present Majesty, for the Preservation of the Health and Morals of Apprentices, and others, employed in Cotton and other Mills, and Cotton and other Factories', *House of Lords Sessional Papers*, XCVI, 90, (1818) pp. 30–43, 52–62, 85–90, 92–3, 98–116, 141–54, 155–65ff.
131 *PD*, 1st ser., XXXVIII (5 June 1818) 1252.
132 *Ibid.*, XXXIX (4, 8, 25 February 1818) 288–9, 344, 399–43, 652–6.
133 Extracts reprinted in Charles Wing, *Evils of the Factory System Demonstrated by Parliamentary Evidence*, 1837 (London: Frank Cass & Co. Ltd, 1967) pp. clxvi–clxxxii.
134 *PD*, 2nd ser., XIII (5, 16, 31 May 1825) 421, 643–9, 1008–11.
135 David Roberts, *Paternalism in Early Victorian England* (London: Croom Helm, 1979) p. 187.

4: The 'Sadlerian School': a Defence of Protectionist, Paternalist Ideals

1 Samuel O'Sullivan, 'Review of the Last Session of Parliament', *Blackwood's*, XXVI, CLV (August 1829) 235.
2 The Diary of Samuel G. Fenton (MS, Central Library, Leeds, 1828–9) 18, 23 February 1829.

 3 *Ibid.*, 21 and 22 February 1829.
 4 *Ibid.*, 3 February 1829.
 5 *Ibid.*, 23, 24, 26 February 1829.
 6 *Ibid.*, 5 March 1829.
 7 *Ibid.*, 8 March 1829.
 8 *Ibid.*, 10–16 March 1829.
 9 *Ibid.*, 17 March 1829.
10 *Ibid.*, 18, 19 March 1829.
11 Lowther to Lonsdale, 17 March 1829, quoted in D.S.G. Simes, 'The Ultra Tories in British Politics 1824–1832' (DPhil, University of Oxford, 1974) p.411.
12 Robert Southey to Grosvenor Charles Bedford, 28 March 1829, reprinted in Kenneth Curry, *New Letters of Robert Southey*, 2 (New York and London: Columbia University Press, 1965) p. 334.
13 Fenton, *op. cit.*, 20 March 1829; Robert Seeley, *Memoirs of the life and Writings of Michael Thomas Sadler* (London: R. B. Seeley & W. Burnside, 1842) p. 115.
14 Fenton, *op. cit.*, 21 March 1829; Thomas Babington Macaulay, 'Church and State', *ER*, 69 (April 1839) 231.
15 Willoughby polled 775, Sadler 746 and Wilde 652.
16 Tallents to Newcastle, 3 August and 1 September 1830 (MS, University of Nottingham, fols NeC6414, NeC6420).
17 Sadler to Newcastle, 4 August 1830 (MS, University of Nottingham, fol. NeC6415).
18 Tallents to Newcastle, 1 September 1830 (MS, University of Nottingham, fol. NeC6420); *PD*, 2nd ser., XXII (1 March 1830) 1081–2.
19 *Ibid.*, 1084–8.
20 *Ibid.*, 1102–3, 1105–19.
21 *PD*, 3rd ser., III (18 April 1831) 1530–68, 1688. For a detailed account of Sadler's views on politics, see Michael Thomas Sadler, *A First Letter to a Reformer, in Reply to a Pamphlet Lately Published by Walter Fawkes … Entitled The Englishman's Manual* (London: Longman, Hurst & Co., 1817).
22 *PD*, 3rd ser., III (18 April 1831) 1531, 1533–5ff.
23 *The Times* (28 April 1831) 4.
24 Michael to Ferrebee Sadler [June 1831], (MS, BLPES, Coll. Misc. 62, vol. 1).
25 Thomas Tooke, quoted in Elie Halévy, *The Liberal Awakening (1815–1830)* (London: Ernest Benn Ltd, 1961) p. 121.
26 Barry Gordon, *Political Economy in Parliament 1819–1823* (London: Macmillan, 1976) p. 76.
27 Second Report (relative to the silk and wine trade) from the Select Committee of the House of Lords appointed to inquire into the means of extending and securing the Foreign Trade on the Country, *PP*, VII, 703 (June 1821) p. 6.
28 *PD*, 2nd ser., XXI (13 April 1829).
29 *Ibid.*, 789–90.
30 *PD*, 2nd ser., XX, 26 (27 February 1829); XXI, 6 (9 April 1829).
31 David Robinson, 'Mr. Huskisson's Speech in Defence of Free Trade', *Blackwood's*, XIX, CXI (April 1826) 478.

32 David Robinson, 'Free Trade', *Blackwood's*, XVII, C (May 1825) 551.
33 David Robinson, 'The Old System of Trade and the New One', *Blackwood's*, XXIV, CXLII (September 1828) 371.
34 Robinson, 'Mr. Huskisson's Speech' (1826) 487.
35 *Ibid.*, 474; 'The Silk Trade' (1825) 750.
36 *Ibid.* 'Mr. Huskisson's Speech' (1826) 471.
37 *PD*, 2nd ser., XXI (13 April 1829) 744–56.
38 *Ibid.*, 745, 747.
39 *Ibid.*, 758, 760.
40 *Ibid.*, 762–3, 776–9, 782.
41 Fenton, *op. cit.*, 3, 4, 11 April 1829.
42 *Ibid.*, 801–2.
43 *PD*, 2nd ser., XXI (13 April 1829) 803.
44 *Ibid.*, 802, 804–5.
45 *Ibid.* (14 April 1829) 822.
46 *Ibid.*, 831, 833, 835.
47 *Ibid.*, 830–1.
48 *Ibid.*, 844–5, 848.
49 *Ibid.*, 861.
50 *Ibid.*, 859–61.
51 *Ibid.*, 862–4, 865–7.
52 *Ibid.* (1 May 1829) 914–1000.
53 *Ibid.*, 934–6.
54 Fenton, *op. cit.*, 14 April 1829.
55 *PD*, 2nd ser., XXI (1 May 1829) 964–5, 968.
56 *Ibid.* (1 May 1829) 956–9.
57 *Ibid.*, 970–82.
58 *Ibid.*, 987.
59 *Ibid.*, 988–9.
60 *Ibid.* (13 April 1829) 742.
61 Third Report from the Select Committee on Emigration from the United Kingdom, *PP*, V, 550 (June 1827), pp. 9–12, 16–17, 38.
62 Sadler, *Ireland*, pp. 3–4, 83, 84, 315.
63 *Ibid.*, pp. 85, 93–4.
64 *Ibid.*, pp. 316–17.
65 *Ibid.*, p. 4.
66 H.J.M. Johnston, *Emigration Policy 1815–1830: 'Shovelling out Paupers'* (Oxford: Clarendon Press, 1972) p. 145.
67 *PD*, 2nd ser., XII (15 April 1825) 1358; XIIII (14 March 1826) 1390, 1361; Report on Emigration *PP*, V, 404 (May 1826), p. 6.
68 *Ibid.*, p. 4.
69 *PD*, 2nd ser., XVI (5, 7, 8 December 1826) 227–9, 298–303, 317–19.
70 *Ibid.* (15 February 1827) 475–513.
71 *Ibid,* XIX (24 June 1829) 1501–18.
72 Wilmot Horton, *The Causes and Remedies of Pauperism in the United Kingdom Considered: Being a Defence of the Principles and Conduct of the Emigration Committee Against the Charges of Mr. Sadler* (London, 1829) pp. 19–20; Report on Emigration (May 1826), p. 11.
73 Barry Gordon, *Economic Doctrine and Tory Liberalism, 1824–1830*

(London: Macmillan, 1979) pp. 67–70.

74 Peter Dunkley, 'Emigration and the State, 1803–1842: The Nineteenth-Century Revolution in Government Reconsidered', *The Historical Journal*, 23, 2 (1980) 359.

75 Horton, *op. cit.*, pp. 21–2; Third Report on Emigration (1827), pp. 30, 35.

76 *Ibid.*, p. 33.

77 *Ibid.*, p. 92.

78 Horton, *op. cit.*, pp. 2–3, 21, 32–7, 59–60ff.

79 *Ibid.*, pp. 65–6.

80 *PD*, 2nd ser., XXI (7 May 1829) 1135.

81 *Ibid.*, 1136–42.

82 Horton, *op. cit.*, p. 76.

83 John Murray, Sadler's publisher, had apparently heard of this from Horton himself. Fenton, *op. cit.*, 9 March 1829.

84 *PD*, 2nd ser., XIX (1 May 1828) 245–6.

85 Robert Southey, 'Ireland: its Evils and their Remedies', *Quarterly Review*, 38, LXXV (July 1828) pp. 54, 55.

86 *Ibid.*, 65, 80–1.

87 *Ibid.*, 78.

88 Johnston, *op. cit.*, 132–3.

89 *Ibid.*, 60 [emphasis added].

90 John Wilson, 'Balance of the Food and Numbers of Animated Nature', *Blackwood's*, XXVIII, CLXVIII (July 1830) pp. 109–35; 'Mr Sadler and the *Edinburgh Review*er', XXIX, CLXXII (February 1831) 292–428.

91 David Robinson, 'A Dissolution of Parliament', *Blackwood's*, XXVI, CL (August 1829) 255.

92 William Johnstone, 'The State and Prospects of the Country', *Blackwood's*, XXVI, CLVII (September 1829) 471; 'Mr Sadler, and the *Edinburgh Review*', XXVI, CLIX (November 1829) 825.

93 Samuel O'Sullivan, 'Review of the Last Session of Parliament', XXVI, CLV (August 1829) 234–5.

94 Fenton, *op. cit.*, 9 March 1829.

95 J.R. McCulloch, 'Sadler on Ireland', *ER*, 49, XCVII (June 1829) 300.

96 Fenton, *op. cit.*, 21 September 1829.

97 Thomas Babington Macaulay, 'Sadler's *Law of Population, and Disproof of Human Superfecundity*', *ER*, 51, CLL (July 1830) 297; 'Sadler's *Refutation, Refuted*', *ER*, 52, CIV (January 1831) 504–29.

98 William Cobbett, 'Sadler's Speech', *PR* (28 March 1829) 385; George Otto Trevelyan, *The Life and Letters of Lord Macaulay*, 1 (London: Longmans, Green & Co., 1878) p. 128.

99 Michael Thomas Sadler, *The Speech of M.T. Sadler, Esq. M.P. at a Dinner Given to Him by the Merchants and Ship-owners of Whitby, on Tuesday September 15th 1829*, Warring, 1829; Thomas Spring Rice, 'Mr Sadler's School – Italian Economists', *ER*, 50, C (January 1830) 344–63.

100 *Ibid.*, 347–8, 349, 350, 352ff.

101 *Ibid.*, 346.

102 *Ibid.*, 347.

103 *Ibid.*, 352.

104 Southey in Curry, *op. cit.*, pp. 342, 344.

105   Seeley, *op. cit.*, pp. 136–7.
106   Fenton, *op. cit.*, 15 September 1829; Sadler, *The Speech of M.T. Sadler*, p. 4.
107   *Ibid.*, pp. 18–19.
108   *Ibid.*, postscript, p. 20.
109   Fenton, *op. cit.*, 15 September 1829.
110   *Ibid.*, 19 September 1829.
111   Samuel Kydd, ['Alfred'], *The History of the Factory Movement from the Year 1802 to the Enactment of the Ten Hours' Bill in 1847*, I (New York and London: Burt Franklin, 1857) p. 133.
112   Norman Gash, *Aristocracy and the People, Britain 1815–1865* (London: Edward Arnold, 1979) pp. 88–9.
113   Simes, *op. cit.*, pp. 125–6, 454.
114   Diary entry (13 February 1830) quoted in *ibid.*, pp. 454–5.
115   Seeley, *op. cit.*, pp. 281.

5:   Ireland, Distress and Social Instability: Sadler Endeavours to Direct the Government 'to a better policy'

  1   *PD*, 2nd ser., XXIV (3 June 1830) 1327–30.
  2   *Ibid.*, XXI (7 May 1829) 1130, 1156, 1158.
  3   *Ibid.*, XXIV (3 June 1830) 1327.
  4   *Ibid.*, 1328, 1330–1.
  5   *Ibid.*, XXI (7 May 1829) 1124–1130.
  6   *Ibid.*, XXIII (16 March 1830) 366–75; XXV (8 June 1830) 82–5; (9 July 1830) 117–21.
  7   *Ibid.*, XXI (7 May 1829) 1127.
  8   *Ibid.*, 1125.
  9   *Ibid.*, XXIV (3 June 1830) 1298.
 10   *Ibid.*, 1327–32.
 11   *Ibid.*, IV (21 June 1831) 86–7.
 12   *Ibid.*, III (30 March 1831) 1211.
 13   *Ibid.*, 1221–4ff.
 14   *Ibid.*, 2nd ser., XVI (9 March 1827) 1088.
 15   *Ibid.*, XVIII (1 April 1828) 1418.
 16   *Ibid.*, XVIX (5 June 1828) 1041.
 17   *Ibid.*, 3rd ser., V (27 July 1831) 390.
 18   *Ibid.*, 2nd ser., VII (24 July 1822) 1737.
 19   *Ibid.*, XVI (9 March 1827) 1089.
 20   *Ibid.*, XIX (5 June 1828) 1040–1.
 21   *Ibid.*, XXI (7 May 1829) 1143–4.
 22   *Ibid.*, III (30 March 1831) 1224.
 23   *Ibid.*, 2nd ser., XVII (29 March 1827) 128–9; XXI (6 April 1829) 406; (14 May 1829) 1161, 1130; XXIII (16 March 1830) 366–7; XXIV (11 May 1830) 533.
 24   *Ibid.* (1 May 1828) 245–6.
 25   *Ibid.*, 3rd ser., III (13 April 1831) 1305.
 26   *Ibid.*, IV (21 June 1831) 87.
 27   *Ibid.*, III (18 March 1831) 533; V (27 July 1831) 395; (10 August 1831)

1124.

28 *Ibid.*, VI (29 August 1831) 799–800.
29 *Ibid.*, 785–9.
30 Report from the Select Committee on Emigration, *PP*, IV, 404 (1826) pp. 3–4ff; Third Report from the Select Committee on Emigration, *PP*, V, 550 (1827) pp. 3–5ff.
31 *PD*, 2nd ser., XXIII (16 March 1830) 368.
32 *Ibid.*, 3rd ser., VI (29 August 1831) 806–7, 815.
33 *Ibid.*, 827.
34 *Ibid.*, 836.
35 *Ibid.*, 818.
36 *Ibid.*, 826.
37 *Ibid.*, 818–19.
38 *Ibid.*, 823–4, 835.
39 *Ibid.*, 847, 848, 850.
40 *Ibid.*, 2nd ser., VII (23 July 1822) 1737.
41 *Ibid.*, 3rd ser., VI (29 August 1831). *Ibid.*, 847–9.
42 *Ibid.*, 851–4.
43 *Ibid.*, 831–3.
44 *Ibid.*, 836.
45 *Ibid.*, III (13 April 1831) 1300.
46 *Ibid.*, VI (29 August 1831) 839.
47 *Ibid.*, 840.
48 *Ibid.*, 828; John Weyland, *The Principle of the English Poor Laws* (London: J. Hatchard, 1815).
49 *Ibid.*, 825.
50 *Ibid.*, VI (29 August 1831) 846–7.
51 *Ibid.*, V (27 July 1831) 394–5.
52 *Ibid.*, VI (29 August 1831) 816–18.
53 *Ibid.*, 854. The vote for Althorp's motion was 64 in favour and 52 against.
54 *Ibid.*, XIII (19 June 1832) 831–5.
55 *Ibid.*, 840, 844, 845, 846, 849, 856ff.
56 *Ibid.*, 835.
57 *Ibid.*, 854.
58 *Ibid.*, 840–71.
59 Edward Edwards, 'The Influence of Free-Trade upon the Condition of the Labouring Classes', *Blackwood's*, XXVII, CLXV (April 1830) 248.
60 William Johnstone, 'The Present Crisis', *Blackwood's*, XXVIII, CLXXII (October 1830) 692.
61 *Ibid.*, XXII (5 February 1830) 156.
62 *Ibid.*, XXIII (16 March) 391–430; (18 March) 548–609; (19 March) 624–72; (23 March 1830) 789–827.
63 *Ibid.* (16 March 1830) 410–11.
64 *Ibid.*, 416.
65 *Ibid.* (18 March 1830) 553.
66 *Ibid.*, 570–1.
67 *Ibid.*, 573.
68 *Ibid.* (19 March 1830) 671–2.
69 *Ibid.* (23 March 1830) 795.

70   *Ibid.*, 585.
71   *Ibid.*, 588.
72   E.J. Hobsbawm and George Rudé, *Captain Swing* (London: Pimlico, 1969) pp. 308–9.
73   *PD*, 3rd ser., VIII (11 October 1831) 499–502.
74   *Ibid.*, 513–14.
75   *Ibid.*, 503–4.
76   *Ibid.* 501, 524.
77   *Ibid.*, 513–22.
78   *Ibid.*, 524–8.
79   *Ibid.*, 534–6.
80   *Ibid.*, 542–9.
81   *Ibid.*, 554.

6:   Sadler's Ten Hours Bill and Leadership of the Parliamentary Factory Reform Campaign

1   Samuel Kydd, *The History of the Factory Movement*, I (New York and London: Burt Franklin, 1857) p. 316.
2   John Roach, *Social Reform in England 1780–1880* (London: B.T. Batsford, 1978) pp. 77–8; E.P. Thompson, *The Making of the English Working Class* (Harmondsworth: Penguin Books, 1980 edn), pp. 374–84; T.S. Ashton, 'The Treatment of *Capitalism by Historians*' in F. A. Hayek (ed.), Capitalism and the Historians (London, 1954) p. 35; David Roberts, *Victorian Origins of the British Welfare State* (Yale: Yale University Press, 1969); Oliver MacDonagh, *Early Victorian Government 1830–1870* (London: Weidenfeld & Nicolson, 1977) pp. 6–8ff.
3   Maurice Walton Thomas, *The Early Factory Legislation: A Study in Legislative and Administrative Evolution* (London: The Thames Bank Publishing Co. Ltd, 1948) p. 39.
4   MacDonagh, *op. cit.*, p. 33; Clark Nardinelli, *Child Labor and the Industrial Revolution* (Bloomington & Indianapolis: Indiana University Press, 1990) p. 11.
5   A.V. Dicey, *Lectures on the Relations Between Law & Public Opinion in England during the Nineteenth Century* (London: Macmillan, 1914 edn) pp. 224–7.
6   Cecil Driver, *Tory Radical: The Life of Richard Oastler* (New York: Oxford University Press, 1946) p. 117.
7   *PD*, 3rd ser., VIII (11 October 1831) 498.
8   Sadler to Oastler, 1 September 1831, in Kydd, *op. cit.*, p. 127.
9   See Nathaniel Gould to Benjamin Sadler, 11 March 1817 (MS, BLPES, Misc. Coll., vol. 1)
10   Quoted in Kydd, *op. cit.*, p. 220.
11   Driver, *op. cit.*, pp. 21–2, 41.
12   Thompson, *op. cit.*, p. 377.
13   Richard Oastler, *The Home* (1851) in Kydd, *op. cit.*, pp. 95–7.
14   *PD*, 2nd ser, XIII (31 May 1825) 1010.
15   *Ibid.*, XXI (1 May 1829) 971.

16 Seymour Drescher, 'Cart Whip and Billy Roller: Antislavery and Reform Symbolism in Industrializing Britain', *Journal of Social History*, 15 (1981) 9ff.
17 Kydd, *op. cit.*, pp. 98–9.
18 *PD*, 3rd ser., II (15 February 1831) 584–5.
19 *Ibid.*, V (27 July 1831) 388–9.
20 *Ibid.* (30 July 1831) 558.
21 *Ibid.*, 2nd ser., XIII (5, 16, 31 May 1825) 421, 643–9, 1008–11.
22 *Ibid.* (5 May 1825) 421.
23 *Ibid.* (31 May 1825) 1008.
24 Kydd, *op. cit.*, pp. 139–40.
25 Richard Oastler, 'Slavery in Yorkshire', *Leeds Intelligencer*, 20 October 1831, in Kydd, *op. cit.*, pp. 118–22.
26 *Ibid.*, pp. 139–40.
27 Anon, *A Letter to Sir John Cam Hobhouse … on 'The Factories Bill' by a Manufacturer* (London, 1832).
28 Sadler to Oastler, 1 September 1831, in Kydd, *op. cit.*, p. 127.
29 Hobhouse to Oastler, 16 November 1831, *ibid.*, p. 139.
30 Sadler to Oastler, 20 November 1831, *ibid.*, pp. 130–1.
31 *PD*, 2nd ser., IX (15 December 1831) 255–7.
32 *Ibid.*, 3rd, II (16 March 1832) 375.
33 *Ibid.*, IX (1 February) 1094–7; X, (7, 9, 10 February) 20–3, 104–7, 190–5; (7 March) 1222–5.
34 *Ibid.*, 3rd ser., XV (28 February 1833) 1294.
35 Driver, *op. cit.*, p. 43.
36 *PD*, 3rd, II, 16 March 1832, 343–5.
37 *Ibid.*, 2nd ser., XIII (16 May 1825) 647.
38 *Ibid.*, 3rd ser., II (16 March 1832) 346–8.
39 *Ibid.*, 358.
40 *Ibid.*, 349.
41 *Ibid.*, 344.
42 *Ibid.*, 358.
43 Andrew Ure, *The Philosophy of Manufactures or an Exposition of the Scientific, Moral, and Commercial Economy of the Factory System of Great Britain* (London: Frank Cass & Co. Ltd, 1835, 1967) pp. 8–18ff.
44 *PD*, 3rd ser., II (16 March 1832) 351, 358–9.
45 *Ibid.*, 348, 354, 368.
46 *Ibid.*, 357, 369.
47 *Ibid.*, 374.
48 *Ibid.*, 367.
49 *Ibid.*, 360.
50 Anthony Forder, *Concepts in Social Administration. A Framework for Analysis* (London: Routledge & Kegan Paul, 1974) p. 9.
51 *PD*, 3rd ser., II (16 March 1832) 360.
52 *Ibid.*, 382.
53 *Ibid.*, 375, 379.
54 *Ibid.*, 376 [emphasis added].
55 *Ibid.*, 385–6.
56 *Ibid.*, 386–7.

57 *Ibid.*, 389–92.
58 *Ibid.*, 393–8.
59 Robert Benton Seeley, *Memoirs of the life and Writings of Michael Thomas Sadler* (London: R. B. Seeley & W. Burnside, 1842) p. 380; Ward, *op. cit.*, p. 63; Driver, *op. cit.*, p. 170.
60 *PD*, 3rd ser., XVII, 3 April 1833, 81.
61 *Ibid*, XVI (22 March 1833) 972; XVII (3 April) 81–2, 90, 92–3.
62 Driver, *op. cit.*, pp. 167–70, 550–3.
63 *PD*, 3rd., XVII (3 April 1833) 83.
64 J.L. and Barbara Hammond, *The Town Labourer, 1760–1832* (London: Longmans, Green & Co., 1925 edn) pp. 159–60.
65 W.H. Hutt, 'The Factory System of the Early Nineteenth Century' in F.A. Hayek, *Capitalism and the Historians* (London, 1954) pp. 161–2.
66 *Ibid.*, p. 164; Thomas, *op. cit.*, p. 41; Frederick Engels *The Condition of the Working-Class in England* (Moscow: Progress Publishers, 1845, 1977) p. 183.
67 Nardinelli, *op. cit.*, pp. 3–4, 26–7.
68 Thompson, *op. cit.*, p. 371; see also MacDonagh, *op. cit.*, pp. 31–2.
69 Kenneth Curry (ed.), *New Letters of Robert Southey*, 2 (New York and London: Columbia University Press, 1965) p. 391.
70 Ure, *op. cit.*, pp. 290–1.
71 Report from the Select Committee on the 'Bill to Regulate the Labour of Children in the Mills and Factories of the United Kingdom', *PP*, XV, 706 (August 1832) pp. 134–5, 225, 249, 295–6, 276, 297, 311, 410, 412, 415ff.
72 *Ibid.*, p. 134.
73 *Ibid.*, p. 411.
74 *Ibid.*, p. 295.
75 *Ibid.*, p. 341.
76 *Ibid.*, p. 421.
77 *Ibid.*, p. 423.
78 *Ibid.*, p. 296.
79 *Ibid.*, p. 412.
80 John Wilson, 'The Factory System', *Blackwood's*, XXXIII, CCVI (April 1833) 445.
81 Report of the Select Committee on Child Labour (1832) pp. 514–15, 524, 560–4ff.
82 *Ibid.*, pp. 572, 565ff.
83 *Ibid.*, pp. 392–3.
84 *Ibid.*, pp. 401, 405.
85 *Ibid.*, p. 135.
86 *Ibid.*, p. 421.
87 *Ibid.*, p. 451.
88 *PD*, 3rd ser., II (16 March 1832) 360.
89 Report of the Select Committee on Child Labour (1832) p. 400.
90 *Ibid.*, p. 406.
91 *Ibid.*, pp. 135, 274, 401ff.
92 *Ibid.*, p. 227.
93 *PD*, 3rd ser., II (16 March 1832) 360.
94 Report of the Select Committee on Child Labour (1832) p. 460.

95 *Ibid.*, pp. 401, 404–5.
96 *Ibid.*, p. 491.
97 *Ibid.*, p. 460.
98 *Ibid.*, p. 424.
99 *Ibid.*, p. 400.
100 *Ibid.*, pp. 457–8.
101 *Ibid.*, pp. 424, 425, 426.
102 John Mayhall, *The Annals of Yorkshire from the Earliest Period to the Present Time*, 1 (Leeds: Joseph Johnson, 1862) p. 393.
103 Driver, *op. cit.*, p. 107.
104 Arthur Stanley Turberville and Frank Beckwith, 'Leeds and Parliamentary Reform, 1820–1832', *Thorseby*, XLI (Leeds, 1954) p. 44.
105 Peter Pearker, 'Letter to Michael Thomas Sadler' (Leeds, [1832], New York: Arno Press Inc., 1972).
106 Anthony Armstrong, *The Church of England, the Methodists, and Society, 1700–1800* (London: University of London Press, 1973) pp. 196–7; Driver, *op. cit.*, p. 108.
107 Thomas Babington Macaulay, 'Southey's *Colloquies on Society*', ER, 50 (January 1830) pp. 532, 538–9, 540–1, 546–7ff.
108 T.B. Macaulay to Ralph Taylor, Secretary of the Leeds Short Time Committee, 16 March 1832, in Kydd, *op. cit.*, pp. 148–51.
109 Address to Michael Thomas Sadler from the Huddersfield Short Time Committee, *Leeds Intelligencer*, 10 November 1831, in Driver, *op. cit.*, p. 114.
110 *Ibid.*, pp. 114–15.
111 *Leeds Intelligencer*, 10 November 1831, quoted in Turberville and Beckwith, *op. cit.*, p. 46.
112 *PD*, 3rd ser., VIII (11 October 1831) 544–6.
113 Ward, *op. cit.*, pp. 46–9ff; Driver, *op. cit.*, pp. 194–7ff.
114 *Leeds Intelligencer*, 15 September 1831, quoted in Turberville and Beckwith, *op. cit.*, p. 43.
115 Quoted in *ibid.*, p. 81. Marshall polled 2,012, Macaulay 1,984 and Sadler 1,596.
116 Report of the Select Committee on Child Labour (1832) pp. 425, 427.
117 Lord Ashley to Richard Oastler, 16 February 1833, in Edwin Hodder, *The Life and Work of the Seventh Earl of Shaftesbury*, I (London: Cassell & Company Ltd, 1886) pp. 152–3.
118 *Ibid.*, pp. 147–9.
119 *Ibid.*, pp. 152–3.
120 Charles Wing, *Evils of the Factory System Demonstrated by Parliamentary Evidence* (London: Frank Cass & Co. Ltd, 1837, 1967) p. iv.
121 Southey to John May, 1 March 1833, in John Dennis, *Robert Southey. The Story of his Life Written in his Letters* (London: George Bell & Sons, 1894) p. 391.
122 J.R. McCulloch to Lord Ashley, 28 March 1833, in Edwin Hodder, *op. cit.*, pp. 158–8.
123 *PD*, 3rd ser., XV (26 February) 1164; (28 February) 1298; XVI (14 March 1833) 640 (22 March) 970, 971, 972; (25 March) 1002; XVII (3 April) 80ff.
124 *Ibid.*, XV (26 February) 1163; XVI (14 March) 641, 642; XIX (5 July) 229;

(18 July) 894.

125   David Robinson, 'Mr. Huskisson's Speech in Defence of Free Trade', *Blackwood's*, XIX, CXI (April 1826) 484–5.

126   *PD*, 3rd ser., XV (26 February) 1160, 1161; XVI (20 March) 880.

127   *Ibid.*, XV (8 February) 392; XVI (20 March) 880; (22 March) 971, 972; XVII, (3 April) 84; XIX, (5 July) 235, 246ff; (18 July) 900–1, 906ff.

128   *Ibid.*, XVII (3 April 1833) 92–4, 101–2.

129   *Ibid.*, 106.

130   *Ibid.*, XVIII (3 June 1833) 305–8.

131   *Ibid.*, VIII (17 June 1833) 914–5.

132   *Ibid.*, XIX (5 July 1833) 229.

133   Driver, *op. cit.*, pp. 227–8ff; Engels, *op. cit.*, pp. 183–4; Evans, *The Forging of the Modern State* (London and New York: Longman, 1983) pp. 229–30; Roberts, *op. cit.*, pp. 36–8; Nardinelli, *op. cit.*, pp. 1–5; Edward Royle, *Modern Britain: A Social History 1750–1985* (London: Edward Arnold, 1987) p.193; Thomas, *op. cit.*, pp. 40–1, 46–60; Thompson, *op. cit.*, pp. 371–2

134   Hutt, *op. cit.*, pp. 160–88, Roberts, *op. cit.*, p. 37.

135   Brian Inglis's analysis of the two reports is one of the exceptions. As part of a broader area of study, this is not particularly exhaustive, but it high-lights some of the areas where the reports converge. Brian Inglis, *Poverty and the Industrial Revolution* (London: Granada Publishing Ltd, 1971) pp. 329–38, 348–68.

136   First Report of the Central Board of His Majesty's Commissioners appointed to collect Information in the Manufacturing Districts, as to the Employment of Children in Factories, and as to the Propriety of Curtailing the Hours of their Labour, *PP*, XX, 450 (June 1833), pp. 10, 13, 18, 21ff.

137   *Ibid.*, p. 20.

138   *Ibid.*, pp. 31–2.

139   *Ibid.*, pp. 34–5.

140   *PD*, 3rd ser., XVIII (17 June) 914.

141   *Ibid.*, XIX (5 July) 221–3.

142   *Ibid.*, XVII (3 April) 86, 90; XVIII, (17 June) 915.

143   Royal Commission on the Employment of Children (1833) pp. 72–3.

144   *PD*, 3rd ser., XIX (5 July 1833) 224–7.

145   *Ibid.* (18 July 1833) 900–2, 907.

Conclusion: Towards a Realization of the Paternalist, Collectivist Idea of the State

1   A.V. Dicey, *Lectures on the Relations Between Law & Public Opinion in England during the Nineteenth Century* (London: Macmillan, 1914 edn), pp. 211–40, ff; Elie Halévy, *The Triumph of Reform* (London: Ernest Benn Ltd, 1927, 1961) pp. 98–129; Henry Parris, 'The Nineteenth-Century Revolution in Government: A Reappraisal Reappraised', *Historical Journal*, III, I (1960) 17–37; Jennifer Hart, 'Nineteenth Century Social Reform: A Tory Interpretation of History', *Past and Present*, 31 (July 1965) 39–61;

Derek Fraser, *The Evolution of the British Welfare State* (London, 1973) pp. 21–2; Howard P. Marvel, 'Factory Regulation: A Reinterpretation of Early English Experience', *The Journal of Law and Economics*, XX, 2 (October 1977) 379–402; Eric J. Evans, *The Forging of the Modern State* (London and New York: Longman, 1983) p. 230.

2 J.L. and Barbara Hammond, *Lord Shaftesbury* (London: Frank Cass & Co. Ltd, 1923, 1969) p. 18; Brian Inglis, *Poverty and the Industrial Revolution* (London: Granada Publishing Ltd, 1971) p. 367; Norman Gash, *Aristocracy and the People, Britain 1815–1865* (London: Edward Arnold, 1979) p. 195; Oliver MacDonagh, 'The Nineteenth-Century Revolution in Government: A Reappraisal', *Historical Journal*, I, I (1958) 52–67 and *op. cit.*, pp. 1–54; David Roberts, 'Jeremy Bentham and the Victorian Administrative State', *Victorian Studies*, II, 3 (March 1959) 193–210; 'Tory Paternalism and Social Reform in Early Victorian England', in Peter Stansky, ed., The Victorian Revolution: Government and Society in Victoria's Britain (New York: Franklin Watts Inc., 1973), pp. 147–64 and *Victorian Origins of the British Welfare State* (Yale: Yale University Press, 1969) pp. 22–34ff; Oliver MacDonagh, 'The Nineteenth-Century Revolution in Government' and *Early Victorian Government 1830–1870* (London: Weidenfeld & Nicolson, 1977) pp. 1–54.

3 *PD*, 3rd ser., XIX (5 July 1833) 249.

4 Halévy, *op. cit.*, p. 114; Maurice Walton Thomas, *The Early Factory Legislation* (London: The Thames Bank Publishing Co. Ltd, 1948) p. 39; MacDonagh, *Early Victorian Government*, p. 33; Clark Nardinelli, *Child Labor and the Industrial Revolution* (Bloomington & Indianapolis: Indiana University Press, 1990) p. 11; Parris, *op. cit.*, p. 31; R. K., Webb, *Modern England* (London: George Allen & Unwin, 1969) p. 242.

5 Halévy, *op. cit.*, pp. 112, 114; Hart, *op. cit.*, p. 42; MacDonagh, *Early Victorian Government*, pp. 34–5, 43–54; Parris, *op. cit.*, p. 31; J. Bartlet Brebner, 'Laissez-faire and State Intervention in Nineteenth Century Britain', *Journal of Economic History*, VIII (1948) 62, 64.

6 Parris, *op. cit.*, p. 31.

7 Jeremy Bentham, *The Constitutional Code*, in John Bowring, ed., *The Works of Jeremy Bentham*, IX (New York: Russell & Russell Inc., 1962) bk. II, ch. xi.

8 See Chapter 1, Section V.

9 Norman McCord, *British History* (Oxford: Oxford University Press, 1991) p. 188.

10 Hart, *op. cit.*

11 First Report of the Central Board of His Majesty's Commissioners [on] the Employment of Children in Factories, *PP*, XX, 450 (June 1833) p. 72 [emphasis added].

12 MacDonagh's observation is pertinent. Although Benthamism was clearly crucial to Chadwick's thinking, Chadwick himself never 'openly acknowledged a debt to Bentham'. Indeed, one of the great difficulties for historians is that those of whom they 'speak of so readily as Benthamites did not often speak of themselves in such terms or attribute their ideas to the great man'. MacDonagh, *Early Victorian Government*, p. 35.

13 Roberts, 'Jeremy Bentham and the Victorian Administrative State', p. 199.

14 Webb, *op. cit.*, p. 242; MacDonagh, *Early Victorian Government*, p. 34;
    Parris, *op. cit.*, p. 31; Halévy, *op. cit.*, p. 112; Nardinelli, *op. cit.*, pp. 132–3.
15 Roberts, *Victorian Origins of the British Welfare State*, p. 37; MacDonagh,
    Early Victorian Government, p. 47.
16 Halévy, *op. cit.*, p.113 n.
17 Althorp was to some extent hoist by his own petard. When the new Act
    came into force on 1 March 1834, the factory reformers launched a
    campaign, albeit short-lived, for an eight-hour day. On that day, all adult
    operatives stopped work at the same time as the children. Halévy, *op. cit.*,
    pp. 117–18.
18 *PD*, 2nd ser., XXI (14 April 1829) 835; (1 May 1829) 934–6.
19 *PD*, 3rd., XX (12 August 1833) 530.
20 'The object of the present publication', explained Wing, 'is to prevent, as
    far as bringing evidence within the reach of the public can do so, a partial
    return to the factory system, as it existed previously to the year 1833,
    since a partial return to that system is in itself an evil, and may be the
    prelude to a total return.' Charles Wing, *Evils of the Factory System*
    (London: Frank Cass & Co. Ltd, 1837, 1967) pp. i–ii.
21 *PD*, 3rd ser., XXXIII (9 May 1836) 737.
22 MacDonagh, *Early Victorian Government*, p. 27.
23 Roberts, *Victorian Origins of the British Welfare State*, p. 38.
24 David Roberts, *Paternalism in Early Victorian England* (London: Croom
    Helm, 1979) pp. 45–6.
25 MacDonagh, *Early Victorian Government*, pp. 32–3.
26 Brebner, *op. cit.*, pp. 60–1ff.
27 MacDonagh, *Early Victorian Government*, pp. 9, 11–12, 50–1.
28 Roberts, *Paternalism*, p. 187.
29 See Chapter 1, Section V.
30 *PD*, 3rd ser., XX, 14 August 1833, 585.
31 Boyd Hilton, *The Age of Atonement* (Oxford: Clarendon Press, 1988)
    p. 213.

Index

Elements of Political Economy, 29
Mill, John Stuart, 4–5, 45
Milton, Lord, 74, 75, 77, 80, 87, 88
minimum wage, 80, 82–3, 112
Monck, John Berkeley, 82–3, 130
monitorial system, *see* Lancastrian
  schools
monopoly, 29, 47, 51, 54, 105, 143,
  146
Montesquieu, Charles-Louis de
  Secondat, 39, 52
More, Peter, 75
More, Sir Thomas, 39
  Sadler's ghost of, 16
Morpeth, Lord, 139, 153, 165
Murray, John, 122

Napier, Macvey, 123
Nardinelli, Clark, 151, 166
natural law, theory of, 52, 53–4
nature, laws of, 17, 51–2, 55, 58
new economy, *see* political economy
New Lanark, 20–4, 84
New Poor Law, 3
Newark, 43, 97, 98–102, 122
Newcastle, Duke of, 3, 97, 98, 99,
  101–3, 111, 121, 125–6
Newport, Sir John, 132, 133
Newton, Sir Isaac, 61
non-intervention, 13, 65, 157
  proponents of, 89–90, 96, 154
Nugent, Lord, 165

O'Connell, Daniel, 140, 142
O'Ferrall, Richard More, 137–8
O'Grady, Colonel Standish, 137
O'Sullivan, Samuel, 121–2
Oastler, Richard, 2, 4, 150, 151–3,
  155, 173, 174
  'Yorkshire slavery', 152, 157, 176
Osborne, John, 27
Owen, Robert, 20–4
  authoritarian paternalist, 84
  community and social
    organisation, 22–4, 84
  educational schemes, 20–3, 117,
    185–6, 192
  employment schemes, 83
  factory regulation, 91

government's social role, 22, 83–4
social reform, 22
Report to the County of Lanark
  (1820), 84

Paley, William, 39, 45, 53–4
Palmer, Charles, 77–8
parish assistance, parish relief, *see*
  Poor Laws
parliament, paternal and social
  responsibilities, 1, 5, 29, 35, 45,
  62, 82–3, 91, 95–6, 108, 111,
  123, 164, 174, 192
parliamentary committees
  House of Commons Select
    Committees: on the 'Bill to
    Regulate the Labour of Children
    in the Mills and Factories of the
    United Kingdom' (1832); on
    Child Labour (1816); on the
    Employment of Boys in
    Sweeping of Chimneys (1817),
    see child labour; on Emigration
    from the United Kingdom (1826
    and 1827) *see* emigration;
    Employment or Relief of Able-
    bodied Persons (1828);
    Labourers' Wages (1928); Poor
    Laws (1817), *see* Poor Laws
  House of Lords Committees:
    Employment of Children in
    Cotton Factories (1818);
    Employment of Boys in climbing
    Chimneys (1818), *see* child
    labour: chimney sweeps; Poor
    Laws (181), *see* Poor Laws
Parnell, Sir Henry, 109
paternal state, concept of, 96, 190–1
paternal government, 5, 19, 96, 191
paternalism, 2, 4, 37, 76, 96
  agrarian, 86
  aristocratic, 185
  authoritarian, 66, 69, 73, 74, 76,
    84
  humanitarian, 74, 76, 96
  'old world', 64, 85–6, 96
  revival of (1820s), 1, 2, 3, 5, 7, 29,
    78
  theory of, 4–5